TRIAL IN THAILAND

Trial in Thailand

George K. Tanham

Formerly State Department
Special Assistant for Counterinsurgency
at U.S. Embassy, Bangkok

CR

CRANE, RUSSAK

& COMPANY, INC.

NEW YORK

Trial in Thailand

Published in the United States by

Crane Russak & Company, Inc.

347 Madison Avenue
New York, New York 10017

Copyright © 1974 Crane, Russak & Company, Inc.

ISBN 0-8448-0318-9

LC 74-75314

Printed in the United States of America

CONTENTS

Preface vii
Foreword xi

CHAPTER 1
Thailand Today 3

CHAPTER 2
Communism in Thailand 27

CHAPTER 3
The Insurgency 47

CHAPTER 4
The Thai Response 71

CHAPTER 5
An Assessment of the Thai Response 95

CHAPTER 6
United States Government Apparatus........ 115

CHAPTER 7
Special Assistant for Counterinsurgency 129

CHAPTER 8
Some Reflections 151
Glossary 169
Index 171

pREfACE

I F the question of "what went wrong" in American policy in Southeast Asia during the last decade is pertinent, so too is the question of what went right, particularly where successes occurred because lessons had been learned from previous errors. This book contains an important chapter in the study of what went well, a chapter delineating both the main issues, and the development of an American role, in the still growing Thai insurgency.

It was inevitable that public attention to Thailand would be linked with that paid to Vietnam. The whole "domino" theory was in part based on an assessment of Thai intentions; Thailand, as the unsinkable aircraft carrier, played an increasingly important strategic role in our Vietnam strategy and now represents our last trump in dealing with Indochina; Thailand was where theories of revolution could be investigated without fear that it was too close to the eleventh hour. Thailand was also where men who had seen things gone awry in Vietnam could seek to get one corrective effort off to a good start.

People usually learn from their mistakes how to make new ones. It seemed almost inevitable that the apparent resemblance of the incipient Thai insurgency in the mid-1960s to that in Vietnam five years earlier would lead American CI experts to overdraw the similarity. It was important that the lessons learned from Vietnam be the right ones, applied by people who had both an analytical and intuitive grasp of what was possible in Thailand. George Tanham, a distinguished student of revolutionary doctrine, strategy, and warfare, had a tour of duty as a senior AID administrator in Vietnam in the mid-1960s, out of which came his well-received book *War Without Guns*. In 1968 he went to Bangkok as Minister-Counselor for Counterinsurgency. On my own first research trip to Thailand in 1969 every Thai official whom I interviewed, without exception, told me that what success attended their joint efforts with the United States in the counterinsurgency efforts was the result of Tanham's sensitive and skillful efforts. That its author was the right person to head the counterinsurgency effort as well as his success in his job is the first reason for underlining the importance of this book.

The first question that had to be asked in Bangkok was one that had never been asked in Vietnam; it was "how much Americans should do," as Tanham stated it in discussing his Vietnamese experience. This asks a highly practical question of who should do what, particularly at the lower echelons. In tight situations "Americans frequently tend to want to take over and do the job themselves." Tanham decided that the Thai government must accept full responsibility for the CI work, keeping their American advisors merely advising. To do this required both an awareness of Thai sensitivities and also an appreciation of the delicate balance of power in the kingdom existing between the different armed service and police commanders. Few Americans understood how power was distributed in Bangkok and how to deal with it. Sometimes seemingly obvious solutions to compelling problems would not be applied despite all the reasoning Americans could offer. This might be the result of a power struggle within a ministry that one general controlled in name but not in fact. Tanham understood the Thais and he solved problems sometimes by serving as the link between what should have been complementary ministries but which were in fact competitive. From Tanham's development of a suitably pragmatic doctrine for counterinsurgency and America's role in Thailand, some explicit guidelines emerged which specified the lines beyond which American help would not go. These guidelines anticipated in substance the essence of the Nixon doctrine by almost a year. Here then is the second reason for paying close attention to this book: it illustrates how a diplomat can steer through treacherous channels to get a host government to do at least some of what it knows it must do but to do which it lacks sufficient will or to do which it has too many competing factions. The book also shows how the home government must be prevented from doing that for which it still has the will but which, in the doing, would be self-defeating.

Its suitably pragmatic doctrine itself is the third reason for looking carefully at this book. Doctrine must be appropriate to the terrain and it must take into consideration *all* the components that have to be orchestrated together. Like Vietnam at various times, and no doubt like any country with an insurgency, Thailand always echoed with arguments within the American and Thai communities respectively as to whether development or suppression must be emphasized; Tanham notes that at times the Thai and American soldiers on the one hand, and Thai and American development specialists on the other, made common cause across national lines. The military sometimes thought the aid specialists "soft," and these in turn sometimes thought their military counterparts to be insensitive fascists. But clearly it was a question of finding the proper mix. Without security no development can occur. Without a realistic plan for development there can be no long-run hope for cooperation between village and government. And in between, one runs the risk in starting development projects of whetting the villager's appetite enough to lead him into the enemy's lair when results did not appear overnight. Working with Thai army and political leaders Tanham developed concepts of cooperation between civil, police, and military forces (which took on the initials CPM). Such cooperation was difficult to implement; Tanham had to convince some army leaders not to rely on pure force, and had to work with them to find a proper balance between political education in the villages and suppression in the mountains and rough terrain. He also had to convince both American and Thai communities that in CI work there must be ample room for innovation. Decisionmakers had to be able to act fast, and if bureaucracy in the embassy or in the ministries could not keep pace, so much the worse for the bureaucracy.

There is yet another reason for drawing attention to this book. The support for American CI efforts is dwindling due to disillusionment with our experience in Vietnam. From the caché CI had in the days of Professor Rostow, General Taylor, and President Kennedy, we come to a time when CI experts and offices rename themselves; foreign service officers involved in CI work run for cover and attend to other duties, fearing Congressional wrath and lack of promotion. Nevertheless, world political patterns are increasingly determined by military action within, rather than across, borders, as dissident ethnic groups, underprivileged classes, take to the hills or to the streets in one country after the other. We should learn from our experiences in Southeast Asia, however unpleasant their memory, how to better defuse insurgencies so as not to tear a nation apart. Almost every country is now learning to deal with potential insurgencies and other forms of low-level violence; many are already having to test their knowledge. The facts remain, irrespective of our ignorance of them, or, more pertinently, our choosing to ignore them. It happens that the American experience in Thailand was one of the first such situations where the resources of a relatively sophisticated research capability could be put to use. Tanham's office was the crossroads of joint research efforts utilizing anthropologists, sociologists, economists, and political scientists. No one could have been better prepared by academic training and professional experience to make use of this influx of data than George Tanham.

It is only now that we can begin to assess the work done in Thailand during the 1960s. The insurgency grows apace in Thailand at the same time that military action declines in Vietnam; thus it is clear that the Thai government has not found a magic formula for coping with problems deriving both from geography and her own past neglect and mistakes. It has taken a long time for the leadership to accept the seriousness of the threat to the kingdom. But one thing is clear: American debts to Thailand increase daily as we come to rely on our bases there for whatever last rounds President Nixon has to engage in across the borders in Laos, Cambodia, and the two Vietnams. Yet the American role in the Thai counterinsurgency effort is not growing, rather it is declining. The Thai capability for dealing with the insurgency is improving. For all the praise Tanham, in this absorbing and lively book, lavishes on those who preceded him, there can be little doubt that the greatest credit for what was done goes to him.

W. Scott Thompson

Cambridge, Massachusetts

foreword

THAILAND, like most other countries of Southeast Asia, is troubled by a communist-led insurgency which is most active in the border and mountainous areas of the country. Most of the movement, though communist-led and inspired, feeds to an extent not only on socioeconomic problems but also on the dissatisfaction of minorities living in these remote areas. In the Northeast, socioeconomic problems and government neglect predominate, while in the North and South, minorities—Meo and other mountain tribes in the North and Malays or Thai Muslims and Chinese in the South—form the primary population base for insurgency. While the insurgency in the various areas of Thailand in 1974 constitutes no immediate threat to the Royal Thai Government, it is a festering sore. It is hurting the Thai government's efforts toward socioeconomic progress even with its limited drain on resources, including scarce human skills. It is also growing slowly and in a few years could pose much more serious problems for Thailand than it does today. It has some limited outside support which may or may not grow depending on the general state of international relations in the area, the policies of Peking and Hanoi, and the viability of the internal insurgency apparatus in Thailand.

The first part of this book is concerned with the origins and progress of this insurgency and the various Thai efforts to contain or destroy it. While I have gone through the literature on the subject, most of the book is based on study and observations made during numerous trips to Thailand, the first being in 1958. Two months with the Southeast Asia Treaty Organization (SEATO) Expert Study Group on Counter-Subversion in 1961 gave me a good basis to build on as well as a chance to visit various parts of Thailand, to get to know Thailand better, and to make friendships and acquaintances which would continue for years to come. Subsequent visits kept me up to date. My two year tour in the American Embassy in Bangkok, 1968–1970, gave me a chance to go more into depth in my study of Thailand and its insurgency problems. I visited almost every one of the seventy-two provinces, most several times, became acquainted with the Thai leadership in Bangkok as well as in the provinces, and made trips to Laos, Burma, and Malaysia to see the insurgency problems from their side of the border. A trip to Thailand in 1972 allowed me to make more recent and first-hand judgments on the situation there, and I have tried to keep up to date from Washington since then. While being primarily concerned with the insurgency and related problems, I have tried not to allow this interest to give me a distorted perspective of Thailand's problems and the insurgency's priority among them. My friendships with many Thais, I suspect, may have led me to hold a somewhat more sympathetic view of Thailand than that held by some though, here again, I hope I have maintained an independent and objective viewpoint. In any case, I have tried to present facts when available as accurately as possible although fact gathering is most difficult when dealing with clandestine movements and a foreign government which pursues its own actions and policy without always revealing them. Often, the data are vague and unclear, and when this is the case, I have said so. The interpretation, assessments, and judgments are my own, and these, of course, are of importance in a work of this nature.

The last portion of this work, probably of greater interest to Americans, is concerned with the role of the United States in helping the Thais over the past eight to ten years (though military and economic aid began over twenty years ago) to counter the growing insurgency. This American aid has raised the possibility of too much direct U.S. participation and a repeat of many of the mistakes made in Vietnam. In fact, the U.S. has tried to avoid this danger and during my own tour I laid down in writing strict prohibitions against U.S. direct involvement in the Thai counterinsurgency effort. This latter part of the book includes a review of the activities of the various U.S. agencies in Thailand—Department of Defense, Agency for International Development, United States Information Agency, and the State Department—associated with the Thai counterinsurgency effort. And, there is a rather long but important chapter on the office I headed in the Embassy, the Office of Special Assistant for Counterinsurgency (SA/CI), which had the task of laying down U.S. counterinsurgency policy in Thailand, coordinating the various aid efforts (both military and civilian), regulating the actions of American advisors in the counterinsurgency field, advising the Ambassador and the Royal Thai Government, and reporting to Washington on the Thai efforts and the insurgency situation. It was an important experiment in coordinating the work of U.S. government agencies in the field with very little guidance or help from Washington and less than warm enthusiasm for the effort from certain other quarters, such as the U.S. Pacific Command. Important lessons can be drawn from this experience; they may be helpful for the U.S. in future similar situations which I suspect may arise again in spite of current attitudes toward overseas involvement now held by many Americans.

The trial in Thailand is obvious: can the Royal Thai Government, with all its other problems, successfully cope with the communist insurgency while pursuing its course of modernization and search for democracy? While Thailand has many assets which other Southeast Asian countries lack—an independence maintained throughout the colonial period, an unbroken royal dynasty for over two hundred years, and a reasonably homogeneous population with essentially one religion, Buddhism—the future poses serious problems which will test the leadership of Thailand and its people. Another part of the trial is how well the low-key, nonoperational U.S. posture coupled with material aid and advice will serve to help the Thai. A final element of the trial is how feasible it is to have a closely coordinated U.S. effort in Thailand, since many factors in Washington, as well as in between and in Thailand itself, work against this principle. This problem of coordinated U.S. policies and actions abroad is a continuing one and deserves greater attention than it receives. My experience in Thailand makes me hopeful, if people of good will and intelligence will work together and concentrate on coordination.

While I take full responsibility for the work of SA/CI and this book, I must express my deep appreciation to members of the staff of SA/CI who were so loyal and hard-working during my tenure, as well as to some who were also helpful in the preparation of this book. In particular, I wish to thank Major General John R. D. Cleland, USA; Colonel George K. Osborn, USA; Jerrold Milsted; John Eisenhour; and especially Middleton Martin for their constructive criticism and helpful suggestions.

I would also like to express my appreciation for the very useful criticisms and suggestions of Robert Asprey and Douglas Blaufarb. William Klausner, an old Thai hand, sharpened my description of the Thais and their ways. I cannot express adequately my thanks to Professor Scott Thompson of the Fletcher School of Law and Diplomacy, who spent so much time and effort on improving my manuscript and who was kind enough to write the Preface.

Mrs. Lee Rademaker Meyer, who has worked with me during the past eight years, has contributed in many ways to this book, by editing, redrafting, typing, and giving general advice and criticism. This has been especially helpful as she was with me in Thailand and knows it well. I want to thank Mrs. Katherine Sproul who, during the pressure of other business on me, helped to make this a more readable manuscript. My thanks also go to Marsha Childs who generously helped adapt the maps of Thailand for use in this book.

This is also a good opportunity to thank the heads of agencies who composed my Tuesday Group in Bangkok, which is described in Chapter 7, and who cooperated so generously in this experiment. They were for most of my tour: Rey Hill, Director of the U.S. Operations Mission (USOM); Major General (now Lieutenant General) Louis T. Seith, USAF; G. Lewis Schmidt, Director of the U.S. Information Service (USIS); Philip Worchel, Director of the Advanced Research Projects Agency's (ARPA) R&D Center in Thailand; and Lewis Lapham, Special Assistant to the Ambassador.

I also want to thank my Thai friends who indirectly contributed to this work and to a few, who shall go nameless, who read and discussed with me portions of the book.

Last, but by no means least, I wish to thank my wife, Barbara, who shared my experience in Thailand and who not only typed many drafts but patiently encouraged me to finish the book, shared the frustrations of working on it part-time, and explained my sometimes difficult behavior to the children. Without her there would be no book.

G. K. T.

TRIAL IN THAILAND

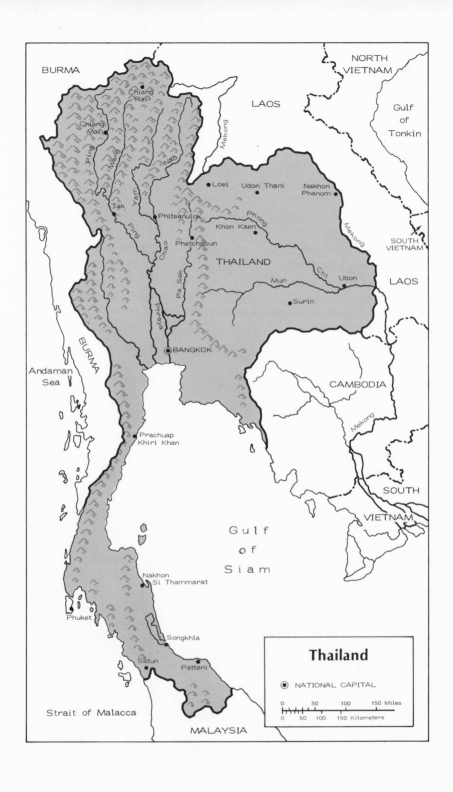

BURMA

Chiang Rai

Chiang Mai

LAOS

NORTH VIETNAM

Gulf of Tonkin

Mekong

Ping

Wang

Nan

Yom

Tak

Ping

Phitsanulok

Phetchabun

Loei

Udon Thani

Nakhon Phanom

Khon Kaen

Phong

THAILAND

Mekong

SOUTH VIETNAM

LAOS

Pa Sak

Chao

Mun

Chi

Ubon

Phraya

Surin

BANGKOK

Andaman Sea

BURMA

CAMBODIA

Mekong

Prachuap Khiri Khan

Gulf of Siam

SOUTH VIETNAM

Nakhon Si Thammarat

Phuket

Songkhla

Satun

Pattani

Strait of Malacca

MALAYSIA

Thailand

⊙ NATIONAL CAPITAL

0   50   100   150 Miles

0   50   100   150 Kilometers

Chapter 1

Thailand Today

Thailand today is known in the United States primarily by tourists and service-men who flit through the capital, Bangkok, for a glimpse of its colorful temples and picturesque canal scenes; they usually learn little of the country's history, government, geography, economic and social problems, and national character-istics, all of which have direct bearing on the insurgency and counterinsurgency efforts that this book explores. While it is true that the Indochina war attracted much attention on the part of the United States public and has been the subject of much research by scholars, Thailand still remains largely a mystery to most Americans, many of whom remember it best as a result of seeing the film *The King and I.*

As background for this book, a brief survey of the history, characteristics, and current problems of Thailand and its various regions will be useful. The survey includes a description of the regions where the insurgents operate, along with the methods and procedures within the Royal Thai Government (RTG) pertinent to an understanding of its counterinsurgency effort, and a synopsis of past and present relations between Thailand and the United States.

About the time of the American Revolution, the first Chakri King and founder of the present dynasty, who ruled as Rama I, was consolidating his power, establishing order after a Burmese invasion, and developing the new capital of Bangkok on the east bank of the Chao Phya River. During the two hundred years since then there have been nine kings, including the present one, His Majesty King Bhumibol Adulyadej (Rama IX), who ascended to the throne in 1946. This continuity reflects one of the main characteristics of Thailand, an inherent stability and conservatism. Despite coups and changes in government, it has been a stability which allowed for adjustments and permitted an amazing adaptation to changing times, especially during the period of modernization under Thailand's two great kings, Rama IV (1851–1868), better known in the West as King Mongkut, and Rama V (1868–1910), better known as Chulalong-korn, and again in the period of great change since World War II. This character-istic probably contributed to the fact that Thailand is one of the very few Asian nations that managed to survive the entire colonial period of the nineteenth century as free and independent—an important factor in its domestic affairs and in its international relationships.[1] Independence and stability have given the Thais confidence, but not to the extent of warping their very realistic assessment of most situations, especially in the international field. These characteristics have also mitigated some of the tensions that are felt and expressed in other more recently independent countries. But in the latter part of the twentieth century Thailand faces new problems of a rapidly changing world fraught with many dangers and unforeseen difficulties, which, even for the Thais, are a challenge.

THAILAND AND ITS REGIONS

Bangkok is a booming and bustling city of some 4 to 5 million people. It has retained some of the older Thai culture, but also has many modern features. In fact, there are almost two Thailands—Bangkok on one hand and on the other hand the seventy-two administrative provinces that make up the rest of the country. Even in the rural areas, however, and especially in some of the provincial cities, there have been considerable change and modernization, some good and some bad. Thailand always seems to move deliberately—in the Thai way, as the saying is—but it has been moving.

Comprising about 200,000 square miles, Thailand is slightly smaller than France and nearly twice as large as the State of Colorado. Although most of it is

1. Thailand's sovereignty was somewhat compromised by treaties with certain nations which gave them special legal and trade privileges. In the early twentieth century, Thailand negotiated the revocation of these privileges, partially at the expense of the cession of outlying areas to Britain and France.

fairly compact, it does extend south, past the Kra Isthmus, about 500 miles, thus making the longest north-south distance about 1,000 miles. The east-west distance across the main part of the country is nearly 500 miles but at the narrowest point on the Kra Isthmus only ten miles. In geographical terms there are six regions: the rich Central Plain of the Chao Phya River, the East and Southeast near Cambodia, the Northeast touching Laos, the North bordering Laos and Burma, the West Central with Burma on the west, and the South with Malaysia as a southern boundary. In overall importance the Central Plain, which includes Bangkok, is paramount, but for the purposes of this book, the Northeast, North, and South are the key regions because the insurgents are most active in at least portions of those areas.

The Northeast, sometimes referred to as the Korat Plateau, is actually a plain broken occasionally by undulating, forested hills, in particular the Phu Phan Range in the northeastern part of the Northeast. The hills are not jungle-clad but are in part heavily forested; their rise of from 2,000 to 3,000 feet is adequate to hide guerrillas as well as to conceal and protect the annual meetings of the Communist Party's Central Committee. The Mun River (pronounced Moon) and its tributaries provide the drainage for most of the region. The area has a wet season, but in the dry season it becomes nearly a desert. Chronic droughts have limited the much-needed rice crop and caused other hardships, and so far no solution to the water problem has been found. The harnessing of the Mekong River projected for later in this century is probably the only answer. The area has no significant natural resources. A few new crops such as corn, cotton, and kenaf (a variety of jute) are being raised and plans for an increase in cattle raising have been made, but rice remains the primary agricultural product.

The Northeast is composed of sixteen provinces and contains about one third of Thailand's 40 million people. Most of the population speak a dialect similar to Lao, but the people are very definitely Thai in their economic and political allegiance. There are some minority groups, however, and each group tends to be cohesive. Several hundred thousand Khmers live in the southern part of the Northeast along the Cambodian border as do fifty thousand or more Vietnamese, many of them refugees from the French Indochina war in the 1950s; other Vietnamese, earlier arrivals, are found in several of the provinces and provincial cities. There is also a scattering of Chinese merchants and some more or less assimilated smaller groups such as the Soh and Phu Thai; many of the analysts of insurgency believe that these latter groups are the most fertile ground for the communists.

Most of the Northeast has a frontier with Laos, the Mekong being the demarcation line except in the southeast corner where the river flows to the east and Laos and Thailand have a land border. But demarcations on the map and realities on the ground are two different things. Like boundaries throughout Southeast Asia, demarcated for the convenience of the colonial powers or by accident, the river is more a thoroughfare than a barrier; the same, we shall see, is true, *mutatis mutandis,* of the mountainous boundaries of the North, inhabited by people for whom mountains are the traditional habitat, the traversing of which is one's daily fare. All this makes nonsense of the notion of boundaries as traditionally conceived in the West.[2] Indeed, the Mekong provides easy transportation up and down many reaches as well as across; in many places there are shallow rapids and in the dry season much of the river is very shallow. People living on both sides, though in different countries, are culturally similar, are intermarried, and have carried on commerce for years. Rather than viewing the river as a boundary they see it and use it as an avenue of communication and commerce; it is a clear-cut border line only on the map.

The Northeast, partially because of its distance from Bangkok, its poverty, and its differences from the plains, has until recently been a neglected area. Bangkok seemed little interested except when trouble arose in the area or difficulties presented themselves in Laos or Cambodia. Until recently, high officials rarely visited the area, and officials posted there are generally unhappy and scheme to be assigned elsewhere. This situation has led to some dissatisfaction and occasional uprisings. The late Field Marshal and Prime Minister, Sarit Thanarat, began in the early 1960s to take an interest in the region and initiated plans to develop it. He even talked of establishing a regional "capital" in Khon Kaen. The rise of insurgency in parts of the area accelerated the plans and development activities. The presence of four major air bases with large U.S. components, as well as numerous smaller installations, has helped the economy, though not always in the most morally correct or culturally acceptable ways. While very serious problems remain, some progress has been made, though more slowly than in some other regions, and there is reason to hope for continuing improvement of the region.

In the North the terrain is much more difficult than that of the Northeast, but the area is, potentially and in fact, a richer region. Heavily forested mountains that range from 5,000 to 8,000 feet are largely inaccessible except on foot (or by helicopter if landing areas can be cleared). The mountain ranges run roughly north-south and are divided by four rivers: from west to east, the Ping, Wang, Yam, and Nan, which flow south and join to form the Chao Phya River. The soil and the rainfall are better than in the Northeast, but both regions are subject to the monsoons. Rice is grown, but the crop has not been enough to feed the region's population. Since World War II the growing of tobacco and fruit has been increased, and other diversifications are being tried. There are some phosphates, and other valuable mineral resources might well be found if the area could be carefully surveyed. Teak, though controlled by the govern-

---

2. See RM-5936-1-ARPA, *Boundary Concepts and Practices in Southeast Asia,* by R. Solomon, The Rand Corporation, Santa Monica, California.

ment, is an important resource of the area and of export for Thailand. Poppies are grown for opium by the hill tribes as their cash crop. The lack of an adequate transportation system in the generally rugged North has been an impediment to exploration and development, but efforts are being now made to expand the road system.

The borders are less well defined than in the Northeast, though a portion of the Chiang Rai province border with Laos is the Mekong. Most of the boundaries, both with Laos in the east and Burma on the north and west, are remote ridgelines, with the Salween River and a tributary providing a border between Tak province and Burma. Thailand has no common border with Red China but the northernmost tip of Thailand is only 70 miles from southern China as the crow flies. A road being built by the Chinese into Laos has been a source of worry to the Thais. (This road is discussed further in Chapter 3.)

The total population of the North's nine provinces is about 6 million. Chiang Mai, capital of a formerly independent princedom, is the key city and an increasingly popular tourist attraction. The North is populated overwhelmingly by ethnic Thais who live mostly in the valleys, but some 300,000 to 500,000 hill people, often referred to as hill tribes, live in the mountainous areas. The shortage of tillable land, which is bringing the region's diverse people closer together as the Thais move into the hills closer to the hill tribes, might lead to better relationships with them, but it could also increase friction, and in some cases has as the hill people are pushed out of their land and their form of agriculture.

The hill people are far from homogeneous. They include representatives from several of the basic ethnic groups inhabiting the great mountain range of South China and the borderlands from India to Vietnam. Some of them, especially the Meo, Aka, and Lisu, have migrated into Thailand only since the turn of the century. The word 'tribes' is somewhat misleading, since there are no strict tribal organizations as such; there are, however, clan relationships within linguistic and ethnic lines. Each village is a separate entity, with its own leadership and responsible to no one else except, theoretically, the local Thai government officials. Most of the mountain people are animists and have no written language. Among the several major groupings, the Karens are the most numerous, followed by the Meo, Yao, Lisu, Aka, and many other smaller groups. Most of the people are seminomadic because they practice dry rice farming, using the slash-and-burn or swidden method, which tends to exhaust the soil and force frequent moves to better land. This way of life leads to problems, since the Thais and the hill people obviously have entirely different concepts of land ownership. For example, the teak forests are government property, and thus, the cutting of a teak tree by anyone except a state forester is against the law, but the hill people do not understand this law. They view all the land as theirs. They also raise most of the poppies from which opium is produced—another source of difficulty with the Thai government which has declared poppy raising and opium transport illegal, though some Thais are involved in the drug traffic. U.S. pressure to halt the production and trade of opium has had only limited results.[3]

Thai policies toward the hill people have been largely characterized by neglect and indifference, but not persecution or calculated oppression as some people have charged. Some cases of local mistreatment and considerable misunderstanding cannot be denied. Since the hill people live in very inaccessible areas and are separated as well by deep cultural and linguistic differences and have very limited commercial contacts with the Thais, many have preferred to live their own lives and to be separate from the Thais. To bring these people into the Thai political and socioeconomic system would require considerable effort and money. The Thais have not made such an effort, and the government has not provided much in the way of communications, schools, or health facilities to the hill people. The Border Patrol Police (BPP) have, however, with support from the Royal Family and the United States, built a few schools, provided teachers, and undertaken some civic action programs for altruistic reasons, as well as to gain information. The Royal Family has also undertaken some pilot programs independent of the BPP in order to help the hill people, such as a rice bank and training in crop substitution. The Public Welfare Department has a few model areas where the hill people are encouraged to settle permanently and where schools, health facilities, and instruction in modern agricultural techniques are provided, but these efforts are small in relation to the number of the people and the magnitude of the problem. However, the hill people compose only a small minority of the population, and social and economic improvements for them are expensive on a per capita basis because of the nature of their home terrain and their widely scattered small villages. The problems of the hill peoples will attract our attention again later when we come to the insurgency in the North.

Although the South region is a single geographical area, for our purposes it is best divided into two sections, the Mid-South and Far South. The Mid-South, that part of Thailand from Prachuap Kiri Khan province in the north to Songkhla and Satun provinces in the south, is inhabited primarily by Thais who speak a southern dialect. For several hundred miles Burma and Thailand share the isthmus and the mountain ridges are the boundary.

Rice is the primary agricultural product, although the region is not self-sufficient in this commodity, and rubber is grown on both small and large plantations and is still an important commodity of the region, although the

3. See *Report of the United Nations Survey Team on the Economic and Social Needs of the Opium-Producing Areas in Thailand*, Bangkok, Thailand, January-February 1967, for a careful survey of the opium problem and the difficulties involved in finding a substitute cash crop.

Thais have not kept up with modern developments in raising the trees. Phuket, a charming island in the Andaman Sea, is the center of the tin industry. Fishing off both east and west coasts is important. In the past due to rich natural resources, the area was quite prosperous, but in the 1960s the declines in rubber and tin prices deeply affected the economy and help is needed to restore its viability.

For reasons not entirely clear, the region has had considerable disaffection and crime. Some left-wing members of Parliament in the 1940s later became leaders of the insurgency in the Mid-South. One former member of Parliament is allegedly in China. The crime rate is also high: Nakhon Si Thammarat province has one of the highest murder rates in Thailand. The recent economic decline, the basic rice shortage, and the feeling of being neglected by Bangkok have created a general uneasiness which probably contributes to the small but growing insurgency.

The Far South is composed of the four provinces bordering Malaysia—Narathiwat, Yala, Songkhla, and Satun—plus Pattani province, which is not contiguous. At one time Thailand extended its domain as far south as Malacca in Malaysia, but in a 1909 treaty with the British, the Thais gave up most of their Malay holdings and agreed to the present frontier. Nearly a million people inhabit the five provinces. The vast majority of these are Malays who speak a Malay dialect and believe in Islam; the Thai refer to them as Thai Muslims. In Satun, however, Thai is spoken. A few ethnic Thais live in the area, and a few thousand ethnic Thais have been deliberately moved in from the other regions of Thailand. A sizable Chinese community is spread throughout the Far South, especially in Haad Yai city and in the Betong district on the Songkhla-Malaysian border. This part of the South has traditionally been a rich area because of the many rubber plantations and tin mines; however, because it is even more dependent than the Mid-South on tin and rubber for income, declines in prices have caused severe economic difficulties in recent years, though the situation was somewhat better in 1973. Fishing, the other important source of income, has become more difficult and expensive as the coastal waters are increasingly fished-out and larger boats are needed to make extended trips out into the seas. Some efforts have been made to introduce palm oil and other income diversifications, but these efforts are moving very slowly.

The Royal Thai Government has followed a laissez-faire attitude toward the Muslim population and has been completely tolerant of the Islam faith. While this policy is commendable on many grounds, its net effect is that little has been done to improve the lot of the people of this region, leaving it far behind in schools, health facilities, roads, and other such social needs. There has been very little attempt at assimilation and almost no effort to involve the Thai Muslims in the Thai political apparatus. Thus, the Muslims are left out of local governments and are governed by people who seldom speak their language or share their faith. Consequently, Muslims in general have had little feeling that they are a part of Thailand. This has led to the development of a weakly organized separatist movement.

In the past few years this separatist movement has caused increasing concern to the Thais. Although it has been in existence for some time, its objectives are unclear, the leadership weak and split, and the organization feeble and small. The movement, in short, is more a "feeling" of irredentism than an organization. However, even in the earlier years, there had been occasional revolts, such as the one in Narathiwat province in 1948. There is a pretender to the old Sultanate of Pattani living across the border in Kelantan State in Malaysia, and at least one of the opposition parties in Malaysia is supporting the separatists clandestinely. The Malaysian Government publicly opposes the movement and has taken action against those found supporting it. However, separatist sentiment exacerbates the already delicate Thai-Malaysian relations, especially as these countries jointly try to deal with the communist insurgency problem on both sides of the border.

Most of the officials in the Far South are Thais, most of whom do not speak Malay and are not of the Muslim faith. The religious differences pose a real barrier, since Muslims are very strict about their beliefs and want their children to be good Muslims; they are not as tolerant as the Thais about intermarriage and prefer the Muslim schools (*panoks*) to the Thai government schools. Religion also generates other social barriers: e.g., the Muslim cannot eat the pig or even food cooked in a utensil that once cooked pork; thus the Far East's especially strong bond of sharing food is not easily formed. There is no real enmity or even strong animosity between the two groups, but the various social barriers keep them apart. Certainly some ill will does exist and could grow if the Thai Muslim feels increasingly neglected and sees his kinfolk doing much better in nearby Malaysia.

The Southern Coordination Center in Yala is an attempt to provide officials newly assigned to the South from other regions of Thailand with some information about the history, religion, culture, and language of this area. The government has also subsidized the religious schools in exchange for the teaching of Thai history and language and plans eventually to take them over. Some efforts have been made to recruit more Thai Muslims for the police, civil administration, and the Community Development program, but progress has been slow because the qualifying examination is given in Thai. Some of the Muslim leaders in Bangkok have also been employed to help with the problems. Despite all of these efforts, one cannot gloss over the very serious racial problems in the South for which no one has yet developed any real solution.

Like the Mid-South, the Far South has major problems with banditry and piracy. Just why extortion, holdups, and robberies are so numerous is not clear.

Partial causes could include the ethnic problems; border area difficulties such as smuggling; the apparently declining standard of living; the dependence on a cash economy; large amounts of gambling; the insurgents' need for money; or a combination of all of these. In 1969 the extortion claims became so high that bus companies were obliged to stop certain runs because they could not pay the demanded sums. Small rubber growers, having been terrorized, stopped production because of the danger. Extortion and terrorism were extended to the fishing industry and hampered its already precarious operation. During 1969 and 1970, the RTG, under pressure from the southern members of Parliament, the press, and key individuals in the South, launched a massive campaign against the bandits. It claimed hundreds arrested and a number killed. The action apparently improved the situation, but one doubts that banditry is permanently wiped out, because the root causes, never basically addressed, still exist.

The whole South, for reasons of its small size and population, its distance from Bangkok, and its racial makeup, probably rates lowest in the Thai regional priorities. The Southern Regional Development Committee seems not to have the drive or perhaps political power to get much increase in funds for the area. [4] Officials in the South feel they have been neglected and are not given the tools to work on the various problems confronting them. In the Mid-South the considerable expansion of insurgency southward adds to the already existing problems. Chin Peng and his Communist Terrorist Organization (CTO), although allegedly concerned with Malaysia, control border areas in the Far South and have increasingly extended their activities in the border provinces. Certainly the Thais could not put all regions in first priority, but this area is in great need of help. Possibly other countries, especially Commonwealth countries with Malaysian ties, might give assistance. Some people concerned with the region contend that the answer is greater assimilation of the Thai Muslims, but that is a very long-term effort which historically has been a hard road with no certainty of success. Furthermore, given the strength of feeling of minority groups today (and certain other factors discussed later) that approach does not seem timely. A better solution might be to allow the Thai Muslims to continue to be as they are but to provide modern facilities for them and allow them to hold responsible positions in the government, particularly at province and local levels. This option would also take time, patience, and understanding and has no real guarantee of success.

The East and Southeast area is relatively small and lightly inhabited by Thais and Khmers. It includes some lovely beaches and hills and may become an important producer of certain gems. In general, it is a quiet area, although one group of guerrillas does slip down into Prachin Buri province every so often from

4. The status of this committee has been unclear since the November 1971 coup.

their lair in the bordering hills of Korat and Buriram provinces. The U.S. uses the naval base of Sattahip and the air base of U-tapao, both of which are significant influences in the area. The rather long Cambodian border not very far from Bangkok and Thai anxiety over events in Cambodia lead the Thais to station quite a few troops and police in the area.

The West and West Central region is also small and thinly populated. A few guerrillas are sequestered there. They do not strike frequently; however, they are very efficient when they do, and this makes people in the neighboring areas somewhat uneasy. The region includes the famous beach resort of Hua Hin where the Royal Family spend the hot season, March to June. The western border with Burma is mountainous; the Karens inhabit the rugged and isolated terrain, but thus far have caused the RTG little trouble.

The alluvial plains of the Central region are the heartland of Thailand. Here the Chao Phya flows slowly toward the Gulf of Siam and helps water the almost unending rice paddies. Here live the central Thais who speak "pure" Thai, in contrast to the northeastern, northern, and southern Thai dialects. The region has been, and is, the richest in the country, and has generally been free from insurgent-instigated strife. One suspects, however, that the communists are not ignoring it, but at least they have so far apparently relied entirely on covert subversion. The Central region, which includes Bangkok and extends from the northern shores of the Gulf of Siam to the hills and mountains of the North, must remain prosperous and secure if Thailand is to survive as a viable nation.

DIVISIVE ELEMENTS

As the above survey of regions has made evident, divisive forces have been at work, on which the communist insurgency, a slowly growing cancer and itself a divisive element, has built and can continue to build. The minorities are certainly one element that the insurgents have already exploited considerably. In the North, for example, the communists, by publicizing the basic problems between the Thais and the hill people, have triggered a revolt among some of the tribal people in the mountainous areas. In the Far South, the separatist movement of the Malays could merge with the communists or be taken over by them; the process may, in fact, already have begun. The Khmers or Cambodians in the southern border areas of the Northeast adjoining communist-dominated parts of Cambodia are a potential source of trouble whenever anyone wishes to foment it. The Vietnamese, many with ties to North Vietnam, are also a separate, unassimilated, and, to a large extent, hostile minority, primarily in the Northeast. The Chinese, though probably better assimilated in Thailand than in most Southeast Asian countries and an important element not only in the country's financial and economic life but also in its politics, are spread throughout the country and could be troublesome if so inclined. Indeed, almost all the top leadership of the Communist Party of Thailand and the insurgency are believed to be of mixed Thai and Chinese blood. Others are ethnic Chinese born in or citizens of Thailand (Sino-Thais), though the actual numbers are very small.

Other factors, though perhaps not as divisive but certainly likely to create greater instability in traditional Thai society, should be mentioned. In 1972 and especially in 1973 and 1974 Thai university students for the first time in the modern era have become a much more activist, better organized group and are not afraid to confront the government on issues they deem important. By means of mass demonstrations, marches, and printed leaflets, the students have protested over such issues as the expulsion of some fellow students for criticizing the government, Japanese economic exploitation of Thailand, corruption in the government, and the lack óf democracy. They have not devoted much effort to foreign affairs, though the few radicals have stated that the Americans must leave Thailand. The students feel they are acting as representatives of the people, though how many they actually represent is certainly not clear. This increased student activity is likely to continue partially due to recent successes and partially because there seems to be a political vacuum to fill.

The laborers, especially those in Bangkok, though not well organized, have also taken on a more active posture and, in spite of legal limitations on strikes and unions, have gone on strike. After negotiations with the government, they have been successful in having most of their demands fulfilled. It is likely that as Thai industry grows, this group will become more important.

It is more difficult to ascertain what is going on in the provinces. In the few university towns the students have acted in concert with their fellow Bangkok students. Perhaps the most serious problem in the provinces is the increasing loss of land ownership by the peasants to often absentee landlords possessing large tracts of land. A landless rural population could cause serious problems and aggravate the difficulties caused by the increasing gap between rich and poor.

Today Thailand seems to be more in a state of flux than it has been for some time. Even in the military and civilian bureaucracy the younger officials are restive and searching for new solutions. Yet one gets the feeling that traditional Thai values are not collapsing overnight; the King, I believe, will support orderly evolutionary change as evidenced by a statement he made in an address to the Thai nation on October 14, 1973: "I ask that all people on all sides unite in support of the new Government that it may administer the nation effectively and quickly bring the situation to an orderly state, heading to tranquillity and progress for the country and all the Thai people."[5]

UNIFYING ELEMENTS

In spite of the factors just mentioned, one could say that, in general, Thailand as a whole in the 1970s appears reasonably stable and cohesive. All the regions,

5. Press Release No. 11/1973, October 16, 1973, Office of the Public Relations Attaché, The Royal Thai Embassy, Washington, D. C.

despite their differences, are bound together by various ties—some intangible, some tangible. The majority of the population in each region are ethnic Thais who, while speaking different dialects, consider themselves Thais and have a loyalty to the Thai nation. The King is almost universally accepted as the head of the state and is an impressive symbol of Thai unity. However, he is a constitutional monarch who has considerable influence but no legal power. [6] Rama IX and his beautiful Queen have traveled around the country often and consistently demonstrate their concern for their subjects' welfare and happiness. Although some of the leading politicians may not be recognized by many peasants in the regions, the King is known everywhere in Thailand. The monarchy plays an important unifying role, as it has over past years. Closely associated with the monarchy is Buddhism, the religion of the vast majority of Thais. It is a tolerant, compassionate religion and one that still binds people together as a way of looking at life and death, which also influences private and official acts and actions. In addition, the leadership role of the Buddhist monks in rural Thailand has served to enhance both progress and stability. A shared history is another unifier, though probably more for the educated than the uneducated. This includes the people's sufferings, the threats from outside powers, and the vicissitudes of war as well as pride in the achievements of the Thais in modernizing the government and the country and in the nation's international status.

The Royal Thai Government, while trying to strengthen traditional ties, has also tried to add new ones. One of the first attempts, early in the twentieth century, was to introduce a more effective system of countrywide government administration. Another, in the 1920s, was to build a railroad system which linked the major regions with Bangkok. Since World War II roads have been built, both major trunk lines to join the major parts of the country, and feeder roads to reach into the rural areas. The Thai Navigation Line provides a coastal water link from Bangkok to several southern ports. A domestic airline linking twenty or more Thai towns and cities now supplements the ground transportation system. Telephone, radio, and telegraph systems reach all provincial capitals and many other towns. These modern means of communication and transportation have encouraged greater travel, commerce, and industry throughout Thailand. The government has hopes that its improvements in governance, plus the physical efforts to bring the country together, will, along with the traditional cohesive factors, help Thailand to continue to develop as a viable modern nation, unified geographically, socially, and politically.

6. The term "constitutional monarch" is a somewhat misleading term but is the best one I can think of to describe the Thai King. The monarchy is constitutional in the sense of the British system, not as a carefully delineated monarchy described in a written constitution.

THAI POLITICAL STRUCTURE

Inasmuch as the insurgency avowedly seeks the overthrow of the Royal Thai Government, a brief look at the sources of strength and weakness within the political structure is in order. Furthermore, some understanding of the Thai political system will throw light on the course of the government's counter-insurgency effort and the relations of the United States with the Thais.

The continuity of the Chakri dynasty reflects the general stability of Thailand, but its role changed drastically after the 1932 revolution, which was carried out by young army officers and civil officials, many of whom had studied in Europe. Field Marshal Phibulsongram became the most powerful political figure, while Pridi Phanomyong was the intellectual leader. The coup group was dissatisfied and frustrated with the royal monopoly of power which, furthermore, was not being exercised efficiently. The world financial crisis at the time also affected Thailand and led to cuts in the military services, a move that made the army leadership somewhat restive. The spread of Western ideas among young educated people had also weakened the concept of monarchy. Unfortunately, King Rama VII's personality did not enhance the monarchy's image at this crucial time. On June 24, 1932, troops seized key personalities and positions in Bangkok, and the coup leaders declared the absolute monarchy at an end. King Rama agreed to rule under a constitution and all was settled in a few days. A permanent constitution, proclaimed on December 10, 1932, established a quasi-parliamentary system. Half of the Parliament was appointed by the government, since many of those involved felt the country was not ready for full democracy. The prestige of the monarch declined and rule by elements of the coup group continued with Field Marshal Phibulsongram the dominant figure a large part of the time. He was Prime Minister from 1938 to 1944 and again from 1948 to 1957. A number of coups and attempted coups occurred after 1932, engendered by men almost always within the system. Thus, the 1932 revolution, although a step forward toward constitutional government, left a legacy of uncertain methods for the transfer of political power, but most of the changes have been accomplished with little or no bloodshed.

The Thais have evolved a way of handling their internal politics that is unclear and confusing to most outside observers. Politics is essentially conducted within the inner circles of the government or the Thai "Establishment," not in outside political parties or organizations. Decisions are made by the government, but there is a tendency for actions and policies to evolve, rather than to be the result of specific and datable decisions. Even when precise decisions are made, implementation sometimes modifies them or they are carried out gradually. This is due to such factors as the Thai desire to arrive at a consensus, to avoid public differences between conflicting personalities and groups and consequent loss of face for those on the losing side, and to go slowly on complex, difficult, and troublesome issues. The Thais have demonstrated that, although the political equilibrium may seem to be fragile, they are quite capable of manipulating and maintaining it during periods of stress, both domestic and international.

From 1968 to 1971, the formal structure of Thailand's government was prescribed in the new Constitution that had been worked on for years and was finally promulgated in 1968. It continued the constitutional monarchy, headed by His Majesty King Bhumibol Adulyadej (Rama IX), and most of the character-istics of the preceding government. But it also introduced limited parliamentary and democratic government by providing for certain municipal elections, some elected officials, and a national Parliament that was composed of two houses, the Senate, the majority of whose members were appointed by the government, and the Assembly, whose members were elected. The Senate was appointed in 1968. A large majority of the senators were military officers and most of the rest were civilian officials of the government who thus performed both legislative and executive functions. The makeup of the Senate, with its heavy weighting in favor of the government, tended to give the government great power in the legislature and mitigated against any unwanted change.

The Thais never attempted to conceal this fact and indeed argued strongly that democracy is a fragile form of government which must grow slowly. The argument was entirely in keeping with the Thai tradition of stability and conservatism with gradual change to meet domestic and international demands and situations. The lower house, as an elective body, represented the greater step toward democracy. Representatives were elected in all the provinces, each of which had at least one representative and an additional one permitted for every 150,000 people in the province. In the first election held in February, 1969, about a third of the eligible voters came to the polls. United Thai People's Party (the government party) elected seventy-five assemblymen, a slim plurality. However, of the seventy-two independents elected, many supported the govern-ment and seemed especially inclined to Field Marshal Praphas, the Deputy Prime Minister. The opposition (the Democratic Party headed by former Prime Minis-ter Seni Pramoj) won fifty-seven out of the total and swept the Bangkok-Thonburi area where the party had already won the earlier municipal election. The remaining fifteen assemblymen, of the total of two hundred and nineteen in the lower house, were in very small, almost one-man parties. However, the real leadership during the Constitutional period, 1968-1971, and during the difficult years of 1971–1973, remained in the hands of the Thai military.

Commentators may easily go to one or the other extreme of believing that the government is on the verge of complete overthrow or that it is so firm and solid that no changes will occur. The best estimate, however, seems to be that neither extreme is likely to occur. However, some changes in the next few years are inevitable, which the Thais may, in their usual fashion, be able to work out quietly within the power structure, though this is not certain. The November, 1971, "coup," which kept the governing group in power but dissolved the Parliament, and the 1972 return to partial constitutional government would seem to confirm this view. An official announcement explained the December, 1972, shift as follows:

"On Friday 15th December 1972, Thailand's interim constitution was announced, ending the thirteen-month old National Executive Council. Two hundred and ninety-nine persons were appointed as members of the National Legislature. Field Marshal Thanom Kittikachorn and Field Marshal Praphas Charusathira were appointed Prime Minister and Deputy Prime Minister respectively. The ministers and deputy ministers of the 13 ministries were named. The new National Legislative Assembly convened its first session on December 18.

"The 14-point policy statement of the government was made on December 22, the main goal of which is to help speed up national affairs.

"Premier Thanom Kittikachorn said that the permanent Constitution of Thailand will be promulgated within three years from December 15, 1975. The interim constitution fixes the term of the 299 members of the National Assembly to three years each."[7]

In spite of these moves toward a more democratic government, the students in October, 1973, precipitated the overthrow of the Thanom-Praphas regime by massive demonstrations in Bangkok. These led to violence and probably over a hundred deaths and much destruction of property. While the students provided the environment, I believe that two men saw it as an opportunity for a needed change in the government, under which young military officers and bureaucrats, as well as the students, had become very restive and dissatisfied. One of these men, His Majesty King Bhumibol Adulyadej, seems to have quietly seized the chance to help make the change in government, and it is widely known that he disliked Field Marshal Praphas greatly. He provided shelter, guidance, and the prestige of his position for the students during their demonstrations. The other man, General Kris Sivara, who only weeks before was made Commander-in-Chief of the Royal Thai Army, seized the opportunity to become the number one military man in the country. Under him the army did not support the Thanom-Praphas regime, nor did it play an active role against the students, save for a few units under Thanom's son, Colonel Narong. This "neutrality" undercut the power base of the regime. Fear for themselves and their families, plus the loss of military support, led Thanom and Praphas to resign from the government and to flee the country in mid-October, 1973. The King immediately appointed a respected judge, Sanya Dharmasakti, as Prime Minister, the first civilian to hold this position in many years. The new cabinet is mostly civilian officials except

7. *Selected News from Home,* No. 146, Dec. 8, 1972–Jan. 25, 1973, The Royal Thai Embassy, Washington, D. C. (Office of the Public Relations Attaché).

for Air Chief Marshal Dawee Chullasyapa as Minister of Defense and Lieutenant General Sawaeng Senanarong as the Minister Attached to the Prime Minister's Office (similar to the Minister Without Portfolio in the British Government). General Kris refused a cabinet position but was appointed Director to Restore Peace and Order, which puts him in charge of all the military and police forces in the country. The new government promised a constitution in six months and more honest and democratic rule.

Most Thais were shocked at the violence which has usually been absent from Thai coups in the past and were surprised at the easy toppling of the military regime. The student leaders, some of whom were radical but most of whom were quite moderate, admitted they had never dreamed of such success, an admission which suggests that the factors noted above may indeed have played a key role. However, the new government is not taking the students' role and potential political power lightly, as they have assigned General Saiyud Kerdphol to serve as the liaison between the students and the government. As of this writing, it is not clear how great a change this coup will turn out to have caused. This depends on the quality and unity of the civilian leadership, the willingness of General Kris and the Royal Thai Army to accept this leadership, and on the general health of Thailand (economic and social) in the months ahead. However, as one observer has written, "The Thai Establishment is alive and well and working with the new government."[8] This does seem to be the case and would seem to indicate that few, if any, revolutionary changes are in store. The Thais will probably continue their evolutionary tradition of change as they strive for a better government and nation. In addressing the new Prime Minister and his cabinet, His Majesty the King said, "Things already created must be improved upon; those destroyed must be repaired. Development must be carried out to make people thoughtful and honest. Aberrations during recent events must be rectified."[9]

A feature of Thai governmental practice which contributed during the Thanom-Praphas regime to stability by concentrating power among a relative few is double-hatting—or even multi-hatting. The former Prime Minister, Field Marshal Thanom Kittikachorn, was Defense Minister, Supreme Commander of the Armed Forces, and also held many other positions. The Minister of the Interior, Field Marshal Praphas Charusathira, was also Deputy Prime Minister, Commander-in-Chief of the Army, Director of the Communist Suppression Operations Command (CSOC) and held a host of other positions and committee chairmanships. Many other examples could be cited from both the lower and the top ranks of officialdom. The following story illustrates the problems that this

8. H. D. S. Greenway, *The Washington Post,* October 21, 1973, p. K1.
9. Press Release No. 11/1973, October 16, 1973, Office of the Public Relations Attaché, The Royal Thai Embassy, Washington, D. C.

procedure can create and also how seriously the Thai can wear each hat. A colonel, serving in one of the departments of the Ministry of Interior was recommended by his division chief for promotion to general. The action was approved by the department head and by the then Minister of Interior (Praphas) who forwarded it to the then Commander-in-Chief of the Army (also Praphas). Acting as Commander-in-Chief of the Army, he turned down what he had approved as Minister of Interior. What seems initially baffling is not really so if one considers that the man tries to act the role needed for each hat. In this case, the colonel, from the point of view of the Minister of Interior, deserved promotion, but from the viewpoint of the Commander-in-Chief, which includes the overall needs of the army and the merits of all officers, this promotion did not seem warranted.

The practice of multi-hatting, usually confusing to Westerners, serves several purposes. By this means the leaders of the political factions can keep a finger on the pulse of government agencies and provide, at least in the upper levels, some degree of coordination. And the representation of one faction in an agency, which may seem to be dominated by another faction, supplies a form of check and balance. The practice is in fact a key element in the delicate balance of power within the government—and also a reason why organizational charts of command and control bear little relation to reality. While this practice was well-known in the Thanom-Praphas regime, it is not clear whether it will be continued in the new civilian government, though one suspects it may in a modified form.

What might appear to be instability—the steps forward and backward to and from constitutionality usually accomplished by a coup d'état—is not necessarily that at all. As Fred Riggs has written, "The successive coups d'etat by which ruling circles are modified and replaced have become as much a constitutional formula for changing elites as the periodic electoral battles which take place in the United States, or the cabinet crises of France during the Third and Fourth Republics. The succession of constitutional charters in the Thai polity have, correspondingly, scarcely more systemic significance than a change of party in England—perhaps less. The effective constitutional structure, which is unwritten, appears to have taken shape as a relatively stable pattern."[10]

That ideology enters very little into Thai politics should be well noted. The ruling elite, composed primarily of military officers and a few civilian officials, generally agrees on the broad political approaches and policies. Even the opposition Democratic Party usually has not based its opposition on ideology but rather on grounds of alleged government corruption, inefficiency, ineptitude, and on personalities. The left-wing parties are very small, and even they have

10. *Thailand, The Modernization of a Bureaucratic Polity*, by Fred Riggs. East-West Center Press, 1966.

rather vague platforms. In politics, as in most other matters in Thai society, it is the individual that is important. Position is respected, especially when combined with age, but the real power does not always show itself obviously. Organizational diagrams, flow charts of power and responsibility, and other such modern management tools are not, therefore, very meaningful. An individual can through personality, power, and wealth build and often maintain a personal following. Since policy and ideology are not involved in these allegiances, however, men can rather easily switch from one group to another if personal differences arise. Groupings centered around personalities can also by changing allegiance en masse sometimes bring about changes in the power structure, often by a show of force or deployment of force, but actual violence is seldom used.

THAI FOREIGN POLICY

Since the 1950s Thai foreign policy has diverted from its traditional effort of balancing various powers against one another. Thailand, for a long time, prided itself on its ability to maintain its independence and to avoid being caught on the losing side, whether in diplomatic or war situations. The keen sensitivity to power shifts or changes in the policies of the major powers, which has seemed a special talent of the Thais, has helped them in this regard. Prior to World War II, the government saw the rise of Japan as the major Asian power and so the country drew close to Japan, especially in trade, yet did not bind itself too closely and thus kept its options open. This policy, which led to the accommodation with Japan in 1942, paid off in the sense that Thailand survived in better condition under the Japanese than other peoples in the area. But fairly early in the war the Thais saw that the Allies might win and made appropriate moves. These included the organization of the Free Thai movement, and later the appointment of a pro-Western Prime Minister and offers of settlement of territorial claims; all this prepared the way for a relatively painless settlement with the Allies at the end of the war.

Thai foreign policy since World War II has generally been based on the idea of friendship with the West, and especially with the United States. Within this general framework, however, there have been frictions and uneasiness over the commitment to the United States. From 1946 to 1948 Thailand tended to support, morally and with some materiel, nationalistic movements in Indochina that were also inclined toward communism, as she favored the development of free Asian nations. The United States generally pursued a similar policy while trying to help develop a friendly and non-communist China. By 1949, however, the communist nature of the movements in Indochina and the collapse of Chiang Kai-chek's regime and its flight to Taiwan began to arouse Thai fears and to create uneasiness in the United States. The outbreak of communist insurgent movements in several Asian countries, especially in Malaya in 1948, seemed further warning to the Thai government of the hostile intentions of the communists. It also seemed that Thailand was surrounded by unfriendly and threatening forces; that the Thais turned increasingly to the United States for assistance and support is not surprising. In late 1950 military and economic aid agreements were signed with the United States, both accelerated by the outbreak of the Korean War earlier that year. Thailand sent troops and other military personnel to the United Nations Command in Korea and still has an infantry company there. In 1954 Thailand was an enthusiastic supporter of the Manila Pact and the subsequent Southeast Asia Treaty Organization (SEATO).

Thailand quite naturally has been particularly concerned about happenings in the border areas, and in 1958 was so disturbed when Cambodia accorded *de jure* recognition to Red China that the government broke relations with Prince Narodom Sihanouk. Relations had never been close with the Cambodians as the expanding Thais, over the centuries, helped to push the Khmers into a smaller and smaller area. When the French took over Indochina in the late nineteenth century, they regained some of the former Cambodian land and thus antagonized the Thais. World War II gave the Thais an opportunity, which they seized, to regain some of the border provinces, but they had to give them up after the end of the war. The strong and bitter Thai reaction to the loss of the temple Preah Viharn to Cambodia through a World Court decision in 1961 showed the depth of feeling about the border issue. That a well-known United States lawyer pleaded the Cambodian case did not help Thai-American relations, but common interests at the time kept the reaction under control. While the Thais and Cambodians are now faced with a common communist threat, the Cambodians, though desperately needing help, are still a little suspicious of Thai support.

The deteriorating situation in Laos in 1959–1961 again worried the Thais, and they tried to get SEATO to take action under its umbrella clause, which included Laos. SEATO revealed its basic weakness, lack of unanimity on such issues, and failed to act. The limited United States action in Laos did little to reassure the Thais. Due to this early failure (at least from the Thai point of view) of SEATO, Thailand was the first nation to have some doubt about the viability and effectiveness of that organization. This led to the 1962 communiqué issued by the U.S. Secretary of State, Dean Rusk, and the Thai Minister of Foreign Affairs, Thanat Khoman, in which the United States explicitly stated that it considered its obligation to Thailand to be unilateral in certain situations. This meant that the United States could, essentially without the concurrence of other SEATO members, come to the assistance of Thailand.

As the United States became more directly involved in the Vietnamese war, so did the Thais. In early 1964 the United States helped expand and build new Thai air bases which could be used if necessary by American aircraft operating over Vietnam. Between 1965 and 1968, and 1971 and 1973, U.S. planes have used these bases to bomb targets in Indochina and otherwise support United States forces in Vietnam. At one time the Thais had a full infantry division, support troops, and air and naval personnel in Vietnam, but all these forces have now been withdrawn. These units also had heavy United States financial support. Direct U.S. military assistance also increased in the mid-1960s to help the Thais improve their military forces, and economic aid also increased to help develop the country and blunt the incipient insurgency in the Northeast. All of this was helpful to Thailand, but also bound it closer to and made it more dependent upon the United States.

Some of the Thais have always been skeptical about the reliability of the American commitment to them. And, as the relationship with the United States grew closer, others became increasingly uneasy over what seemed to be a radical break with Thai tradition—that of not becoming too closely involved with one great power at the expense of freedom of action and the ability to shift position and policy as external situation changed. In addition, while many Thais welcome American economic aid, both civil and military, which has contributed significantly to Thai prosperity, a few have grown concerned about the degree of the American influence on the Thai economy. A more numerous group, however, worry about the cultural and social changes being accelerated by the Americans.

The most obvious and sharpest problem has been connected with the presence of large numbers of American military personnel stationed in Thailand—at one time nearly 50,000. The Thais on no account can be considered prudish, but Thai culture frowns on public exhibition of affection between the sexes. Americans, on the other hand, love to walk down the street with their dates, holding hands or arm-in-arm, but this is "not done" in Thailand. While the sex problem is obvious in the bars and brothels, the Thais are also concerned about the cultural differences in other areas. To the Thais, Americans seem not to respect age as much as the Thais do, appear at times crassly materialistic, and value family and religion much less highly than the Thais do. Thus, the Thais have been caught in a dilemma: they have wished to avoid or at least control the impact of the Americans on Thailand, yet they have wanted the Americans to stay and help provide security from outside threats as well as continuing financial assistance.

Another factor causing concern was the domestic opposition in the United States to the Vietnam war, as manifested during the Johnson administration and the first Nixon administration. In Congress and in the press, attacks were made on the war and on those who supported it inside and outside the United States. The Thais, who felt they had been loyal allies to the point of abandoning their traditional middle of the road policy, were angered and hurt by the attacks. They felt that those who had done nothing to help the United States were rewarded, while they, who had tried to help the United States, were being attacked and vilified. It is true that the Thais were well paid for their help, but they respond by saying that they were supplying the men while the United States was only providing the money.

Given the basic Thai ambivalence over the American presence, their continuing anxiety about the reliability of the U.S. commitment to them, and their concern that the U.S. might withdraw completely from Southeast Asia, the Thais seem to be going through a slow but steady reappraisal of their own foreign policy.

Congressional opposition to any U.S. military activities in Southeast Asia, which forced the President to stop all operations in Cambodia in August, 1973, has reinforced this trend. As early as 1969 the then Foreign Minister, Thanat Khoman, began to talk about a gradual rapprochement with Peking and the need for a more flexible foreign policy. While the Thai military leaders did not support Thanat publicly, neither did they silence him as they easily could have done until their 1971 coup, when they closed the door on him and, for the moment, his search for accommodation with Peking. Furthermore, it is reasonably certain that at least a few of them were quietly establishing, or perhaps even strengthening, contacts with the Chinese. In 1974 there are increased contacts and talks between Peking and Bangkok. There has been also more talk of closer commercial relations with the Soviet bloc in Europe. The Brezhnev proposal in 1970 for a Soviet-led pact in Southeast Asia, while drawing little or no support from the Thais or other Southeast Asia countries, was a recognition of the growing ferment and anxiety in the area. While Henry Kissinger's discussions with the Red Chinese in 1971 and Nixon's visit to Peking in early 1972 reinforced the Thai search for greater freedom in their foreign relations, Nixon's firmness in the Paris peace negotiations and continued bombing and mining of North Vietnam tended to reassure the Thais about the firmness of purpose of the U.S. in the area. The U.S. air buildup in Thailand in late 1972 and the year-end bombing against North Vietnam were reassuring to the Thais, but present U.S. policy is unclear to them and this strengthens their search for their own future policies.

The Thais have responded by trying to develop a policy with more options but without cutting their close links with the U.S. These efforts have been intensified as a result of the peace in Indochina. They have established trade relations with several Eastern European nations, have had somewhat more cordial dealings with the Soviets, and have begun to improve their relations with the Chinese. In all cases, especially the latter, they are proceeding cautiously. They sent their own table tennis team, which included at least one negotiator, to China in the summer of 1972 and have since pressed on with closer commercial and cultural ties. The Thais hope that the Chinese will cease support of the insurgency in Thailand but are by no means certain this will happen. This has not occurred as yet, though Chinese propaganda broadcasts on behalf of the insurgent cause have been reduced. In early 1973 the Thai Deputy Foreign Minister, General Chartchai Choonhavan, said, "China is a great wall, we should not hurry and run smack into it. We should walk cautiously toward it."[11] He also reflected the slowly changing Thai policy when he said that Thailand is prepared to have friendly relations with North Vietnam after a peace settlement and indeed seeks "friendly relations with all countries without hostile designs against Thailand."

At the same time the Thais are turning to regional cooperation as a source of support, often psychological, and a forum for discussion of problems of common interest to Southeast Asian countries. The most active organization in 1973 was the ASEAN, Association of Southeast Asian Nations, composed of Thailand, Indonesia, the Philippines, Malaysia, and Singapore. In this forum Malaysia has been pressing for neutrality for the area with a guarantee by the Soviet Union, China, and the United States. The Thais have supported this position in the ASEAN declaration of Kuala Lumpur in late 1972, but without great enthusiasm.

In this fast-changing world the Thais are debating their future policy without yet showing clearly what direction it will take, except that it will be more flexible and not tied as much to the U.S. The Thanom government permitted the 1972 U.S. air build-up on Thai bases, allowed the Americans in early 1973 to establish a new command, the U.S. Support and Advisory Group (USSAG) in Nakhon Phanom, to replace MACV and 7th Air Force Headquarters in Saigon, and negotiated a reduction of U.S. forces in Thailand during 1973. All might have continued for a few more years on this congenial track had a regrettable incident not turned Thai-American relations almost upside down, giving vent to the frustrations of many Thais who resented one aspect or another of their government's links with the United States. In brief, the U.S. Central Intelligence Agency (CIA), always a good scapegoat and this time grievously at fault, was found to have intervened in Thai internal matters in contradiction to every principle of American counterinsurgency policy in Thailand. The incident, a faked letter from the Communist Terrorists to the Royal Thai Government, which is discussed in Chapter 6, was closely tied to our counterinsurgency support effort, but its repercussions spread into every area of Thai-American relations and thus raised the question of whether the new government would be able to prevent a very rapid disintegration of its old foreign policy.

At the time of this writing, it is unclear how far public pressures will force the hand of the Sanya government (or that of his successors); however, a late January, 1974, report from Bangkok suggests that the Thai students are becom-

11. Press Release No. 2/1973, Office of The Public Relations Attaché, The Royal Thai Embassy, Washington, D. C.

ing increasingly anti-American and are protesting that the U.S. Mission in Bangkok is violating Thailand's sovereignty. Besides the American relationship problem, the present Thai government faces many of the dilemmas of its predecessor: How real is détente? Will the U.S. preserve some presence in Southeast Asia, and if so, how can the nations in the region develop some common front to reinforce their individual stances? Will the Chinese slow the insurgency or keep it going, and how will the Soviets react? How will Hanoi behave and will it unite all of Indochina, thus posing quite a sizable neighboring power? There are no easy answers, and the Thais will undoubtedly take time in arriving at answers and indeed may avoid some of these questions purposely as they have similar ones in the past. The Thais are going through an awkward period as they try to assess the world situation as it affects Southeast Asia and themselves.

Chapter 2

Communism in Thailand

Communist interest and activity in Thailand began in the early 1920s. This was a result of decisions made by the Russian communists soon after their successful revolution of November, 1917. They had initially hoped and believed that the European proletariat would rise, even during the war, and throw out their capitalist governments. When this did not happen, the Russians began to look to Asia for support in maintaining the revolutionary momentum. Lenin's evolving theory held that Asia, the pawn of the European imperialists, was a major reservoir of manpower and other vital resources. If these resources could be removed by revolution, Lenin argued, then the European imperialist powers would fall more easily. There was, however, a serious dilemma for the communists in the situation in Asia: the anticolonial movements. Lenin rightly saw that these movements were the most potent for insurrection, but in this case they were not composed of workers but mainly led by the small middle class. Lenin noted also that Asia literally had no proletariat in his terms, but he saw the peasants as the mass base for his efforts. However, the peasants were not then revolutionary, and developing a revolutionary spirit took time. Thus, the problems were: should the communists join the nationalist anticolonial movement and, if so, how? Or, if not, how could the masses be organized to lead their own communist revolution?

The decision, not too clearly made, was to maintain and develop communist unity within the anticolonial movement. The communists would support the first step, independence, retain their organization, and try to take the leadership in the new nation so that the next revolutionary step to socialism could be assured. Some of the leaders feared that the communists could not gain the leadership and would be lost in the nationalist movements, and this tended to happen except in the case of China and Vietnam. At the Fourth Comintern Congress in 1922 the idea of Asian revolution was fully advanced, so as to undermine the European powers, and a manifesto, calling on the workers and oppressed nations to arise, was issued—an attempt to combine the national and communist approach. Borodin was sent to be an advisor to Sun Yat-sen and the Far East Bureau of the Comintern was established in Shanghai. After a few years during which the European proletariat still failed to rise, and the Asian revolution made very slow progress (and indeed experienced setbacks), Stalin announced the theory and policy that socialism was to be developed in one country first.[1] This decision directed Soviet energies and leadership inward and meant considerably less attention for Asia. By the end of the 1920s, the outside efforts of the Russians were therefore reduced but by no means abandoned. In spite of the lessened Soviet interest, various communist organizations concerned with Asia and Southeast Asia continued their activities. Thailand, although not at all first priority, was not overlooked by the communists even in those early years.

ORIGINS OF THE THAI COMMUNIST PARTY

The beginnings of communist activity in Thailand are somewhat obscure, and indeed, the first few decades can only be very sketchily described. The history of the Thai Communist Party is even less well known. The first initiatives emanated from the Far East Bureau in Shanghai; apparently, one year after its founding, the Bureau dispatched six members of the Chinese Communist Party to Thailand, with rather general instructions to lay the basis for a party among the Chinese in Thailand. We know very little about the activities of these six Chinese—or if, in fact, they were really sent, but in 1927 the Thai did arrest one Chinese who was accused of being a communist agent and of trying to organize a

---

1. ChiangKai-shek's break with the communists in 1927 and his assumption of power indicated a failure of the Soviet approach in China, at least for the time being.

Communist Party. In 1925 it was reported that Ho Chi Minh sent a group of Vietnamese from his Vietnam Revolutionary League, headquartered in Canton, to work among the Vietnamese living in Thailand's Northeast. Again, we know little about this visit. The immediate results were obscure, except that the Vietnamese generally remained loyal to their ancestry and proved to be fertile ground for communist appeals. Ho Chi Minh himself was alleged to have lived in Thailand during the 1928–1930 period and, if so, this undoubtedly would have strengthened his hold on the Vietnamese living there.

Significantly, from the days of their earliest efforts in Thailand, the communists apparently concentrated on the Chinese and, to a lesser extent, the Vietnamese minorities. Whether this was because the Thais seemed so indifferent to communism or because the Chinese were such an obvious and easy group to reach is not clear. Certainly the large Chinese minority, not always well treated in Thailand and in many ways loyal to China, did seem to offer a logical and receptive target. However, even a large minority was unlikely to dominate a proud and nationalistic Thailand and could only serve as a cadre and a first step to a Thai party. The effort directed toward the Vietnamese seems to have been the by-product of fate: there were a few thousand Vietnamese in Thailand and one of the great Asian communist leaders, Ho Chi Minh, was a Vietnamese. The communists had long evidenced a special interest in minorities, but there is little evidence that they were active among the other Thailand minorities, such as the Khmers or tribal peoples in those early days. It would appear that, since the Soviets were concerned primarily with China, the overseas Chinese were the logical group to use as a basis for many of the communist movements in Asia. Additionally, the overseas Chinese minorities had been susceptible to being organized by Chinese from China because of obvious ties, and this may have given them greater feelings of security in alien lands. Secret societies were an honored tradition among the Chinese for centuries, and so the clandestine nature of communist activity, almost always illegal in Thailand and the colonies of Southeast Asia, was for the Chinese a natural form of activity and organization. Given their characteristics of being hard workers and great organizers, plus their minority status which they sought to improve, they appeared to be good material for a revolutionary movement. However, in Thailand this association of communism with the Chinese was probably a hindrance rather than an asset to the movement because of the long-standing Thai suspicion of the Chinese and legislation against them.

As noted earlier, the origins of the Thai Communist Party and even its proper name are very unclear. Initially, Thailand seems to have come under the direct responsibility of the Far East Bureau but was soon transferred to Singapore when the South Seas General Labor Union was created there in 1926. Reportedly, a Siam branch, sometimes referred to as a party, was included in the

Singapore organization as early as 1927. Whether the Chinese agent arrested in 1927 came from Singapore or China is not known. In 1928 the name of the Union was changed to the South Seas Communist Party. Its goal was to spread communism among the overseas Chinese in Southeast Asia, thus seeming to confirm the Chinese approach in Southeast Asia. Around 1930 a Malayan Communist Party was formed. It apparently took some responsibility for Siam through a special office or committee, though the relationship with Siam seems to have been intermittent and vague. The reason that Siam, larger than Malaya, was put under the Malayan Party seems again to underline the Chinese approach—i.e., the Chinese minority in Malaya was almost the size of the Malay population, while the Chinese population in Thailand was perhaps a tenth of the total. Another reason may have been a desire to appeal, in a quite distant future, to the large group of Malays and some Chinese living in southern Thailand. In any case, a separate Thai Communist Party probably did not exist in the 1920s, and Thailand, not then considered fertile ground, thus came under the various changing communist agencies for Southeast Asia.

In 1931 the Chinese Communist Party Siam was reportedly formed along with the Youth League of Siam. Based in Thailand, this organization apparently took over responsibility for Thailand from the Communist Party of Malaya, and thus organized communist activities along what would become nationalist lines. That the first formal party in Thailand was called the Chinese Communist Party indicated the continuing heavy emphasis on the ethnic basis for communism. At the time of the 1932 revolution in Thailand, this shadowy Chinese-dominated party claimed partial credit for what was purely a Thai coup; in fact, the party played no role. It is interesting to note that in its claims it referred to itself as the Communist Party of Siam, not Chinese Communist Party of Siam.[2]

During 1933, the Royal Thai Government, perhaps uneasy over the excessive claims of the communists, passed the first anti-communist law, but did not strictly enforce it. The World Communist Youth League claimed that it had members in Northeast Thailand, and in 1936 the communists, many of them Vietnamese, paraded openly in Khon Kaen province; some clashes with the police resulted. However, most of the so-called communist groupings were very small and not well organized, and enjoyed little popular support. Sometimes tying themselves to local grievances, particularly those of the Northeast area, the communists tried to parade as leaders of the people and defenders of the oppressed. Actually, the groups were small and not very important in the overall dissident movement, which itself was very loosely organized and poorly led. Even in Bangkok, a main target area, the communists had little success. In 1938 the Royal Thai Government was strongly nationalistic and took measures against

2. There is some confusion among scholars as to whether there ever were two Communist Parties in Thailand.

the Chinese, thus making the communist job even more difficult. By the beginning of World War II, the communists had made very little progress in Thailand either ideologically or organizationally. For the most part, the Thais were simply not interested, and what the communists had to say had little or no meaning for them. Even the Chinese in Thailand seemed at that time to show very limited interest, as the numbers involved were only in the hundreds. No leader worth mentioning emerged and the whole movement seemed insignificant.

During World War II the Royal Thai Government and most of the people accepted the fact of Japanese dominance. However, some Thais formed an anti-Japanese movement, mainly in the Northeast; the movement was also supported by the Thai Minister in Washington, who called it the Free Thai Movement. It lacked the driving force of other anti-Japanese movements in Southeast Asia, namely the desire for national independence, since Thailand had been free for centuries and was, in the eyes of the belligerents, a national state. Nevertheless, the communists tried to take advantage of the situation in Thailand as they did elsewhere in Southeast Asia. In 1942 the first Congress of the Communist Party of Thailand was held. The party was declared to be open to all Thai citizens, but the Thais did not show much interest in joining and the members were mainly Chinese, with perhaps a few Vietnamese. Some members of the party worked with the Free Thai Movement and thus could claim participation in the anti-Japanese movement of the Thais after the war. However, very little was done by the Free Thais during the war, and there was no real communist-led nationalist movement as there was in Vietnam, Malaya, and Indonesia. But it is interesting to note that some the the present-day insurgent camps are geographically based on former Free Thai strongholds.

COMMUNIST ACTIVITIES AFTER WORLD WAR II

After the war, Thailand successfully negotiated a peace with the Allies without any penalties, except for the surrender of land seized during the war. In 1946, however, as the price for Soviet agreement to its entry into the United Nations, Thailand was obliged to abolish its anti-communist laws. This permitted the party to operate openly insofar as it chose to do so and to participate in politics. It published a newspaper called *Masses Weekly* and issued numerous leaflets. A communist member of Parliament, Prasert Sapsunthon, allegedly the Secretary General of the party, claimed a membership of 50,000. This was obviously nonsense; the party then at best had less than 1,000 members. The ideas and success of Mao did have some appeal for the young Chinese, but for how many no one knows. The coup of Field Marshal Phibulsongram in 1947 put an abrupt end to the freedom of the Communist Party. In 1948 many communists were arrested, though a number also escaped, including Prasert Sapsunthon, who reportedly went to China. Field Marshal Phibulsongram had not officially declared the party illegal, believing that such action might antagonize the Soviets. But he also said the party was too small to worry about, and this seemed to be true.

Outside Thailand certain significant events were developing that would eventually bring repercussions in Thailand. In 1948 the Communist Youth League met at Calcutta, where it was decided or announced that national liberation movements should be launched in the various parts of Southeast Asia. Violent communist outbreaks were in fact already underway in Indochina, Burma, and Indonesia, and began soon in Malaya and the Philippines. Thailand was apparently considered not ripe as little or nothing occurred there. In 1949 the communists took over all of China and forced the nationalist government to flee to Taiwan. Thus, the largest country in the world and one which had strongly influenced most of Southeast Asia off and on for centuries was solidly communist. This fact was soon turned into action when the Chinese communists began to assist the Vietminh in a number of ways. The assistance greatly strengthened Ho Chi Minh and certainly hastened his victory over the French. The Vietnamese conflict spread to Laos and thus became of even greater concern to the Thais who had controlled much of Laos in the nineteenth century. Communist control of Laos would mean that the buffer between China and Vietnam on the one hand and Thailand on the other would disappear and that the communists would have direct access to the long, ill-defined, and poorly protected Thai border. The Chinese established an autonomous Thai area in China in 1953, as well as the Institute of Minorities, a revolutionary center for the various tribes, some members of which lived in Thailand. Both actions appeared ominous, even if little further action followed immediately.

All of this led the Thais to seek firmer ties with the West and to scrutinize even more carefully the activities of the Chinese in Thailand. There was a crackdown on left-wingers in 1951, but the Siam Communist Party, led by Prasong Vongvivat, reappeared in 1952. Although it was still small, weak, and composed primarily of Chinese, it held its Second Congress early in 1952. However, its primary activities seemed to be issuance of manifestos and publication of leaflets. Mao's influence became increasingly evident when the Congress argued over the proper form of revolutionary activity and a central committee was formed with the Maoists in majority. The pro-Mao element was apparently also able to infiltrate a short-lived National Liberation Organization. The party did send cadres out to the rural areas to recruit peasants, but the immediate results of these labors were unknown. Nevertheless, a few cells formed from 1949 to 1952 in the Northeast seem to have continued meetings for years. An anti-communist cycle occurred again in Thailand with the Act of Communists of 1952, which made communism unlawful, and a few left-wingers were arrested late in the year. The party somehow managed to struggle along, although congratulatory messages to the Chinese in 1956 and 1958, plus attendance at occasional communist meetings abroad, were the only overt signs of its continued existence.

In 1955 the Royal Thai Government decided to permit political parties and, in 1956, labor unions, some of which the communists claimed to have infiltrated. This decision coincided with the communist policy of peaceful coexistence and the "spirit of Bandung." At the Bandung Conference in 1955, Chou En-lai had minimized all problems with China's neighbors, emphasized China's peaceful intentions, and denied China's encouragement of insurgency. This combination of events gave the communists an unusually good opportunity to try one of their favorite strategies—the Front.

As could have been anticipated, a number of parties were soon organized in Thailand around leaders who announced very vague platforms. Many dissidents were freed in 1957 on the occasion of the 2,500th anniversary of Buddha's birth and by then there were at least twenty-two parties. A number of socialist-inclined parties appeared, though their platforms seemed to stress foreign-policy issues rather than economic ones. The Labor Party, Economist Party, Socialist Party, the Hyde Park Party, the Social Democrat Party, and the Free Democrats included vague socialistic ideas in their platforms, such as the Socialist Party's espousal of agricultural cooperatives. All were neutralist and anti-West in foreign policy. In 1956 the Socialist United Front was formed by all the parties mentioned above, except the Labor Party. There was really very little to hold these parties together in the Front, except a vague common foreign policy and opposition to the government. The traditional factors governing Thai politics tended to make this effort most difficult. Exactly what role the communists played in this effort is not clear, though the tactics were certainly a part of their strategy for this period, and we might assume that they tried to orchestrate the Front's efforts. The activity was enough to stimulate Thailand to another period of suppression of political parties and of arrests of communists and other dissidents after the Sarit coup in 1958.[3]

PREPARATIONS FOR OVERT ARMED INSURGENCY, 1961–1965

Arguments have been advanced that armed insurgency in Thailand was a new idea introduced by the Chinese Communist Party in 1964, in response to the United States development and use of Thai airfields. This notion ignores the fact that insurgency is not created overnight, and indeed there is ample evidence that it certainly was not so created in Thailand. The Thai communists, as noted

3. In 1957 Field Marshal Sarit led a military coup which ousted Prime Minister (Field Marshal) Phibulsongram and forced him to flee Thailand. About a year later Sarit suspended the constitution and declared martial law.

earlier, had at least talked about "liberation forces" ever since their Congress in 1952. The National Liberation Organization, which apparently came under communist control about that time, appeared to do little, but our knowledge of it is very limited. We do know that, beginning in the late 1950s, a few Thais were taken out of the country and trained in China, Laos, and Vietnam. Those who went to China generally received political indoctrination, and this certainly featured the ideas of Mao, including the armed struggle. Those who went to Vietnam and Laos received some political indoctrination but also very practical basic military training.

In 1961 the Communist Party of Thailand held its Third Congress clandestinely, probably in or near Bangkok. The decisions of this meeting clearly revealed the Maoist control of the Thai communist movement. A formal resolution was passed declaring that armed struggle was the proper strategy for the revolution in Thailand, and plans were laid for the implementation of the resolution. There was, however, realistic recognition that the foundations of the support base must be laid and guerrilla bands trained before the overt insurgency could be launched. The bands were ordered not to initiate incidents, but they could react if attacked. In 1962 a Northeast Region Jungle Headquarters was established to direct the planned insurgency, and a Farmers Liberation Association was formed in the Northeast to support the jungle guerrillas. Similar organizations were initiated in the West Central and Mid-South areas, though they were less advanced than the Northeast groups. Thus the formal decision was taken, and implementing actions were begun in 1961 and 1962 to lay the foundation for an active insurgency in Thailand.

By 1961 other dissident groups, some with a tinge of Marxism, were active in the Northeast. The so-called Solidarity Movement headed by Krong Chandavong was one of the largest. Krong was a follower of Tiang Serrikkhand, who apparently had favored some sort of union between the Northeast and Laos and was reportedly killed by the police in 1952. Krong's political faith is not entirely clear, but he was certainly organizing against the government. As a result, he and some 100 of his followers were arrested; Krong was executed in May, 1961. Some of his followers fled to the hills and formed anti-government bands which later joined in the communist-led insurgency movement. The following year Ruam Wongphan, who described himself as one of the top leaders in the Thai Communist Party, was arrested and executed. His headquarters were in Suphan Buri, west of Bangkok. Both Krong and Ruam have since been hailed by Thai communists as their "hero-martyrs."

In 1961 an allegedly communist document called "Prediction" was circulated, which called for the expulsion of the United States from Thailand and the overthrow of the government. In 1962 a communist radio station calling itself the "Voice of the Thai People" began broadcasting, probably from China; in late

1964 the hours per day were increased. In 1963, in true communist fashion, announcements began of the creation of a series of fronts, such as the Nationalistic Movement for Freedom, which never seemed to function. This was followed by the Neutralist Front, which was unsuccessful and short-lived. The Communist Party of Thailand also came out in favor of the Chinese and against the Russians. In December, 1964, the Thai Independence Movement (TIM) was organized. The parade of new organizations continued in 1965. A Thai Peoples Front was formed, and then the Patriotic Front of Thailand was organized to support TIM. In May the Thai Front of the Working People was added. At the end of 1965 some attempt seemed to be made to coordinate these various organizations when TIM announced agreement to cooperate with the Patriotic Front of Thailand. The others appeared to fade away.

It should be emphasized that none of these organizations was successful in the sense of establishing firm and viable roots in Thai society. The small and scattered Farmers Liberation and National Liberation organizations, however, appeared to have some staying power, particularly in the Northeast. The frequent appearance of new organizations actually reinforced the idea of failure rather than success, although the communists' propaganda claimed that the proliferation of organizations was an indication of a widespread and growing movement. These fronts, whether pure propaganda or serious attempts at recruiting supporters, all had the purpose of encouraging dissatisfaction and developing a fertile base for insurgency and subversion.

The Communist Party of Thailand was not touted as the leader of these fronts, given its great lack of appeal in the past and its need in the incipient period of the insurgency to avoid suppressive actions by the government. The Thai communists, having opted for Mao's doctrines, were clearly trying to follow his formula. The same tactic of concealing the role of the party had been followed in Vietnam when, in 1946, Ho Chi Minh had declared the party disbanded and had taken on a nationalist role; the party merely went underground for a few years. Developments in Thailand continued to follow the usual communist liberation pattern. Since 1961 there has been a steady evolution of communist revolutionary warfare in Thailand which steadfastly sought communist objectives, although initially the role of the party was disguised and the role of fronts and liberation forces was highlighted.

REASONS FOR SLOW DEVELOPMENT
OF COMMUNISM IN THAILAND

Antithetical Thai Characteristics

The development of the communist movement in Thailand in the years up to 1965 was very slow. Certain national Thai characteristics and aspects of Thai history and culture, which may be called passive factors, made the early communist effort in Thailand particularly difficult and have continued to make the country a unique case in communist experience. These factors not only limited Thai vulnerability to communist appeals but also were strongly relied on by the Royal Thai Government as insurance that the communist movement in the country could never expand much beyond a nuisance largely confined to aliens and minorities in remote areas.

Generally speaking, the Thais have never had a great interest in ideology or abstract ideas. One of the major characteristics of communism is that it is an ideology—i.e., an all-encompassing belief that is the central core of the movement. Dedicated communists are in a sense the ultimate "true believers." To execute their ideological goals and attain political power they need to devise means of organization and controls of individual behavior that would help them develop a highly disciplined and motivated apparatus. The individual is subordinated so completely to the ideology and to the organization that he is in some ways lost in the drive to achieve certain objectives. Nevertheless, his personal ambition also becomes associated with these goals so that personal drive does become a part of the movement. Such a tight-knit group can thus be used in a variety of ways: as the cadre to organize mass movements, to engage in guerrilla warfare, to undertake psychological operations, or to launch political campaigns—different strategies and weapons, but designed to achieve the same overall objectives.

The Thais do not fit readily into tight groups motivated by devotion to an ideology. In the first place, they are in general realistic and pragmatic. Abstractions and theories hold little appeal for a people who are much more interested in day-to-day life and the problems involved in it. They view communism as something alien and are excessively nationalistic. Second, the Thai intellectuals are relatively few and have been so largely integrated into the ruling elite that they are concerned primarily with real problems, not ivory-tower ideas. Third, and by no means the least important, is the influence of Buddhism. Over the centuries, Buddhism has provided a satisfactory and stable belief. It is not so much a religion as a way of life, and a tolerant one, with little emphasis on ideology and much more on the practical ways to "gain merit." The all-encompassing materialistic and intolerant ideology of communism, with its disciplined organization, has in general come off second best in competing with the more comfortable atmosphere of Buddhism.

Thai political organization, as noted earlier, is seldom based on strict ideological grounds but tends to form around a leading personality. This allows a certain ease in shifting from one political grouping to another; the shifts are matters of individual allegiance, often based on calculation of personal gain by the person involved. This leads to loosely organized groupings rather than disciplined, highly structured political parties. For example, although the government's United Thai People's Party has been struggling to form a modern political party, its history since the 1969 elections seems to show that traditional Thai factors are still dominant. The government has had difficulty keeping its members in line, and within the party there appear to be factions leaning toward several different leaders. Other parties have been experiencing similar difficulties. Thus it is not surprising that the communists have had difficulties, since their concept of organization is almost opposite to that of the Thais. Marxists strive to develop highly disciplined organizations, calling for complete self-sacrifice of the individual to the ideology and leadership of the party. In theory, at least, communism is highly impersonal. Personalities, of course, play a role in all organizations, but the Marxist emphasis on impersonal loyalty, disciplined obedience, and strict organization are neither in the Thai political tradition nor compatible with the Thai personality.

Communist and Thai party organizations differ widely in organizational composition. The Communist Party itself is selective in its leadership and membership and tries to develop a tight elite organization, but the communist front organizations try to gain as many members as possible with almost no criteria for selection. Through this emphasis on a broad mass base they try to provide a façade of wide popular support and the trimmings of popular democracy.

In Thai political parties, on the other hand, leaders and key members come from a small segment of society, the bureaucracy, and are held together largely by common personal interests. The memberships are usually small. However, the ruling elite over the years, in trying to restrict political power to itself, has maintained an apolitical population, and has attempted to provide enough services and security to keep the people content. Inciting the masses to political action, trying to organize them in large groups, and developing a greater popular awareness have not been part of Thai politics. Rather, the leaders have tried to keep the people away from political matters and have them concentrate on their own mundane affairs. The positive, though very limited, steps toward democracy taken between the declaration of the new Constitution in June, 1968, and the coup of November, 1971, which resulted in martial law, may have aroused greater political concern on the part of the people, though this is by no means obvious even with the further steps toward democracy taken in late 1972 and the promises of the new civilian government in October, 1973. In fact, it seems that there is little fundamentally new in the Thai political situation, and the prospects for any major changes seem unlikely in the next few years.

Most true communists tend to be highly motivated activists who are anxious, even while pursuing protracted causes, to overthrow the prevailing society and to make fundamental changes in the political, economic, and social structure of a country. But the notion of collective responsibility and activity to improve the welfare of others is not in keeping with Buddhist teaching, which lays great emphasis on the individual road to salvation. It is through one's own efforts that the good life is led and an improved status in the next incarnation can be attained. No one can do it for anybody else. Because of the Buddhist religion, a keen sense of reality, and the slowness of change, the Thais have a generally relaxed and easygoing attitude toward life. They are not in a hurry and are patient in dealing with complex problems. A hot, humid climate for most of the year also seems to contribute to this attitude. Thus, the ethnic Thai philosophy and outlook contrast starkly with the communist desire to save others and to recruit people into disciplined organizations promising fundamental changes in the Thai society that seems thus far to have been so satisfactory to the majority of the people.

Economic factors have also contributed to this easygoing, relaxed approach to life. Tin and rubber in the South and teak in the North have provided significant exports, but the central valley is the economic base which not only produces more than enough food for the population, but has also provided generous rice exports. Most of the peasants in the central plain own their own land and cultivate it. Approximately 70 percent of the population are small landowners; consequently, a large landlord element has been very rare in Thai society. Recently, however, there has been some evidence that the situation is changing and that the number of small landowners is decreasing. The population has always been low density; recently, however, it has been increasing at a very high rate. There has always been plenty of land for all, but with the population increase this is changing. The Thais still have a homesteading act (somewhat like that of the United States) that permits people to occupy land, improve it, and take legal ownership after a few years. There are very large forest preserves which the government has wisely set aside and, if used properly, they could provide some cushion for the population increase. Nature has helped Thailand become a relatively well-to-do country with only modest effort.

Because of economic plenty, the philosophy of Buddhism, and the easygoing nature of Thai society, socioeconomic mobility is considerable. People feel free to leave one job and take another, to try to climb the social and economic ladder. Men of rather limited background have been able to reach high levels in the world of business and in the government, both as military men and civilians. Lower economic groups are provided opportunities for free education, even through the university level. Although a certain level of education is an essential requirement for government service and thus the great majority of the population are shut off from that avenue, this is not true for the business sphere. In the Northeast particularly, it is customary for young men and women to take parts of several years off to see Thailand and "live a little." Many of them go to

Bangkok or some of the smaller cities, usually returning later to their native environs. Recently, however, an increasing number have stayed in the urban areas, thus forming a new urban class. The opportunities to rise in society and to travel have been, to a certain extent, safety valves that prevented social pressures from building up. The Buddhist monkhood also serves as a class-leveling institution, since all are considered equal. The relative economic well-being of the peasants and the lack of strong and impenetrable class distinctions have contributed to a society considerably free of the kind of tensions that communism utilizes in its drive for power.

The Intellectuals

Inasmuch as the communists usually make intellectuals one of their primary targets, it may be useful to discuss this class separately. The Thai intellectual community is small, and mainly centered in the universities, of which there are several in Bangkok. (The Royal Thai Government has recently been developing three new regional universities, one each in the South, Northeast, and North.) Traditionally, Thai intellectuals have been primarily concerned with poetry, drama, and religion—especially Buddhism—and much less with the sciences, philosophy, and the more speculative areas of intellectual endeavor. A number of other factors also contribute to the intellectuals' characteristics. For example, the universities have traditionally been owned and operated by the state; the professors are therefore officials of the government and subject to its guidance and discipline. Many of them also have additional jobs within the government. Thus, the universities are part and parcel of the government and not free, independent institutions as in most Western countries.[4] In addition, those intellectuals who have a particular interest and skill in politics have generally been incorporated into the ruling elite. However, a very small independent well-educated group has also existed, primarily made up of speculative scholars, who perform a traditional academic role, and writers, journalists, researchers, and so on, but their small numbers make their influence minimal.

The intellectuals associated with the government necessarily deal with a variety of real-life problems, and this seems to increase their pragmatic tendencies and lessen their inclination toward theoretical solutions of problems. In short, most members of the group appear to have little taste for exploration of ideas and also little dissatisfaction with their status, are relatively well employed, and to a certain extent feel that they are part of the political process. They also share many of the traditional Thai beliefs and customs. Thus, it is not surprising that the communists have had little luck in converting the members of this small community.

4. However, a 1969 law permits private colleges and universities, and a few are in the process of organization.

Thai National Pride

Another very important factor working against the communists has been the Thai people's strong sense of nationalism and pride in their country's history of independence. The communists, as we have seen, realized in the 1920s that a revolution of the proletariat in Asia at that time could not happen because there was almost no such class. In regard to Thailand, they believed that the peasants constituted the population mass needed, but for a long time no theory or method for involving them in a revolution was developed, because even the poorly educated peasants shared some of the pride in the country's history. In other countries the communists could concentrate on anti-imperialism, trying to ride popular and ongoing causes, and some Asian communist parties played an important role in the European-held colonies. In Indochina the communist cry was anti-French, in Burma and Malaya anti-British, in Indonesia anti-Dutch, and in the Philippines anti-American. Since the Royal Thai Government was independent, the only role for the communists in Thailand was anti-government, but the government was a Thai government and the communists in Thailand were almost exclusively Chinese and a few Vietnamese. Not surprisingly, in the early years of the insurgency the communists gained only a minimal following among ethnic Thais.

Royal Thai Government (RTG) Suppressive Measures

In addition to these passive factors which made the communist task of preparing Thailand for a war of "liberation" difficult, the RTG during the years prior to the surfacing of the insurgency took, as we have seen, positive and sometimes rather harsh actions against communists, alleged communists, and left-wingers. These suppression measures followed a cyclical pattern. The first anti-communist law and activity occurred in 1933, but relaxed enforcement followed. Immediately after World War II the anti-communist laws were revoked because of Soviet pressures. Then in 1948 and 1951–1952 there were again crack-downs and new anti-communist legislation. A few years of relaxation, particularly during 1955–1957, were followed by a period of sharp repression after the Sarit coup in 1958. The times of repression were reactions to periods of considerable opposition to the government; however, the communist threat was also often used as an excuse for action against other forms of dissidence. The Chinese, as an obvious alien group, were most often the target of repressive acts (as well as the initial primary target for communist recruiters).

Tactical Mistakes of the Communists

We may surmise also that the communists themselves made some tactical mistakes. Certainly, as we have seen, they failed to perceive the need for or the means of adapting their approaches to the Thai passive factors. And, granted that the Chinese were their most obvious and easiest target, was that approach the most productive in the long run? The Chinese were a minority primarily located in Bangkok and the larger towns where the RTG could easily watch and control their activities. In fact, they had been, even before the advent of communism, closely monitored. Could such an obvious group, relatively easy to identify and traditionally suspect, be an effective cadre for a movement designed to seize political power or overthrow the RTG by force? Given the long-term aim of getting at the heart of Thailand, would the movement have had better success if its first and chief target had been the ethnic Thais, even though Thai cadres were harder to recruit and indoctrinate? All evidence shows that the choice to recruit Chinese as leaders tended to restrict the communist appeal and to limit its expansion, to attract repressive measures even when not warranted, and to hamper the movement's possible ability to play on Thai pride and nationalism.

The leadership difficulty is an example of how the communists, especially in the earlier years, seem to have disregarded the unique Thai characteristics and the strong belief of the Thais in their own way of life. So far as we can judge from the periods when communism was not forced underground in Thailand, the communists failed to develop a dynamic and appealing leadership that would be a key to all Thai institutions, political and otherwise. This resulted in part, of course, from the emphasis on Chinese cadres, but even the few local Thai leaders appeared not to be well known or to have any wide appeal.

For whatever reason, the communist priority list for Asia was slow to include Thailand. Perhaps the communists realized that Thailand with its history of independence and strong culture was a difficult target. Perhaps the reliance on Chinese as cadres led to an emphasis on other areas where the Chinese seemed to offer a more tempting target, for example, Malaya. Possibly there was a hope that if all the surrounding areas became communist, Thailand would simply fall like a ripe plum. In any case, the communists in Thailand, compared with those in other Asian countries, received scant attention and assistance and had to operate largely on their own for a long time.

THE DECISION TO LAUNCH THE INSURGENCY IN THAILAND

Sometime in 1963 or 1964 the communists apparently decided to launch an overt Thai insurgency in 1965.[5] However, we really do not know exactly when the decision to launch overt revolutionary warfare was made. Where the decision to act was made is not known either, though it seems likely that it emanated from the Chinese Communist Party in Peking, since a Western ambassador in

5. In December, 1961, a SEATO study group, of which I was the American member, predicted the outbreak would come in two or three years. This, of course, was several years before the American buildup in Vietnam or Thailand.

Peking made it known in January, 1965, that armed insurgency in Thailand could be expected before the end of the year. The communists date the beginning of the outbreak from August 7, 1965, and since they launched it, that is a reasonable date to accept. Without this clue, however, it would be difficult to be sure of so specific a date, because violence had been increasing in the Northeast for at least four to five years. Not all the violence was communist, to be sure; it included banditry and cattle rustling and noncommunist dissidence, but we have it on communist word as well as from observers in the field that communist violence in the Northeast did increase markedly in late 1965.

Before asking why the decision was made just then, a summary of the position of the Thai Communist Party at the time will be useful. The party was still small and weak in 1965. Its total membership was probably under 1,000. It seems to have had the usual Politburo, Central Committee, and Party Assembly as its principal elements of organization. There appeared to be four branches of the Central Committee, one in the Northeast, one in the North, one in the Central area, and one in the South. All communist theory suggests that there must have been central control and guidance, but in 1965 little was known about the top echelons of the party. The top leadership, almost all of whom were ethnic Chinese but Thai citizens, that is, Sino-Thais, were believed to be composed of hard-core communists, many of whom had been trained in China and had had many years of experience. Some of them were in China, others in Bangkok and elsewhere in Thailand, but Bangkok seems to have been the location of party headquarters. The party tended to follow China's leadership, receiving policy and doctrinal guidance from Peking.

The regional branches of the Central Committee were apparently quite independent of the Central Committee as a whole, but under the control of one or more of its members. Each region pursued its own independent armed revolution, choosing tactics and techniques that it considered suitable. The leaders of some districts (subordinate units of the regions) acted rather independently, although there was more coordination at the regional than at the national level. This description suggests that control was loose within the party, but we cannot be certain that it was, because central control might have existed and information about it was not picked up. However, what was known tended to indicate considerable decentralization in Thailand. Why? Obviously the full answer to this is not known to us either, but a number of hypotheses can be advanced. In the first place, until very recently communications in Thailand had not been good. One railroad and one main highway plus commercial air service and the usual mail and telegraphic service connected the regions with Bangkok, but there were few communications between the regions without going through Bangkok. Couriers were used by the party, but given the transportation system this method was slow. However, other underdeveloped countries probably have similar communications, and in many of these the communist parties operate under highly centralized control. A more important factor is that the individual regions of Thailand vary considerably in their proximity to certain other countries, in their ethnic makeup, in their terrain, and in their socioeconomic problems. These differences could cause the Thai communists, at least initially, to allow considerable local autonomy so as to attract followers and build a local organization using local issues and conditions. Still another possibility might be that the traditional Thai political factors were in operation, particularly the idea of following a personal leader rather than an ideologically inclined party. Perhaps this personal aspect accounts for the continuing reports of dissension and rivalry among the communist leadership. All of these factors may have contributed to the generally ineffective—because less cohesive and centralized than in other countries—communist apparatus in Thailand.

Given this situation, the pertinent and debated question is still why mid-1965 was chosen as the time to launch the overt insurgency. We can only surmise communist intentions and what actually went on behind the scenes. One hypothesis maintains that the decision was made by the Chinese Communist Party, with the intent of using the threat of insurgency and then the insurgency itself to deter the RTG from assisting the United States in Southeast Asia. If so, the move was decidedly belated, for work on expanding Thai bases for American use had been going on for many months. The Chinese may have seen advantages in an insurgency that could be embarrassing and hampering for the RTG and for the U.S. forces in Thailand. The Chinese have not, however, provided the kind of support for it that would be expected if this were an important part of the policy. Furthermore, the insurgents did not interfere with the Thai troops that were trained for duty in Vietnam nor conducted any serious campaign against any Thai military forces. Although anti-Americanism has been one of the constant and strongest propaganda themes, the insurgents have rarely attacked Americans. It was not until July, 1968, that the first attack on an air base used by the United States was launched and this was a small primitive effort, poorly executed. Two other attacks were obviously for psychological reasons, one coming on the anniversary of the earlier attack and the other on the day of President Nixon's arrival in Bangkok in 1969. The relatively few other attacks have not been successful as the Thai warning system seems to have worked well. All these attacks appear to have been carried out by special sapper teams sent into Thailand, not by the indigenous guerrillas. If vigorous attacks on the Americans and on those elements of the RTG closely associated with them had been mounted early in the insurgency to demonstrate the danger and destruction the Americans were indirectly causing by their presence, considerable pressure probably would have been brought on the Thais to review and change their policy. The lack of such actions by the insurgents casts some doubt on the idea that the increased use by the United States of Thailand as a platform for air operations in Southeast Asia was the primary reason for initiation of the insurgency. Rather, these facts suggest that, although the Chinese may have ordered an acceleration of the insurgency timetable with the hope of deterring the Thais or at least of creating a troublesome domestic situation, they were, in the main, regarding the overt insurgency as a step in their long-term and gradually increasing effort to bring about a totally communist Thailand.

Another possible explanation for the timing is that the Chinese Communist Party initiated the armed struggle in Thailand to counter the possibility that North Vietnam, which in 1964 and early 1965 seemed headed for victory in South Vietnam, would take over Thailand as part of its sphere of influence. However, there is a rumor that in 1966 the North Vietnamese conceded to China that Thailand should be part of the Chinese communist responsibility. It is also possible that the Chinese, foreseeing a communist victory in Vietnam, reasoned that even a limited success in a concurrent insurgency in Thailand would ensure that Thailand would be swept promptly into the communist fold after Vietnam had been gathered in.

A former U. S. Ambassador to Thailand, Graham Martin, stated in a speech to the National War College on January 9, 1969, that in 1965 the communists in Thailand received instructions "to telescope a much more lengthy timetable and start the offensive." This would imply that the order came from the Chinese Communist Party and was not initiated by the Communist Party of Thailand. There is some evidence that the Thai party, or at least some of its leaders, felt that the movement was not ready for such a step as open violence in all the regions where it had been organized. It seems to have decided, therefore, that armed attacks should at first be initiated only in the northeastern corner of the Northeast where conditions were thought to be most ripe for action. This was an area where Tiang and Krong had proselyted and in which many of their followers continued to live. Men who had been sent out of the country for communist training had now returned; a limited village support system had been organized; and there were small jungle bands to serve as nuclei for expansion. Some evidence suggests that these bands were growing restive under the restrictions against violence imposed in 1962 by the Thai Communist Party, and this contributed to the Party's decision.

In spite of some evidence and good reasoning to support the different hypotheses about the decision to launch the insurgency in the summer of 1965, it seems reasonably clear that no one really knows. There is not adequate information about Hanoi to give a definitive answer. However, we can say that the communists have been active in Thailand for about fifty years, that the Thai Communist Party follows the Maoist line and is dominated by Sino-Thais, that many hundreds of Thais have been trained abroad in communism and guerrilla warfare, but that progress has been slow and the party apparatus was not strong in 1965.

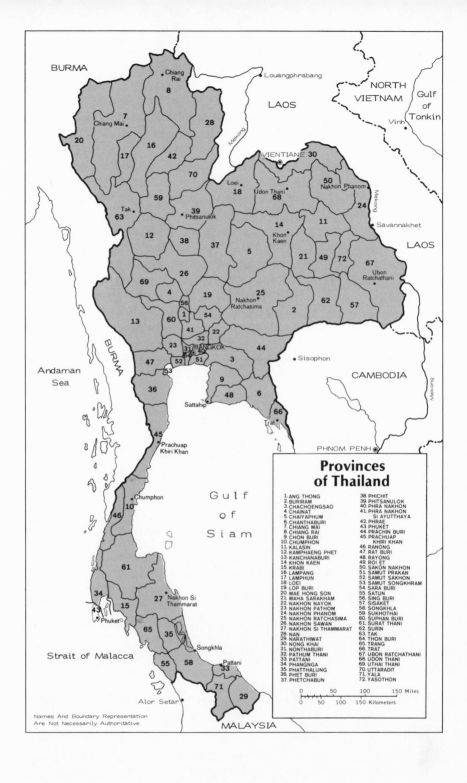

BURMA

Chiang Rai
8

LAOS

Louangphrabang

NORTH
VIETNAM

Gulf
of
Tonkin

Vinh

7
Chiang Mai
28

20

16

17

42

70

VIENTIANE 30

Loei
18

Udon Thani
68

50
Nakhon Phanom

24

59

Tak
63

39
Phitsanulok

14

Khon
Kaen

11

Savannakhet

LAOS

12

38

37

5

21

49

72

67
Ubon
Ratchathani

69

26

4

19

25
Nakhon
Ratchasima

2

62

57

13

60

56

1

54

41

32

22

23

31 BANGKOK

44

Sisophon

CAMBODIA

Andaman
Sea

BURMA

47

52

51

3

53

36

9

48

6

Sattahip

66
Trat

45

Prachuap
Khiri Khan

PHNOM PENH

Chumphon

Gulf

of

Siam

46

10

61

34

43

15

27 Nakhon Si
Thammarat

Phuket

65

35

55

58

Songkhla

Strait of Malacca

Pattani
33

71

29

Alor Setar

MALAYSIA

Provinces
of Thailand

1. ANG THONG
2. BURIRAM
3. CHACHOENGSAO
4. CHAINAT
5. CHAIYAPHUM
6. CHANTHABURI
7. CHIANG MAI
8. CHIANG RAI
9. CHON BURI
10. CHUMPHON
11. KALASIN
12. KAMPHAENG PHET
13. KANCHANABURI
14. KHON KAEN
15. KRABI
16. LAMPANG
17. LAMPHUN
18. LOEI
19. LOP BURI
20. MAE HONG SON
21. MAHA SARAKHAM
22. NAKHON NAYOK
23. NAKHON PATHOM
24. NAKHON PHANOM
25. NAKHON RATCHASIMA
26. NAKHON SAWAN
27. NAKHON SI THAMMARAT
28. NAN
29. NARATHIWAT
30. NONG KHAI
31. NONTHABURI
32. PATHUM THANI
33. PATTANI
34. PHANGNGA
35. PHATTHALUNG
36. PHET BURI
37. PHETCHABUN

38. PHICHIT
39. PHITSANULOK
40. PHRA NAKHON
41. PHRA NAKHON
   SI AYUTTHAYA
42. PHRAE
43. PHUKET
44. PRACHIN BURI
45. PRACHUAP
   KHIRI KHAN
46. RANONG
47. RAT BURI
48. RAYONG
49. ROI ET
50. SAKON NAKHON
51. SAMUT PRAKAN
52. SAMUT SAKHON
53. SAMUT SONGKHRAM
54. SARA BURI
55. SATUN
56. SING BURI
57. SISAKET
58. SONGKHLA
59. SUKHOTHAI
60. SUPHAN BURI
61. SURAT THANI
62. SURIN
63. TAK
64. THON BURI
65. TRANG
66. TRAT
67. UBON RATCHATHANI
68. UDON THANI
69. UTHAI THANI
70. UTTARADIT
71. YALA
72. YASOTHON

0   50   100   150 Miles

0   50   100   150 Kilometers

Names And Boundary Representation
Are Not Necessarily Authoritative

Chapter 3

The Insurgency

The Thai insurgency has developed, not as one unified effort, but with varying characteristics in the different regions. This reflects the apparent lack of an effectively centralized communist movement in Thailand, and at least makes it necessary for us to examine the insurgency by region. It also calls for some further examination of the Chinese role and attitudes toward the insurgency.

Recent Chinese revolutionary doctrine has stressed that the indigenous party apparatuses must carry out the revolution themselves, with only limited support from the socialist nations. The concept was fully developed in Lin Piao's 1965 speech, and since then the Chinese have generally adhered to it. However, this does not mean that they provide no help whatever to the revolutionary movements. For the Thai insurgents, they offer a safe haven for some of the leadership; they train and inspire cadres; they support propaganda campaigns, mostly radio, both in Thailand and in the outside world; they provide an ideological and doctrinal framework as well as moral support; and they give limited amounts of material assistance, not only guns but recoilless rifles and mortars. Insurgency training for the Thais continues in Laos, probably in China, and perhaps in Vietnam. However, as far as we know, the Chinese have not sent in masses of equipment. Very recently, there have been reports of foreign advisors and technicians, but earlier the Communist Party of Thailand was reluctant to accept such assistance. In any case, aside from radio use, all Chinese efforts have been small and low-key. However, the Chinese undoubtedly back the insurgency and the Thailand effort is much higher on the priority list than it was a few years ago.

As the Thai communist apparatus improves its leadership, organization, and capabilities, more weapons and materials are likely to be sent to them by the Chinese. As we shall see, in 1971–1973 there was a large increase in the number of Chinese weapons in the North and to a lesser extent in the Northeast. The development of secure communist bases in the North and Northeast also facilitates training, possibly by the Chinese or North Vietnamese, and provides good depots for more advanced weapons. If the insurgent movement continues its progress, covert Chinese support, especially in material things, will very likely increase in the next few years.

THE NORTHEAST

As we have seen, the insurgents, generally referred to as Communist Terrorists (CTs), a name borrowed from the Malaysian Emergency, had planned for armed insurrection in Thailand for some years and priority appears to have been given to the Northeast. A number of young Thais from that region had been sent to schools in Laos, Vietnam, and China via a well-developed underground railroad in Laos. Some of these, when they finished school, were provided practical experience with the Pathet Lao in Laos; in fact, some observers believe that the Thais were recruited merely to serve in Laos. (This was probably true in some cases but not in all.) The exact numbers of the recruits are unknown, but it has been estimated that at least 500 attended schools abroad and returned to the Northeast in the mid-sixties. The Thai government estimates a couple thousand more have been trained abroad since then. Most important of all, these young people were mainly Thais, not Chinese or Vietnamese. The attempt in the Northeast has been to work directly with the ethnic Thais and the assimilated minorities such as the Soh and Phu Thai. Some observers believe that the minorities are more fertile ground than the ethnic Thais, but few persons are well enough acquainted with the Northeast to draw this conclusion. However, it may be significant that the district of Sawang Daen Din in Sakon Nakhon, which has been a dissident area since Krong's time in 1961, is also heavily populated by a local minority, the Phu Thai, and that Na Kae in Nakhon Phanom, another strong CT district, has a heavy Soh minority.

While the cadres and future guerrillas were being trained, a parallel effort was made to develop village support. This was mostly carried on among the families of those who had attended the communist schools or were already deeply involved in the movement—such as those who had gone into the Phu Phan hills as members of jungle bands. The "Voice of the Thai People" concentrated its broadcasts on the Northeast, trying to create or increase unrest and dissatisfaction there. By 1965 cadres had been trained abroad, small guerrilla groups had been formed around these cadres, and a start had been made to develop support bases among the villagers.

After the call to arms in 1965, the number of CTs in guerrilla bands increased noticeably in late 1965 and in 1966, and the size of the individual bands, which had been five or ten, rose to between twenty and fifty or more. The larger bands made possible in some cases a more sophisticated specialization of duties in the classic communist pattern of political, military, and support sections. During this period, armed attack on Thai police and other officials broke out in several areas in the Northeast but were at first most frequent in the provinces of Nakhon Phanom and Sakon Nakhon. Na Kae, Pla Pak, and Mukdahan districts, all partially in the Phu Phan hills, were the most active in Nakhon Phanom and have continued to be. It has been reported that the Central Committee meets somewhere in the Phu Phans and occasionally in Laos, but the precise whereabouts is unknown, and indeed probably moves periodically. Sawang Daen Din and Waritchaphum districts, in Sakon Nakhon, are old areas of dissidence and have continued to be insurgent strongholds. CT activities also broke out to a lesser extent in Loeng Nok Tha district in northern Ubon, Nong Bua Lam Phu district in Udon, and Lahan Sai district in Buri Ram, in Nong Khai province, and several other places. The new areas of violence probably were added partly to avoid government suppressive reactions in any one area and partly to oblige government forces to disperse their efforts.

Although the CTs have continued to be most active in these known areas, especially in building a covert village support system, past experience and some general intelligence suggest that they have begun to develop in other areas of the Northeast. Because of limited governmental intelligence capabilities and an inadequate surveillance and reporting system in the whole region, such activities are rarely detected early, much less acted against. This permits the CTs to develop an apparatus, to decide when they want it to take overt action, and thus to surprise the government, which may still be focused on the older areas of insurgency. Therefore, to describe all of the present active locations in the Northeast precisely is extremely difficult.

The CTs, as noted earlier, have tried to follow the classic Mao pattern. They have recruited in the more remote villages where the government presence was negligible. During the insurgency, Thai suppression forces have discovered villages hostile to them, a fact sometimes unknown to the provincial or even district authorities. Often the local officials or villagers have known of this hostility but either were afraid to report it to higher levels or did not know how to. A good example of this was the discovery by an army unit of CT villages in Wanon Niwat district of Sakon Nakhon in early 1968. Many local officials, including the Community Development worker, knew about this development but had never reported the situation to the higher levels of provincial government, largely out of fear of reprisals by the CTs. All those involved in the communist movement said they had been forced to join the CTs and to be silent about it.

Techniques and Tactics

The communists have used certain general techniques in all regions of Thailand but have taken pains to adapt them in detail to local situations. Both in written propaganda and face-to-face recruitment they have used local practical issues to attract followers. Instruction in communist ideology has been reserved for the later stages of indoctrination of the more promising recruits. In the Northeast, as in other regions, they have made much of alleged corruption and indifference of certain local officials, have decried police oppression and the inadequate justice provided the peasants, bemoaned the government's failure to provide satisfactory schooling and health facilities, and harped on such chronic local problems of farmers as the water shortage in the Northeast. The very young have been offered opportunities for travel and education, both very attractive to those who are ambitious but frustrated. And in general, promises, very seldom fulfilled, have been made of tractors, food, regular salaries for guerrillas, and official status within the movement. As clever and appealing as these approaches may seem, they have not produced the desired results as quickly as the communists hoped.

In the Northeast (as well as in the other regions) terror has therefore also been used—that is, threats or acts of violence to arouse fear. It has seldom been used indiscriminately, but rather as a deliberate weapon to obtain certain goals—for example, to call attention to the movement and make it seem larger and more powerful than it actually is, or to intimidate the people in a certain village so that they will not report communist activities to officials. Terror is also used to force peasants to work for the communists and thereby become involved and finally so entangled in the movement that they must either continue to support it or take the risky step of turning themselves in to the authorities. In some cases government reactions and reprisals following terrorist acts have harmed villagers and tended to make them more sympathetic with the insurgent cause.

Both persuasion and terror have been shrewdly used by the communists to build up feelings of isolation and insecurity among the villagers, to make them feel that the government has no concern for them and cannot protect them, and that they have no choice but to go along with the communists. Key people, such as village leaders and teachers, have been harassed to the point that they could not or dared not perform their duties. Others have been assassinated or threatened with death. There have been some attacks on government offices and police posts, most of them carried out by small bands in guerrilla type operations; however, in December, 1965, a government police and army sweep force met a band of at least 200 insurgents in Nakhon Phanom. Early in 1966 the CTs in the Northeast began to conduct armed propaganda meetings, which combined propaganda with terror. On these occasions a guerrilla band would appear in a village, intimidate the population by show of arms and sometimes violence, and then deliver long lectures on the failures of the Royal Thai Government (RTG) and the unhappy life of the people.

Developments 1966–1974

Although statistics can be misused, they can also, with discretion, be used to complement the word picture of the insurgency. For the early days, the figures are probably less reliable than they have been recently. The best estimates are that there were 200 or so guerrillas in the Northeast in 1965 and that this rather vague number rose to perhaps 600 in 1966. The number of sympathizers and supporters is not known though some people use a ratio of ten to one guerrilla or six to one (the average size of a Thai family) to make very rough guesses. In any case, the variations in the kinds and devotion of the sympathizers are such that precise figures are not very useful. These few hundred guerrillas were involved in perhaps fifty to a hundred incidents in 1965 and the figure rose in 1966 to over 500 reported.[1] The latter figure probably, though we do not know, includes a higher percentage of government-initiated incidents, because the Thai military forces became active shortly after overt insurgency broke out. Adequate information on the incidents is lacking, so that their size, intensity, nature, and objectives are unclear. All of which makes it most difficult to get anything close to an accurate picture of the insurgency.

As will be detailed in Chapter 4, the response of the RTG to the terrorist incidents was to launch a series of sweeps in the affected provinces in the Northeast. In December, 1965, the Communist Suppression Operations Command (CSOC) was formed in Bangkok to coordinate the central government suppression activities, and a joint civilian-police-military headquarters (CPM-1) was established, first at Mukdahan in southern Nakhon Phanom and later at Sakon Nakhon, to coordinate suppression activities in the Northeast. CPM staffs

---

1. There is also a tendency, once insurgency begins, to include all regular crimes in the incident counts.

also were set up in the most sensitive provinces in the region, and other provinces were directed to organize more loosely structured Communist Suppression Committees. During 1966, as comprehensive plans to protect villages and destroy jungle bands were being worked out, major emphasis was placed on large-scale sweeps with artillery and air support. These were not successful in destroying the jungle bands, but they disrupted to some extent the Thai Communist Party's plans for the increased armed struggle and forced the bands to move frequently.

There was an upsurge of violent incidents in February and March of 1967, particularly in armed encounters between government forces and insurgents and in armed propaganda meetings conducted by insurgent forces. To some extent, the government's selection of target areas on the basis of intelligence was validated by the violent reaction to increased government activity. After March, however, the incident level dropped off again and remained on the average only slightly above that in 1966. Apparently, the insurgents had discovered that they could evade the government forces, which tended to be tied down to target areas, simply by slipping away, temporarily or permanently, into unprotected areas. Some bands may then have moved permanently into the hills, but incidents continued to occur in old insurgent strongholds such as Na Kae in Nakhon Phanom and Sawang Daen Din in Sakon Nakhon. By the summer of 1967, there were more frequent reports of insurgent efforts to collect food by begging or seizure, possibly indicating that the support mechanism had been degraded by government activities. However, 1967 was a drought year in much of the Northeast, and many villagers suffered from a food shortage themselves and so had less to give the guerrillas.

The armed propaganda meeting, a much-favored insurgent activity during the latter half of 1966 and the first few months of 1967, declined increasingly in frequency after March, 1967. The reasons for the rise and fall in the numbers of such meetings are not really known, although one could surmise that the insurgents decided the meetings had aroused too much resentment among villagers.

By late 1967 and early 1968 it seemed reasonably clear that the insurgency in the Northeast had not made the progress its leaders had planned and indeed seemed to be stalled. Observers saw several explanations for this. First, the communist apparatus had not been fully ready in 1965 for overt insurgency, because the guerrillas were too few and not adequately trained and equipped, properly led, or keenly motivated. Second, and very important, there were indications that the support system, so essential to the logistics of guerrillas and also necessary for any increase in their numbers, was woefully inadequate. Although some villagers were providing food and clothing for the guerrillas, they were not numerous and their relationship to the guerrillas was based more on kinship or friendship than on a common cause. (As we shall see, these deficiencies became more apparent later on in 1968). Third, although the communists supported some appealing causes and tried to take advantage of reasons for unrest, particularly among the youth, Thai rural society to a large extent was unmoved or untouched by either appeals or terrorism and remained more or less loyal to the government. Few actively supported the guerrillas, and this is significant, since the assumption often is that where there are grievances insurgency almost automatically prospers.

The valid issues, of which there were some, were clearly not strong enough in this case to win many sympathizers and were no substitute for good communist leadership and organization. Furthermore, the movement did not or could not mount a significant campaign of mass terror which could markedly change people's behavior, especially as the villagers were already accustomed to a certain level of violence. Additionally, the insurgency in the Northeast, as in other regions, suffered from the arrests of February and August, 1967, which deprived it of some support from the party in Bangkok; in particular two key functions, the financial and courier systems, seem to have been badly hurt. Lastly, some of the Thai counterinsurgency activities were beginning to have some effect. Most of the military operations were local sweeps in specific target areas. These netted few casualties but did have the effect of keeping the CTs on the move and off balance, made it harder for the CTs to obtain and stock supplies, and generally created living conditions in the jungle camps which many of the guerrillas came to like less and less. Furthermore, on the constructive side (as we shall see in Chapter 5) Thai developmental activities, such as road and pond building, were beginning to be visible and a more effective government propaganda effort was under way.

The CTs themselves were becoming more aware of their own difficulties and the lack of progress. The guidelines put out for 1968 were a clue to this. The first prescribed task, to build up stores of supplies, indicated that logistics was an increasing source of concern. The second task, to develop armed units, was startling, since this was after two and a half years of overt insurgency. Further, these units were told to increase their defensive and offensive capabilities and when this had been done they were to ambush isolated government patrols and officials but to refrain from attacking government strong points. All of these instructions suggested that the movement was still very much in a building stage and had not moved ahead smoothly.

In fact, 1968 was a difficult year for the CTs. Their initiated incidents dropped off sharply after the first quarter of the year. This might be explained to some extent by the coming of the wet season, except that incidents did not increase when the wet season ended, and a study of incident rates over the years has shown little or no seasonal cycle. All evidence available suggests that the communists were very much on the defensive and were more concerned with building and strengthening their organization and the capability of the guerrillas than in engaging in paramilitary actions. The leaders, however, were reluctant to reduce the number of incidents to a level that would appear to suggest a slowing-down of the movement. Any indication of slowing-down could, and as a matter of fact did, have repercussions on the guerrillas as well as on the peasants whose support the communists sought. During the latter part of 1968 the CT defection rate increased sharply, though most of the defectors were low-level and recently recruited and none were really hard-core. Most of them complained of scarcity of food and clothing, of a hard life and frequent moves, all brought about by RTG activities and a poor support structure. In general, at least among the rank and file, morale seemed to be low.

There are indications that some of the defections were not entirely voluntary. In the process of tightening up the organization, the communist cadres may have pushed a number of the weaker elements out, telling them to go home for a while. (This was apparently done in the South when Chin Peng in the early 1960s reportedly sent the older and weaker members of his terrorist organization back to their villages and retained only the young and motivated.) The insurgents had also begun to alienate some of the villagers through their tougher behavior and extortion of food. Many villagers could clearly see that the insurgents had not kept their promises of bringing a better life, had not driven the government out, and were not winning. The Thai peasant, in common with many other country folk, is a very sharp observer of the ebb and flow of events and also rather keen on being on the winning side. In 1968 not many believed that the communists were going to be the victors.

However, little real damage had been inflicted on the basic structure of the insurgency except for the high-level arrests in 1967 and some government success in northern Ubon and a portion of Udon. The military and police activities in the Northeast had inflicted few casualties. Intelligence activities had been slow in producing accurate pictures of the situation. Although improving in 1968 and beginning to give a good picture in a few provinces, particularly Sakon Nakhon and Nakhon Phanom, intelligence had not led to as many or timely actions as were needed. In short, government activity was successful in limiting the spread and growth of the insurgency, but not in eliminating it.

The insurgents recognized that most of their weaknesses were inherent in their apparatus and set out to correct them, as later developments demonstrated. The CTs in the Northeast admitted that the government was now stronger than it had been several years before—stronger in army and police activity and, in certain areas, in village defense. They also admitted that some of the developmental activities were helping the government's cause. The situation for the insurgents was considerably more serious than it had been, and the guerrilla bands were instructed to be very careful in their activities. The party seemed to be urging a reduction in armed activity without saying so explicitly. This notion was reinforced by an instruction to conserve the strength of the trained and dedicated cadres and to concentrate on recruiting, training, and general preparation for the future.

Although 1969 was also a year of retrenchment for the CTs, interestingly enough there was an increase in certain insurgent activities which generally draw little attention but are significant in the organizational building period. For example, there was an increase in food gathering, in covert visits to villagers in an attempt to get information on government forces, and in low-level, low-key propaganda activities. These incidents usually involved two to four people rather than fifteen or twenty and were aimed at improving the CT organization. At the same time, the RTG presence in the villages was greatly expanded as villagers, usually led by a few policemen, were being recruited to defend themselves. This system, when it worked properly, made it more difficult and dangerous for the guerrillas to enter the villages in order to obtain food and information. It also meant that the government's reporting channels had a broader base and that more insurgent activities were reported to higher echelons. Since, as suggested earlier, the villagers were aware that the communists were not winning, and that protection was somewhat better, they were now more willing to provide information to the government. This is a critical development in an insurgency as the villager is the best and most important source of information for either side, and guerrillas cannot survive in an environment where large numbers of villagers feel secure in informing the government about insurgent activities.

In many ways 1970 was a continuation of the insurgents' 1969 building effort, but with some changes. The usual emphasis was put on strengthening the village base and increasing communist indoctrination. The overall strategy was to lie low in most areas, but apparently a decision had been made to increase attacks in the Northeast areas where the CTs were strong, particularly in Nakhon Phanom and Sakon Nakhon. A switch in strategy also seems to have been made to deemphasize persuasion and to stress coercion and fear. The Communist Party of Thailand appeared to be trying to develop a new image as a powerful military organization that should be feared and respected, although this did not mean that all peaceful efforts of recruiting or gaining supporters were discontinued. Why the communists decided on this significant change at that time is not known, but it was probably based on the fact that the organizational efforts of 1968 and 1969 had finally begun to pay off, so that the leadership was more confident. The change may also have indicated that persuasion was not working very well or at least too slowly. If organization is good, coercion and terror carefully used can speed up progress.

The new emphasis on greater action was soon implemented. On February 28,

1970, an estimated eighty or ninety CTs operating in six groups burned nine bridges, blocked two roads, attacked village protection units, and laid an armed ambush against the army, all in one district of Nakhon Phanom. In March, 1970, about 150 incidents occurred in the Northeast, a new high for that area. About one-third of these were armed encounters, and most of the activity occurred as planned in Sakon Nakhon and Nakhon Phanom. As 1970 unfolded, the CTs turned more and more to armed encounters and attacks on communications. A number of bridges were burned, ambushes were laid on the main Sakon Nakhon-Nakhon Phanom highway, and the first armored personnel carrier was mined. Similar armed violence and increased terrorism took place in Sakon Nakhon province and to a lesser extent in Kalasin. There was much propaganda about a dry-season offensive but this did not materialize. Aggressive action by the Thai Second Army helped forestall the offensive, but the whole idea may have been a propaganda effort to help maintain morale. While the insurgents continued to be very active in Nakhon Phanom and Sakon Nakhon, large insurgent bands were also sighted in Buri Ram, Udon, and Ubon provinces. Also, apparently following instructions, the CTs moved into quieter areas where they undertook recruiting, training, and organizational activities.

The limited growth of the CT movement continued through 1973. An increased level of CT-initiated incidents was anticipated but did not materialize partially as a result of Thai army action in the area which disrupted CT bases. The CTs claimed, and most observers admit, that the communists have developed bases in the Phu Phan Mountains. These are used as headquarters, training bases, and depots. In addition, such bases allow easier reception and storage of weapons and supplies from outside Thailand and have considerable psychological value as a symbol of achievement, indicating a growing organization that can keep the government forces away. There was one report of a Peoples Liberation Army platoon in the Northeast and the Thais claimed to have one defector from this platoon, but this report is still questionable and not fully accepted as being factual. Another significant development was the creation and training of village militia who, though not now armed, can help the movement in many ways and are a future potential military force. This is part of the communist attempt to involve the villagers so completely that they cannot desert the movement; if the effort should be successful, there can be no campaign to "root out the infrastructure," because the people and the infrastructure are the same. Finally, money seems to be more plentiful for the party, which makes recruiting and buying of supplies much easier; since shortage of funds had long plagued the CTs in the Northeast, this was an important development. The CT guerrillas seem not to want to attract attention by spectacular military moves, but they do carry on subversive and small irregular activities. The emphasis seems to be on organizing the people, developing and improving the organization, and inciting the people against the government.

After about eight years of effort in the Northeast, the CTs have not only survived but also improved their organization and long-term threat. Their leadership, probably hiding in the Phu Phan hills, has managed to elude the government in spite of search activities by police and military. They have established bases in this area. Insurgency strength has grown, admittedly with some ups and downs, from a few hundred to approximately 1,500 to 2,000. That the organization and indoctrination efforts have been successful and that these guerrillas are better prepared than those of 1965 seems very clear. Perhaps a hundred or so villages could be called CT-dominated (or "red" in Vietnamese terminology). On the other hand, despite the rapid increase in armed violence in 1970 and 1971, with a leveling off in 1972 and 1973, the movement has not grown impressively, though we have no firm figure for the number of members and sympathizers. The mass of the people seem uninterested in the CTs and the campaign of terror has not touched many; but recent evidence suggests that communist organization and propaganda techniques, improved and refined over the past several years, may be beginning to break down traditional Thai resistance but not at a great rate. So long as the CTs can retain the initiative, they will likely build deeper roots in this area and continue to gain strength, and this could pose a problem of ever-increasing seriousness for the government. However, the rate of progress has been and is slow with many basic factors still impeding CT efforts. CT guerrilla strength in early 1974 is about 1,600 with perhaps 1,500 or more unarmed village militia.

THE NORTH

In 1967 active fighting broke out in the mountainous area of the North along the Laotian border. This is some of the roughest terrain in Thailand and is contiguous to the Laotian province of Sayaboury, most of which is under the control of the Pathet Lao, not the Royal Laotian Government. Guerrilla bands can move back and forth across the border with almost no interference and maintain training centers and headquarters undetected or untroubled by Thai or Laotian forces. The majority of the insurgents are tribespeople, particularly Meo, who live in the area and know it well. This presence of a mountain population friendly to, or coerced by, the communists is in addition to the advantages provided the guerrillas by this difficult terrain and together make it a difficult area for the RTG to control.

The first clash in Nan province between government and guerrilla forces took place in February, 1967. Government forces broke up the bands, and the area was quiet until September, when an increasingly serious outbreak began. Again, we do not know why the communists selected 1967 to expand the insurgency. At the time some believed that it was primarily a diversion to draw government attention and resources from the Northeast where the insurgency was not going well. The timing may well have been designed to help the Northeast, but increasing evidence has suggested that the communists had also planned for a long time to start action in the North when those forces were ready. Ever since the late 1950s, tribesmen had been taken outside the country for paramilitary training in North Vietnam and Laos and a few of these gained experience by fighting in Laos. Furthermore, some of the tribal villages had received communist agents who had tried to intensify the differences and difficulties between the Thais and the mountain people. By late 1967 this small guerrilla organization, although perhaps not fully prepared, was in good shape. The incidents in early 1967 had hinted at trouble in the North, and some intelligence sources had also been predicting that the tribesmen, at communist instigation, would rebel. Trouble had started in May, 1967, in Chiang Rai province, but what had been considered to be the actual insurgent outbreak there in late 1967 was in fact a reaction to Thai Border Patrol Police intrusion into a subverted village. Thus the timing may have been forced by the government. Nevertheless, the insurgents were clearly better prepared than those in the Northeast had been in 1965, and if the Northern insurgents had not been ready for combat, it seems unlikely that the communists would have risked another premature effort in Thailand, even though the terrain and population in the North were more friendly than in the Northeast.

In late 1968 overt insurgency broke out in another part of the North where the provinces of Phitsanulok, Phetchabun, and Loei meet, sometimes referred to as the Tri-Province area, or the Phu Lom Lo, which is the name of the high mountain dominating much of the area. There is a sanctuary close by in Laos and tribespeople live on both sides of the border. The area is mountainous and densely forested, with a few scattered villages and almost no roads; travel is mainly by foot trails. The cover provided by the rugged terrain is an advantage for guerrillas and a disadvantage for the RTG. The government also is at an administrative disadvantage in that the area is the dividing line between the Second Army in the Northeast and the Third Army in the North, the boundary between the Fourth and Sixth police regions, and the junction of the three provinces—making it almost a classic area for guerrillas.

Tak province is the third area in the North where the hill peoples have rebelled against the government. The background here is a little different. Originally the outbreak seemed to be purely a confrontation between the government and the tribespeople; it was based on alleged bad behavior of the police and for some time bad feeling tended to smolder rather than develop into open violence. However, a bitter situation, which profited the communists, finally developed despite the governor's wise policy. In early 1969 the governor had been able to prevent suppressive operations by the police and army because he wanted to try to maintain communications with the Meo leaders and to convince them that the government intended to treat them justly. He patiently worked at this strategy for months and seemed to have been making some progress. In December, 1969, however, the government decided to resume building of the Mae Sot-Umphong Road in Tak, whereupon the CTs ambushed the road-building crew, killing four and preventing reinforcements from going to the scene. They continued to make the area very dangerous, but some construction, with strong police protection, was recommenced in early 1971. By the end of 1971, however, all work was abandoned. The area had become extremely dangerous due to the alienation of the local inhabitants and guerrilla activities, and the present situation in Tak is still poor.

In inciting the hill people against the RTG the communist leaders, usually Thais or Sino-Thais, have focused very little on communist doctrine but have concentrated on local issues, as was done earlier in the Northeast. They are appealing to the Meo and other hill people on various grounds, all designed to increase antagonism against the RTG and the Thai people. They have aggravated old tribal fears that the RTG wants to dispossess them of "their land" (all the mountainous areas in which they slowly migrate), stop their slash-and-burn agricultural methods, and halt the growing of poppies for opium, their main source of cash income. The RTG does in fact wish to educate them in the legalities of land ownership, to stop the burning of forests, and to halt the opium trade. As we shall see in Chapter 4, these issues raise complicated problems with no easy solutions. The communist cadres also make much out of alleged corruption, unfairness, and brutality of Thai officials. They stress that the RTG helps the ethnic Thais, but not the hill people, and that few schools, medical facilities, roads, etc. are built in the mountains.

The immediate objectives of the insurgency in the North are less precisely evident. The CTs talk of an autonomous Meo area in Thailand or of combining all the Meo in China, Laos, and Thailand into one kingdom. Both of these options would involve an actual seizure or at least limitation on the sovereignty of Thailand in certain areas. Both could be a part of the Chinese effort to create disaffection among all the hill peoples in countries from India to Vietnam; the Chinese have hinted at the creation of some vague tribal autonomous state in these rugged regions. Whether the real Chinese objective is the development of a defensive buffer, or perhaps a springboard for expansion, we do not know. A more likely objective might be the de facto creation of liberated areas in the North region of Thailand which would be useful in a variety of ways. The areas could serve as local irritations to induce the expenditure of Thai manpower and resources and to remind the government what the communists could do if they wanted to. They could also be used as training areas for ethnic Thais and headquarters of the communist effort and so serve as the base for the campaign in the North. However, as the movement has continued, it seems more likely that the tribal insurgency is not aimed at forming a Meo state but is a first step in a much larger effort. Recent evidence has strongly indicated that a campaign to subvert the Thais is under way and that the true goal is the overthrow of the Royal Thai Government. Certainly, Thai adherents would not be of great assistance if an autonomous Meo region were the eventual goal.

From the beginning in the North the CTs seized the initiative and employed basic guerrilla tactics. The tribesmen cooperated through harassment to frighten and intimidate villagers and to keep police and army outposts off balance. Sometimes, using the heavy cover of the mountains, they would invest a village or post for days, almost a siege but largely an invisible one. The tactic had a demoralizing effect on villagers and police and even on the military. It forced the government to resupply with helicopters, not always an easy task, given the weather, terrain, and the enemy. The CTs also ambushed police and military units. The various tactics were almost always successful and inflicted heavy casualties on the government at practically no cost to the guerrillas. Word of mouth and the "Voice of the Thai People," broadcasting in Meo, announced (and undoubtedly exaggerated) the guerrilla successes and further encouraged opposition to the government.

Beginning in 1969 and continuing into 1970 the insurgents in the North and Tri-Province areas appeared to be building bases and making plans for protracted conflict. They forced the local inhabitants to grow extra food so that this might be stockpiled in bases. They seemed to be setting up training camps and there were indications that they were moving all of the Thai-oriented communist apparatus from Laos into Thailand itself. They continued to maintain the initiative by constant ambushing, harassing, and attacking isolated posts and units in this difficult terrain. In April, 1970, they shot down a T-6 attack aircraft and destroyed a helicopter trying to rescue the crew. In September the governor of Chiang Rai and two or three other Thai officials were killed in an ambush. The tempo of violence remained high and mostly favorable to the guerrillas for all of 1970.

As in the Northeast, 1971 revealed considerable CT progress in the North and increasingly overt activity. Battalion and company-size units were reported operating as such. More guerrillas were armed with AK-47 rifles, and some units had mortars, mines, and rocket launchers. The CTs continued their well-executed attacks and followed the favorite communist tactic of ambushing the reaction or relief forces. They had, by the end of the year, established several secure bases, especially in eastern Chiang Rai and eastern Nan. The government admitted the existence of these bases and did not enter them. The CTs were increasingly trying to win over lowland Thais to the cause, especially by moving into the valleys of Chiang Rai and Nan. Success in this effort would make the threat even graver. The CTs also seemed to be moving south, especially along the mountains on the Burma border.

In some contrast to actions in the Northeast, the CTs in the North seemed to want to attract attention by very visible military actions. This resulted in greater Royal Thai Government activity in the North, without much success so far.

In January, 1972, the RTG moved the First Division from Bangkok to the Tri-Province area for counterinsurgency operations, but there were no positive results and indeed serious losses on the government side, and the division was withdrawn in April, 1972. A similar exercise in early 1973 incurred few casualties but few positive results. The CTs in spite of considerable effort to penetrate the lowland Thais have not had much success. Furthermore, reports in late 1972 and 1973 suggested increasing dissatisfaction on the part of the Meo in the "liberated areas"; they apparently do not like the regimentation and indoctrination of the communists. Some want to leave the areas. But in general, 1972 and 1973 saw some CT progress in the North.

The Northern guerrillas have received more outside assistance than those in the Northeast. This is probably because all kinds of supplies are strictly limited in the mountain area nearby but accessible in communist-dominated parts of Laos, but possibly also because the North segment of the Thai insurgency was better trained and organized before overt insurgency began and therefore needed and was considered eligible for greater aid. Certainly their professionalism has stood out, and very early in the insurgency there were reports that they had AK-47s, one of the most modern communist rifles. Recently they have had a considerable number of bloc weapons, mostly Chinese. The guerrilla areas are along the Laotian border, which of course is not very well delineated and in any case is meaningless to the hill people who live on both sides of it. This situation permitted the communists to build bases in Laos, some of which have been moved into Thailand, and to develop many simple exfiltration and infiltration routes. One of the most significant of these has been in the Pakbeng Valley which runs into the Mekong not too far from the Thai border. An old French lumber trail there made the passage by foot relatively simple. In recent years the Red Chinese have been building a motor road down part of the Pakbeng Valley, though the Chinese themselves deny this. This on-again, off-again activity causes considerable concern in Bangkok, as it seems to be directed straight toward Thailand. The supply needs of the present insurgency in the North, or even a considerably increased effort, would not require such a road, but it might be part of a long-term attempt to prepare for the ultimate hoped-for success of the Thai insurgency or possible Chinese incursions, though the latter does not seem to fit into current Chinese policy.

A number of other factors might explain this Chinese activity. The North Vietnamese have habitually laid claim to Laos, have occupied two of its northeastern provinces, and have installed a number of troops in the Plaine des Jarres. It could be that the Chinese intended to use the road to assert their supremacy in northwestern Laos, either by agreement with the North Vietnamese that China should have direct access to Thailand, which the Chinese consider their area of interest, or because the Chinese wish to stake a claim to this part of Laos and to exclude the North Vietnamese from it. A more likely possibility is that the road and its apparent threat are intended to put pressure on Thailand to alter its pro-Western foreign policy and its active support to anti-communists in the Indochina peninsula. That the road could be used by Chinese troops in a conventional war is not overlooked in Bangkok, however unlikely such a move might seem at the present time. Some observers have suggested that the road has no specific significance to Thailand but is simply part of a Chinese plan for economic development aid to Laos. Whatever the purpose, the road and its bringing the Chinese closer have deeply worried the Thais. The on-again, off-again activity on it has not helped to clarify its purposes.

Partially because of the road and partially because of the intensity of the insurgency and its gradual movement into new areas, the Thais have become increasingly worried about the situation in the North. There is less and less security for more and more people, particularly in Chiang Rai and Nan provinces. The CTs, in the mountainous border areas at least, have been operating with relative freedom and go where they wish when they please. They are penetrating the largest hill tribe, the Karens. They have established liberated areas and increased the areas where visiting officials from Bangkok do not venture. They are tying down numerically superior Thai forces, both police and armed troops. The Royal Thai Government suppression operations, described in Chapter 4, have inflicted very few casualties on the enemy and have scarcely hampered their activities.

Only recently have the Thais begun to gain fairly sound knowledge of the CT organization and its leadership. On the other hand, there is dissatisfaction in the liberated areas, very little progress with the lowland Thais, and few CT operations outside the mountainous areas. Estimated CT guerrilla strength in early 1974 is about 2,500 with about 800 village militia.

WEST CENTRAL REGION

A small group of terrorists, perhaps between fifty and a hundred, have operated in the provinces to the west and southwest of Bangkok. These provinces, Prachuab Khiri Khan, Phetchaburi, and Ratchaburi, also have borders with Burma on the west, where there are mountains and very few people. Most of the activity of the groups has been clandestine organizing, with occasional ambushes.

Organization seems to have started early in the 1960s. The first successful ambushes were two very professional jobs carried out in 1967 in which policemen were killed. There was also a similarly professional and successful one in 1968. In late 1969 the communists increased their terrorism and activities against the villagers. They also carried out a very successful ambush in Ratchaburi province in December, 1969. It was very carefully prepared and the CTs had good concealment and an excellent field of fire. They killed six police and wounded three who were in two jeeps on the way to investigate the murder of a village defense man. However, since 1969 there has been no repetition of the carefully planned ambushes of previous years. Although a few incidents show up in the statistics, most of them were food gathering and information gathering, with only one assassination. Continued inactivity in this area seems to indicate that the movement for some reason is languishing. The numbers of incidents are so small and so little is known about the group that the figures do not mean much, except to show that an organized group is in the area that can carry out very professional operations when it wants to. The group appears not to have expanded after 1969, but the government's intelligence on subversion and insurgency in that area is not very good. That it is not, is somewhat surprising, since the area hosts the King during the summer at Hua Hin and is not far from Bangkok. It is estimated that there are about 100 guerrillas in this area in early 1974.

THE MID-SOUTH

Overt insurgency broke out in the Mid-South about the same time as in the Northeast. The insurgents, like those of the Northeast, are mainly ethnic Thais, with a sprinkling of Chinese. The two main areas of operation are the Khao Ban Tad Mountains along the Trang and Phattalung provincial border and the somewhat hilly border areas in Surat Thani and Nakhon Si Thammarat provinces. Here again the guerrillas have tried to select terrain most suitable to their operations, since it straddles the most important administrative boundaries. In 1969 and 1970 they spread into the lowland areas of Phattalung and extended their activities southward into Satun and Songkhla provinces. Satun is a Muslim area, although unique among the southern provinces in that it is also a Thai-speaking area. It had been thought to lie in the domain of the Malaysian-oriented Communist Terrorist Organization (CTO), the Far South communists. Why the Communist Party of Thailand has extended its activities further south is somewhat puzzling. There may be a secret agreement between the Thai Party and the CTO that as the latter moves back into Malaysia the Thai communists will take over some of the CTO areas in Thailand. Evidence of some training of CTs by the CTO and some liaison between them seems to support this thesis. Also, recent CT expansion into ethnic Thai areas but less so into the Muslim areas, where the CTO has recently been more active, tends to substantiate the hypothesis of an agreement. However, the CTO has to a certain extent moved northward particularly in its proselyting efforts and shows no signs of giving up areas long held in the Far South. Actually, no secret agreement may exist; nationalism may simply be injecting itself into the communist efforts so that the Communist Party of Thailand is in fact moving south to prevent the CTO from trying to dominate more of Thailand.

For most of its history in this part of Thailand, the Thai communist insurgency has pursued a low-level but steady organizational effort. Serious recruiting seems to have begun in 1961. The groups seem not to have developed new able leadership nor did they grow very much until 1969. Over the years the level of violence (small harassments and selected assassinations) has remained fairly even, ranging between forty and seventy incidents per year. In 1969 the violence increased but appeared to have the purpose of improving the capability of the guerrillas. The attacks had the usual objective of intimidating the population and discrediting the government. The main increase was in the attacks on the Village Protection Units (VPUs), which the RTG had organized to protect the villagers, and the main purpose seemed to be to gather weapons, radios, and other supplies. In every attack the CTs were successful in this objective. The communists also appeared to be launching a campaign against the small development projects which the RTG had begun in the area. Two Mobile Development Units were attacked, their leaders killed and the camps burned. The "Voice of the Thai People" also joined in the attack on the small development efforts. Why the communists bothered to campaign against these very small and nascent activities only they themselves know, but the purpose was probably, as usual, to discredit the government and forestall any larger efforts to help the people.

Periodically the RTG has become concerned about the Mid-South situation and conducts a sweep against the guerrillas. During one police suppression operation launched in late 1969, the CTs abandoned their usual custom of trying to evade the forces or retreating into their hideouts. Instead, they went on the offensive and hit several villages and police posts. In February, 1970, seven out of a total of eight incidents in the Mid-South occurred in two districts where major suppression operations were taking place. One of these included a noon-day attack on a police station along National Route 4, the main north-south road. In March, ten incidents were reported in Phattalung province alone, and the increase in violence spread to Surat Thani and Nakhon Si Thammarat.

One important trend in the Mid-South in 1970 and 1971 was the extensive geographical expansion of the insurgency—both organizational activities and armed operations—to the east and west coastal plains out of the north-south mountain chain in peninsular Thailand. A new CT group was also established in southern Nakhon Si Thammarat province, which linked up with the Phattalung insurgency. At the same time, all over the Mid-South the insurgents greatly increased their harassment of village security and police elements, forcing them out of large areas of the countryside.

During 1972 General San, the Thai army commander in the southern provinces used army units more vigorously to pursue the guerrillas and to reintroduce a government presence in certain areas. This presence, however, tended to be temporary as there was no follow-up to establish competent civil authority and continued protection. The army stayed in an area for two weeks and then departed, allowing the CTs to move right back in. In some areas a new feature of the insurgency was CT willingness to stand and fight these army incursions rather than taking evasive action. The increase in CT attacks and control in certain areas has had a serious psychological effect on the population and local officials, though their primary purpose is only to obtain supplies. For example, the CTs have moved into the flat land in the capital district of Phattalung province; the people are being intimidated and provincial officials are reluctant to go into this area right outside the provincial capital. Should this continue, a part of Phattalung province will be lost to the RTG. Although the few hundred insurgents in the Mid-South are by no means an immediate threat to the government, the increase in violence and propaganda in the area in which the insurgents are active, plus their ability to intimidate the population and officials is serious. It would not take too great an effort to sever north-south communications in this narrow part of Thailand, and this could be done almost any time. The links with the communists in the Far South also are ominous for the future. However, General San's actions have to some extent restricted the actions and expansion of the CTs. The 400 guerrillas do not constitute a serious menace to the Thai government but must be kept under continuous surveillance.

THE FAR SOUTH

The security situation is complicated in the Far South's five provinces, which are composed of approximately 75 percent Malays, 20 percent Thais, and 5 percent Chinese. It is a region with considerable banditry and extortion and some piracy on the adjacent sea. There is also the ill-organized Muslim separatist movement which wishes to rejoin Malaysia or perhaps set up an autonomous region. Lastly there is the Communist Terrorist Organization (CTO), which operates under the direction of the Malaysian Communist Party. The CTO was originally made up of those communist terrorists who moved into Thailand in the late 1950s seeking sanctuary after the British had defeated them in Malaya. The CTO is probably the best organized and led communist group in Thailand. Their well-defined political and military organization is headed by the Secretary General, Chin Peng (still believed to hold that office), who provides the political and military leadership as he did during much of the Malaysian Emergency.

Beneath the Secretary General's group are three major political organizations called State Committees, which provide the political guidance in their area of responsibility. Below the committees are Districts and below them Branches and finally the Village organization with its cells. This political element is well run, aggressive in its propagandizing, and active in the use of various fronts and auxiliary organizations. It collects taxes and administers justice. It holds propaganda meetings in the villages and is very active in recruiting members for the armed bands in the jungle camps. There is the Malaysian Communist Youth League (MCYL), composed of several thousand youths between the ages of eighteen and twenty-five, some of whom have received guerrilla training. A few of the League's members join guerrilla bands while the others remain in the villages as a reserve. There is also the Young Vanguard organization which prepares the youth for the MCYL. The movement is particularly strong among the Chinese communities both in the rural areas and in the towns. On the military side, located with the State committees, are three regiments, the 8th and 12th being primarily Chinese and the 10th composed of Muslims. They make up the bulk of the Malayan Liberation Army. This communist apparatus is a significant power in the South with its 1,200 to 1,500 guerrillas, several thousand organized youths, effective political structure, and control over practically 100,000 inhabitants in the area.

The stated intention of the CTO is to return to Malaysia, and it has steadfastly maintained that it is merely poaching on Thai territory. It has emphasized that it has no quarrel with the Royal Thai Government and does not wish to jeopardize its safe haven. It has been very clever in pursuing this line. For example, in the summer of 1969, just before a meeting between the Malays and Thais on border problems, the CTO sent messages to top officials of the RTG, emphasizing that the CTO was merely awaiting the proper opportunity to return to Malaysia and that it had no quarrel with the Thais or territorial claims against Thailand. It added, clearly with malice in mind, that it could not of course speak for the current Malaysian government which it implied might have certain territorial designs. The communists have acted according to the strategy by not being very aggressive and rarely initiating actions against the Thai forces, though in mid-1969 they began to take a more aggressive stand against the Thai Border Patrol Police. This may have been in retaliation for the combined Border Patrol Police-Malaysian Police Field Force actions against them. The Thais have permitted a small number of Malaysian police to operate inside Thailand in conjunction with their own police, as the Malaysians have been naturally anxious to destroy the CTO, which has designs against their own country.

In 1969 activity in the Far South took a significant jump. Thai and Malay security forces were more active, and some of their operations which discovered and destroyed large CTO camps may have begun to hurt. For example, in May, 1969, the Thai Border Patrol Police (BPP) occupied a large CTO base camp capable of accommodating 300 guerrillas. Camps such as these were well planned and designed. They had barracks, dining halls, small parade grounds, and command posts. In almost every case the guerrilla forces managed to escape with most of the important papers and supplies, but they lost several comfortable and elaborate camps. Also, 1969 appeared to be the year when the CTO began with greater determination to pursue its avowed aim of reestablishing itself in northern Malaysia. On the Malaysian side of the border, increasing numbers of armed uniformed CTO elements have been cited, and propagandizing, recruiting, and organizational activities have been on the rise. The CTO has intensified its propaganda appeals to the Muslim community in southern Thailand to widen the potential support base. The propaganda tends to follow communist lines—emphasizing the revolutionary forces of the workers and peasants rather than ethnic differences and thus correcting one of the weak points of CTO propaganda during the Emergency. Reportedly, some transfer of Muslims has been made to the Chinese regiments, to give credence to this propaganda effort.

The CTO has also increased its overt insurgency efforts on both sides of the border, but particularly just inside the Malaysian border. On October 24, 1969, explosives were planted on the main highway between Kedah and Songkhla just one mile inside Malaysia, as cadres of the 8th Regiment had earlier boasted that they would do. A government military convoy was ambushed with casualties, and the road was closed for almost a week while mines and booby traps were dug up. In mid-December, 1969, a railroad bridge was sabotaged in Malaysia at Padang Besar. Two charges were detonated under the bridge, and a red flag and propaganda leaflets were left behind. This action cut the main railroad line between Singapore and Bangkok and necessitated busing around the cut area. In the same month they attacked a Malaysian police station, the first such attack since 1960. Some of these actions were serious in themselves, but it would seem that the main objective was to prove the strength of the CTO and to demonstrate publicly its desire and ability to operate in Malaysia. Although the insurgency in Malaysia seems to be increasing in intensity, there are no indications as yet that the CTO is ready to abandon its bases and support structure so laboriously built up in southern Thailand. These are still essential to its strength and for operations inside Malaysia. It may also be that the CTO, despite its claims, does not intend to give up this area inhabited primarily by Malays and Chinese.

In November, 1969, a new clandestine communist radio transmitter began operations, calling itself "Voice of the Malay Revolution," using the same facilities as the "Voice of the Thai People," and probably broadcasting from southwest China. The station broadcast seven days a week in Malay and Mandarin and in January, 1970, began Tamil broadcasts. Thus it seems to be following the earlier CTO line of appealing to the various races. It calls on "enslaved Indian rubber tappers," "exploited Chinese workers," and "oppressed Malay peasants" to unite and support the revolution. The programs stress alleged abuses and oppressive measures against working people of all races "by the Raman-Razak clique and the Lee Quang Yu puppet clique, both running dogs of U.S.-British imperialism." A New Year's message reviewed all CTO actions in northern Malaysia and claimed that they were victories of the liberation army on behalf of the people of Malaysia.

Although the number of reported CTO incursions and activities in Malaysia decreased during the first part of 1970, the CTO remained a source of considerable concern to the Malaysian government. In mid-April, for example, they ambushed a group of Malaysian rangers, killing seven. Its reconnaissance operations as well as its propaganda efforts continued. The seriousness of the situation was reflected in a Thai-Malay border meeting in March, 1970, when the right of hot pursuit was extended, to enable the armed forces of the two countries to track down the insurgents effectively; provisions were made for combined headquarters on both sides of the border and for increased use of air power. The Thais, on their side, also improved their command structure and dispatched a few aircraft to the South, but made little effort at that time to increase the number or improve the capability of the relatively weak BPP.

Malaysian frustrations have continued to mount as communist activity in their northern provinces increased and as Thai actions against the CTO decreases.

The CTO in early 1974 numbers nearly 2,000 regulars and about 3,500 MCYL members. It had been improving its ability to reestablish a guerrilla presence in northern Malaysia, and some reports suggest that there may already be a permanent armed presence south of the border. They can, and do, insert units as large as fifty men for periods of up to two weeks, thirty to sixty kilometers inside the border. The last significant Thai actions against the CTO were General San's capture of the Sadao Camp in February, 1970, and the capture of three camps in Yala in April and May, 1970. Since then, RTG activity against the CTO has been minimal. On the other hand, not only has CTO cooperation with the CPT increased, but the CTO has been making a major effort to recruit Thai Muslims. This is in line with the CTO strategy of returning to Malaysia under a broad ethnic banner, but it also increases the potential threat of the CTO to RTG authority over the Muslim provinces of south Thailand. The Far South is by far the lowest priority of the RTG which is doing almost nothing against the CTO, since it is viewed as a Malaysian problem.

INSURGENT PROSPECTS

After eight years of overt insurgency, scattered here and there in most of the regions of Thailand, the communists have made progress. They have expanded the geographical area of their activities within regions and have been operating openly in all regions except the Central Plain—and recently have been moving in that direction also. Their armed elements have grown from a few hundred guerrillas to perhaps 5,000 or over 6,000 if the CTO of the South is included. The number of their more or less committed village supporters is not known but could be as many as 50,000. Insurgent activities and actions have increased from a few scattered incidents in 1965 to several thousand in 1973.

The communists claim to have a Liberation Army and a Supreme Command, and in 1970 announced the first liberated areas in the Phu Phan range and in Nan province in the North. They have the usual three-layered military force: regular force, guerrillas, and village militia. They have striven to improve their organization and the quality of its members; they have worked hard to develop a stronger and broader political and logistics base to support the guerrillas. They are supported by the "Voice of the Thai People," which broadcasts not only in Thai but also in several hill-tribe dialects, and by the "Voice of the Malay Revolution," broadcasting in Chinese, Malay, and Tamil to the South. The increase in material assistance from outside is significant, especially in the provision of AK-47 rifles, and now the units have crew-served weapons, mortars or machine guns. More money is also available. The insurgents continue to force the Royal Thai Government to devote an increasing amount of resources to the insurgency problem. In sum, the insurgency is better known, larger, and more effective than it was in 1965, but in spite of its growth and build-up, the current insurgent movement still does not pose a serious threat to the authority of the Royal Thai Government.

With this brief overall assessment in mind, I would predict that in the next few years the CTs will probably continue their recruiting, training, and motivational efforts, especially aiming at ethnic Thais, and will continue to improve their organizational apparatus. They will try in the rural areas to further erode the government position by more selective use of terror, especially by attacking and assassinating local officials and key personages such as teachers. Terror will be accompanied by carefully contrived propaganda pointing out the basic weaknesses and inadequacies of the government. The communists will try to expand their area of control and to develop larger "liberated areas." They will try to move into lowland Thai areas in the North, but there will probably not be any large dramatic moves anywhere in the country. China will continue to encourage and assist the insurgency in spite of a limited détente with Thailand but will not greatly increase its material aid until the movement is going ahead convincingly or the Chinese for their own objectives need to put the insurgency to greater use. The effort seems to be growing, and if unchecked, could in a few years pose serious problems and probably will remove more areas of the country from government control. However, the progress is slow, the basic Thai resistance to communism still seems strong, the communist leadership is weak and partially alien, and more effective Thai countermeasures could to a large degree prevent further communist gains.

Chapter 4

The Thai Response

Well before the surfacing of the insurgency in August, 1965, the Royal Thai Government (RTG) had information which suggested that overt insurgency was impending. Various government intelligence services as well as the police had evidence of subversion in the Northeast, the West Central region, and the Mid-South, and of the Communist Terrorist Organization (CTO) in the Far South. As mentioned in Chapter 2, a 1961 Southeast Asia Treaty Organization (SEATO) study group, of which I was a member, and which spent most of its time on the Northeast, predicted the outbreak of an insurgency in two or three years and recommended certain actions to the RTG. To many in the RTG, however, there appeared to be only the usual dissidence and banditry and no unusual spate of killing or other violence. I discovered that in the insurgency field preventive measures seemed to be almost as difficult to institute as they are in medicine. In reporting to Washington on the 1961 SEATO study, I urged action, both suppressive and developmental, before the active armed insurgency

actually broke out. One top official's reply was, "But no one is getting killed"—
i.e., why worry about something that had not happened yet.

As we shall see in the next four chapters, where the eventual response of both
the American and Thai governments are discussed and assessed, there were
always to be at least two basic dilemmas.[1] If counterinsurgency is always going
to combine some elements of military suppression on the one hand and some
elements of longer-range economic development on the other hand, what is the
best mix? What is the philosophy or the doctrine of the counterinsurgency
work? The second problem had to do with who would do it, assuming there was
some agreement as to what actions were called for. There was to be a continuing
problem of coordination, as between competing Thai hierarchies with the added
complication of sometimes competing and interacting American hierarchies. The
combination of different roles by key figures adds to the confusion. This chapter
essentially was written before the October 14, 1973, change of government in
Thailand. It is too early to know whether the new civilian government will
continue the counterinsurgency doctrine and organization described in this
chapter, though there are indications that the Thai military organization will be
restructured.

THAI COUNTERINSURGENCY DOCTRINE (CPM)

The first question, with which this chapter deals in part, is one that has long
plagued students and practitioners of counterinsurgency. The conventional wisdom all too often in America today is that suppression just breeds more
insurgency and deals merely with symptoms, while development, e.g., satisfying
village needs for water, better roads, or schools, both deals with and removes
causes. Reality, as usual, is more complicated. In the first place, we cannot use a
simple "suppression-development" continuum and locate a particular undertak-
ing on it, because it is often impossible to separate the military and economic
components. A road built into a village not only serves as a feeder road to the
market and opens the area up, but as we shall see in Chapter 5 it also allows both
insurgents and the army in, too.

Nor is it easy to determine with any certainty what is the best strategy. The
data we have do not conform very neatly to the conventional wisdom. Studies
done on the Northeast are not conclusive, but as was suggested in Chapter 3,
some imply that there is a correlation between an increase in developmental
efforts and the propensity of a village to come under the control of the
Communist Terrorists (CTs). Nor is it difficult to understand why this would be
so. In the village, it is not deprivation that matters, but relative deprivation or

---

1. For a more detailed, general description of the dilemmas involved in counterinsurgency, see "Some Dilemmas of Counterinsurgency," by George K. Tanham and Dennis
Duncanson, *Foreign Affairs*, October 1969, New York.

perceived deprivation.[2] Isolated villages, with no contact with the government in Bangkok, and little even with the provincial administration, continue living as they have for centuries—a continuity often noted by anthropologists. The famous 'J' curve of rising expectations, noted by De Toqueville in historical form and more analytically by social scientists in recent times is important;[3] that is, the propensity to rebel increases after conditions have improved and then begun to deteriorate, or even when the rate of increase simply declines. With this in mind, it is not surprising that one observer, Professor Van der Mehden, hypothesized that in Thailand economic and social development were not effective weapons against insurgency; that villagers preferred a military and governmental presence to economic and social benefits in insurgent areas; and that in areas of high insurgency, government should work to control resources, rather than concerning itself with agriculture or commercial development. He did not test these hypotheses, and proposed them only for heuristic purposes, but they are fascinating. What it does demonstrate is that the answers are not easy to find, and in practice decisions had to be based on an intuitive sense of what mix would work—given the particular human and material resources available at the time.

Despite its initial reluctance to deal with the incipient insurgency, the Thai government began taking steps to deal with it as early as 1962. Some of the ensuing organizations and projects were civil, some police, and some purely military, hence the abbreviation CPM to describe the Thai counterinsurgency organization and doctrine. Before examining the problem of trying to coordinate the various efforts we will take a brief look at the efforts made in each of the three areas.

CPM IN PRACTICE: THE CIVILIAN SECTOR

Department of Community Development

The first new institution created was the Department of Community Development, founded in 1962, whose philosophy was one of self-help.

Its objectives were to facilitate communications between the government and the rural population, to improve the peasants' economic status, and to help develop local leadership. The Community Development (CD) Department selected and trained workers to go into the villages to discover what the local peasants needed and wanted; then, armed with money and resources from the government, the workers tried to persuade the villagers to supply the labor for the project, which might be a small dam or canal or market place. Village

2. See *Why Men Rebel*, Ted Robert Gurr, Princeton, 1971.
3. See "Toward a Theory of Revolution," by James C. Davies, *American Sociological Review*, February 1962.

committees were elected to approve projects and indirectly develop local leadership. The CD worker was also intended to be a catalyst, to bring together the officials and resources of other agencies in behalf of the peasant. The program started in a few provinces on a low key. The idea was novel for Thailand, and some of the CD workers tended to force their ideas on the villagers rather than help them develop their own. Furthermore, to the strongly individualistic Thais the idea of a community effort was somewhat alien, though they do customarily help the wat (temple) and a few other collective ventures especially in the rural areas where planting, harvesting, and house building are done on a reciprocal basis. However, the program did expand throughout the country and has done considerable good, though it and its work have largely been overshadowed by more recent and larger programs in the countryside.

Accelerated Rural Development

The self-help method was supplemented by another approach in which the government provided all of the improvements without seeking the help of the population. The Accelerated Rural Development (ARD) program was a follow-up of the CD. As early as 1962 there had been discussions between the United States Agency for International Development (AID) officials and interested Thais on the developmental problems in the Northeast. Prasong Sukhum, then an official in the Budget Bureau of the RTG, was one of the first Thais to become seriously interested in and concerned about the area. As indications of a developing insurgency increased, the need for preventive action, as well as development for its own sake, grew. By early 1964 those involved had arrived at a concept for speeded rural development which was officially adopted May 12, 1964, and became the basis for the ARD. The Thai Department of Local Administration (DOLA) and the National Security Command (NSC), which is discussed below, shared responsibility for the new program the first year, but in 1966 it became a separate agency under Prasong Sukhum in the Office of the Prime Minister, until moving back to the Ministry of the Interior in 1972. The objectives of ARD have been to help increase the income of the rural population, improve ties between the government and the people, and strengthen local government. The last objective led to considerable decentralization and the delegation of authority and equipment to the provincial governors. It was hoped other agencies would also follow this principle, but they have not done so. Indeed ARD itself has in recent years followed a more centralized approach.

The initial ARD emphasis was on feeder roads because most of its planned activities and those of other government agencies depended on being able to reach the people. The governors started with almost nothing, but today have up to 250 people on their staffs, a million dollars or so worth of equipment, and a vastly increased budget. In each province where ARD operates there is a deputy governor, a planning staff, a resident engineer, engineering equipment, and maintenance facilities, all in the province. It has also expanded its activities to include Mobile Medical Teams, a District Farmer Group Program (cooperatives), a youth program, a Potable Water Program, and an information effort. It provides the major rural effort of the RTG. It has had serious problems: getting a release of funds on time, recruiting adequate staff, developing the managerial skills needed, and maintaining equipment. Many of the difficulties were due to ARD's rapid growth and the lack of trained personnel. Recently they have been dealt with in a more systematic manner. Despite the difficulties, ARD has built over 2,000 kilometers of all-weather roads and many small dams, storage ponds, wells, village roads, and paths. It has loaned the equivalent of over $2 million through the credit cooperatives, organized at least thirty youth groups, and carried out over a hundred film showings a month in the provinces. Its direct impact on the population has been small, since it reaches only a few people, but as it expands and word of its activities spreads, it will hopefully reach more. Looking five years ahead, ARD hopes to expand economic growth in the villages, strengthen the developmental capacity of the provincial government, and reduce—or even eliminate—insurgency through the development effort. Provinces are now given priority according to the amount of the threat to security; most intensified efforts will be to those most threatened. ARD also is experimenting with COMAC (Comprehensive Rural Development Action Program) to develop selected districts very rapidly. The Asia Development Bank is assisting this new program. ARD has continued to experiment with new ideas for rural development. However, its future is not entirely clear as the Thai government debates the future shape of its entire counterinsurgency organization.

Department of Local Administration

Several departments in the Ministry of the Interior have played an important nonsuppressive counterinsurgency role. The Department of Local Administration (DOLA) is the administrative heart of the RTG. It is responsible for governing down to the village level, is responsible for the activities of the village headmen as well as the Khamnan, who is the leader of the tambon (cluster of villages), and appoints and supervises the district officers. The governors are appointed by and responsible to the Minister of the Interior, but DOLA also has influence over them. DOLA officials in the field and the governors lack authority over officials from other agencies of the government, but they try to coordinate government activities, some fairly successfully, some not. DOLA recognizes that this is a shortcoming and is trying at least to reinforce the coordinating role of the district officers and the governors. For example, it has dispatched mobile teams that hold meetings at district and province level and which emphasize the coordination role and the range of the resources of the different agencies in the provinces. These meetings seem to help develop a better integrated government effort. The significance that DOLA attaches to the effort is demonstrated by the fact that it pays the per diem for officials from other agencies. (This is significant in a country where per diem is often hard to come by.) DOLA also established in 1965 the Nai Amphur Academy, located just outside Bangkok. This very fine school trains about fifty officers a year in a ten-month course. Upon graduation, they are most likely to be appointed district officers (Nai Amphurs). The training curriculum includes not only technical subjects necessary for the job, but also gives attention to special motivational subjects, psychological operations, and the coordination role. There is also a deputy Nai Amphur course of three months held at the academy. Finally there are tentative plans for a course for governors. Thus DOLA is engaged in one of the most important aspects of counterinsurgency, that of developing an honest, effective, and responsive bureaucratic apparatus.

Public Welfare Department

In the Ministry of the Interior the Public Welfare Department also has played a counterinsurgency role. It has been responsible among other things for the welfare of the hill people. Before the outbreak of the insurgency in the North, Public Welfare had developed a few nikoms, which are areas where it is hoped the hill people will settle down to a stationary existence. New agricultural methods are taught, health facilities and schools are provided, and it is antici-pated that these measures will improve the lot of the tribespeople and slowly bring them into the Thai community. However, there are far too few nikoms, and they tend to be show places rather than really serious attempts at assimila-tion and are generally not well run. The Department has also played a role in handling the refugees who came down from the mountains or were forced down after the insurgency broke out. The camps, called reception centers, are usually in the plains and on terrain the tribesmen would not choose. Some of the centers, however, have done very well. The one in Pua district of Nan province has arranged for legal landholdings for the hill people, has a good school, and a small but thriving handicraft industry. The Public Welfare Department has by no means been the most aggressive agency in the Ministry of the Interior, and, given its broad charter of public welfare of which the hill people are only a small part, the results generally have been rather unsatisfactory.

Psychological Operations

The RTG has also undertaken information programs and psychological opera-tions in its counterinsurgency effort. The Psychological Operations (Psy Ops) Division of the Communist Suppression Operations Command (CSOC), which was organized in December, 1965, has probably been the most active agency in that field. When the first counterinsurgency plan was launched in 1967 by CSOC, Psy Ops prepared leaflets and a few radio programs for it. Subsequently it has supported two sets of psychological teams. The Modular Audio-Visual Units (MAVUs) are manned by Royal Thai Army personnel with the mission of operating in the target areas of the 09/10 plan and supporting the Army Forward Headquarters, the Joint Security Centers (JCSs), and the provincial CPMs. The Mobile Information Service Teams (MISTs) are civilian units designed to operate under the control of the governors and in support of provincial programs. Both units have money, posters, and pamphlets. The MISTs are accompanied on their trips to the villages by officials from other agencies, especially the agriculture and health ministries, as well as district and provincial officials, so as to match words with deeds. These officials can provide information on follow-up action which will be helpful to the people. CSOC also continues to prepare radio programs, national leaflets, booklets, and other messages designed to inform the people of the government's efforts to help them and to weaken the morale of the CTs. It also conducts a National Open Arms and Rehabilitation Program for arrested and surrendered CTs. The main effort is in training courses to retrain persons who had joined the CTs so that they may have a better and more productive life when they return to normal society.

The Public Relations Department also engages in some propaganda efforts, particularly radio broadcasts, and is supporting a radio station to reach the hill people in the North. ARD, CD, and the National Police Department also have information programs. The NSC, as noted earlier, operates Radio 909 in the Northeast, and this has been a great service, not so much in information, as in getting the CTs to defect. The NSC has other radio stations, and its MDUs continue to be active in the information effort. The Royal Thai Army has its own psychological operations units which operate with the troops and contribute to the overall effort.

The National Information Psychological Operations Organization (NIPSO) was established in 1969 to provide overall guidance in the psy ops field. Its specific responsibilities are to determine psy ops policy, consider and approve various psy ops plans and programs, cooperate with suppression and development agencies in the counterinsurgency campaign, evaluate the effectiveness of psy ops and rehabilitation efforts and direct the National Psy Ops Working Group. The working group on the operational level was established to develop its own plans and coordinate those of other agencies, evaluate effectiveness, gather information for use in psy ops, and cooperate with neighboring countries. A National Psy Ops Center was created to do the actual work and support the NIPSO and its working group. In the latter part of 1971, NIPSO's name was officially changed to the Office of National Psychological Operations (ONPO), which now has forty-two audio-visual teams with complete vehicle and projection equipment. Thirty-seven of the teams are presently operating in the provinces, while five are held in reserve. Although this organization for psy ops was well conceived, in reality very few of its designated responsibilities have been implemented, and it is still a very weak effort.

National Development Programs

The above very brief review of some of the major government offices and the coordinating agencies greatly oversimplifies a complicated and overlapping counterinsurgency effort. As noted in Chapter 1, the Royal Thai Government has been very much a vertically organized government, and cooperation and coordination are weak elements. (The RTG is not alone in this; many other governments also have the same weakness.) This tendency also means that Thai ministries and agencies constantly strive to broaden their activities, in part because they see a need and do not know, sometimes do not try to find out, what other agency of government might be properly dealing with it. Also, strong personalities are constantly trying to expand and enlarge their responsibilities and offices. There are numerous agencies outside the Ministry of Agriculture trying to help the farmers: ARD, NSC, Land Development, etc. Many agencies besides the Highway Department are building roads: ARD, MDUs, CD, the Army, etc. The medical field also includes numerous agencies outside the Ministry of Health doing medical work and health improvement.

My review has not touched on the important work being done by the Ministries of Education, Health, and National Development, as well as a number of other Thai agencies. The programs of these ministries have significant implications for counterinsurgency, but they also represent normal governmental efforts to improve the lot of the population and are not strictly counterinsurgency programs. However, drawing the line between programs that are highly useful to the people and programs created to counter the insurgency is difficult. Schools, for example, are a real need of the people and are highly useful in a counterinsurgency role, but they are not merely a counterinsurgency program.

CPM IN PRACTICE: THE POLICE SECTOR

Several divisions of the Thai National Police Department (TNPD), which is under the jurisdiction of the Ministry of the Interior, have played important roles in the counterinsurgency effort. On the suppression and intelligence side, the TNPD has five elements involved in counterinsurgency; out of a total strength in the Department of over 70,000, the Provincial Police number 42,000, the Border Patrol Police (BPP) over 8,000, the Marine Police nearly 1,500, and the Special Branch, Division Seven, a few hundred. The Police Air Division assists counterinsurgency operations by providing transport for men and supplies. The Provincial Police divide the country into nine regions. The BPP follows this organization except that there is no BPP in Region 1, because there are no international land borders. Each region has some 4,000 provincial policemen and all except Region 1 have roughly 1,000 BPP. The Provincial Police have grown rapidly in the last few years, providing a presence in as much of the country as possible and particularly in the areas threatened by insurgency.

The major program to achieve this goal has been the Tambon Police Station Project, which provides for a police station with twelve to twenty policemen in an increasing number of tambons (cluster of villages). It was hoped that 1,000 of the 5,000 tambons in the country would have stations by the end of 1971, but the program has fallen far behind schedule and the goals have not been achieved by early 1974. At first the plan was to rotate the police monthly to the stations, but this turned out to be unsatisfactory, because the police developed no understanding of the region or rapport with the people. Dependent housing is recently in the process of construction, and the plan is to station the police more permanently so that hopefully they will function more effectively. A second major Provincial Police effort has been the formation of fifty-man Special Action Forces. These units have been specially trained and have their own transportation that can provide a quick reaction force able to respond to criminal or insurgency incidents. Although the units were intended to be mobile forces, in many cases they have become involved in static operations.

In addition to these major programs, the police have been experimenting with a tambon Police Patrol Project. The program takes draftees, who volunteer for it in lieu of their military service, and trains them for two months. They are assigned to a tambon, where their mission is to patrol among the villages (mubans) of the tambon, thus extending police presence down to the village. They have been tried in six provinces and the experiment seems to have been successful. For a variety of reasons, however, primarily shortage of money and instruction, the program has been suspended. The police have also been experimenting in Korat with a youth program that provides physical education and sports facilities with police supervision. They further have a medical program and have recently become interested in an information program.

The Border Patrol Police (BPP), which began in the mid-1950s with U.S. assistance, is a paramilitary force responsible for the surveillance of Thailand's 3,000 miles of border area. The BPP's main task is to work closely with the villagers, especially the hill tribesmen, in remote areas. The purpose of these activities is not only to improve the life of the villagers and gain their loyalty, but also to develop useful sources of information about the activities and organization of the communists. By the early 1960s the BPP were operating some 200 schools in remote areas, carried on a medical program, and had an active civic action program. In the mid-1960s, due to the increased communist threat, they expanded their activities to new areas. In 1969 the BPP began the formation of thirty-man border security teams composed of hill people. This was an effort to bring the hill people over to the government's side and to help them protect themselves from the CTs. The program has encountered some funding problems as well as training and operational difficulties, but as of this writing it seems to have done very well and one can hope that it will continue. The BPP has played a leading role in establishing and manning five new counterinsurgency training centers in Udon, Ubon, Chiang Mai, Songkhla, and a larger national one at Hua Hin.

The Marine Police have had a limited counterinsurgency mission—patrolling the territorial waters of Thailand and the Mekong River. They have been active on the Mekong; how the relationship between them and the new naval forces will work out remains to be seen. The new arrangement on the Mekong seems to put' the Navy in charge, even though it does not have the experience or the resources on the river that the Marine Police do.

The Special Branch has Division Seven which is charged with upcountry police intelligence operations directed against the CTs and other subversive elements. Its staff of only a few hundred is far too small; it should be increased because field intelligence is absolutely critical to a successful counterinsurgency operation.

The image of the police in the countryside has not been all one would wish; reports of corruption, bad behavior, and incompetence are too frequent. The Thai National Police Department is increasingly aware of these problems and is trying to improve its conduct and its relations with the people. Its budget, while increasing, does not permit sufficient growth of personnel to carry out its goals of providing a good police presence throughout the country. Furthermore, improvement in assignments is much needed, so that the best qualified personnel will be sent to the right job. Some platoons are left in the field for years and have no officers and few noncommissioned officers. Training is improving but still needs more attention, and the police, like many other agencies, suffer from the per diem problem.[4]

CPM IN PRACTICE: THE MILITARY SECTOR

Royal Thai Armed Forces

Within the Ministry of Defense the Royal Thai Army (RTA) is, of course, the dominant service and it also plays a key role in counterinsurgency efforts. The RTA has a headquarters in Bangkok with the usual staff and a tactical operations center which issues orders and directives to the field units. The First Army is

---

4. Per diem payments are given to military, police and civilian personnel when they are on government operations or travel. Neither the military nor the police in Thailand have their own kitchens as the U.S. military units do. There has always been a shortage of money for per diem payments in spite of the U.S. efforts to help with this problem.

responsible for Bangkok and the Central and Western areas; it is normally referred to as the "anti-coup" army. It also supplies the King's Guard and units for various ceremonial affairs in Bangkok. It formerly had an advance headquarters near Hua Hin which was responsible for the counterinsurgency effort in the Western region. This headquarters has been closed since 1971. The First Army has one division with four regimental combat teams and is probably the best led and best manned of the three field armies. The Second Army is responsible for the Northeast. Its headquarters is in Korat, but Second Army Forward, which is responsible for the counterinsurgency operations, is located at Sakon Nakhon. The Second Army also has one division with three understrength regimental combat teams with headquarters at Ubon, Korat, and Udon. About four of its nine line battalions have taken part in counterinsurgency efforts although most of these troops have been pulled out for possible need along the Cambodian border. The Third Army has its headquarters at Phitsanulok. It has one division with two understrength regimental combat teams, some units of the Cavalry Division, and the 26th Regiment. The Fifth Military Circle in the South, with headquarters at Nakhon Si Thammarat, has one regiment, the Fifth, with four battalions, all understrength and in need of new equipment. In addition to these field forces, there is the Cavalry Division with headquarters in Bangkok but with units stationed around Bangkok, in the Northeast and in the North. There are also the Special Forces numbering over 1,000 and currently expanding; their center is at Lopburi. They conduct operations against the CTs and train the regular army in counterinsurgency operations. Each army has a counterinsurgency training camp, the Second Army at Nam Pung Dam, the Third Army at Lamphun, and the First Army at Hua Hin. The basic counterinsurgency course is from nine to twelve weeks at each camp and is given to company-size units.

The Royal Thai Army is composed of professionals and two-year draftees. Most of the officers have attended the Military Academy and go on to advanced schooling at the staff school and war college. The draftees, taken in twice a year, go into the battalion stationed near their home areas and are trained by the battalion and serve their two years with it. The Thai feel it is best for a draftee to serve in his home area and with one unit for his entire tour. The Americans believe this is an inefficient procedure, because the basic training varies from battalion to battalion and the training responsibility weakens the combat effectiveness of the unit; the Americans would prefer one central basic training center for all draftees. Over the years, the Thais have stuck to their system despite American pressure. No matter what system is used, the training for the RTA could certainly be improved. The tendency has been to use older officers in the combat companies; this is often because bright, aggressive young officers see promotion opportunities much greater in Bangkok. The effectiveness of the combat units would greatly increase if the officers were younger and more aggressive. The perennial Thai problem of per diem is also found here—usually not enough of it to allow field maneuvers and combat. The per diem problem pervades the entire Thai government, and I know of cases when a unit has been pulled out of critical operations because the "per diem ran out." In any event, better training and younger leadership at the lower unit level would greatly enhance the RTA's capabilities.

Until 1970 the Royal Thai Navy had no counterinsurgency role, but since then it has been given total river patrol responsibility. Several Marine battalions are also available for use in counterinsurgency operations but have not yet been assigned to any. The Royal Thai Air Force is capable of, and has supported, counterinsurgency operations, through fire support, transport, and reconnaissance. It has also provided helicopters in support of RTA and police operations. While the support roles of the Navy and Air Force do play a role in the counterinsurgency effort, it is not necessary to go into the organization of these forces as they are not as intimately involved in either politics or the counterinsurgency effort as the Army.

National Security Command

The beginning of armed attack by the insurgents showed the RTG the need for better organization and for new institutions both in Bangkok and in the field. Indeed, at the same time that they created the Community Development program, they also created the National Security Command within the Ministry of Defense and charged it with the responsibility for countering "covert aggression" or insurgency and subversion. It was intended that this command would coordinate the actions of other agencies involved in countering insurgency and would concentrate on the developmental and psychological aspects of the problem, underlining anew the difficulty of demarcating the three areas as neatly as one might like in theory. In fact it never worked that way, and was simply one more organization, within the military sector, providing specific services. One of the most important of these was the organization and deployment of Mobile Development Units (MDUs), specifically devised to counter the incipient insurgency during the largely covert period in the early 1960s. This was a particularly significant step, regardless of the results, since few countries have taken action so early in what promised to be a protracted conflict. The concept was to combine the efforts of the military and civilian agencies into one type of field unit that would provide a government presence to reassure the population and to help improve the life of the rural peasant. The primary effort and effect of the MDUs has been in the information and psychological fields, with some effort in small engineering projects, schools, and health facilities. The MDUs also helped to gather information for larger developmental planning and undertakings. The leader of an MDU is usually an Army officer who has under him a few soldiers and officials from health, education, development, public welfare, and similar agencies. The military provide the leadership and the planning officers and were the key element in organizing the MDUs. The size of the units varies but has ranged from fifty or sixty to well over a hundred. MDU headquarters in Bangkok, in cooperation with provincial authorities, works out the details of the MDU to be sent to a given province. There the MDU is divided into subunits which try to help the villagers in their area. Though originally designed as mobile units, they have in fact generally become somewhat stationary. The first MDU (referred to as MDU-1) was established in the Northeast in Kalasin province in the summer of 1962; MDU-2 was formed in Sakon Nakhon in March, 1963, and three new numbered MDUs have been formed every year since.[5] Most of the early MDUs were formed in the Northeast, then some were created in the South; by 1970 they could be found in all regions of the country except the Central Plains.

The National Security Command and other rural programs moved slowly, partly because the threat was not obvious to all officials, partly because of the political situation in Bangkok, and partly because the participants were learning as they went along. Furthermore, getting other agencies to release personnel to new and different organizations which seemed to exist on an ad hoc basis was difficult. Officials were not anxious to go into the MDUs and other suborganizations, feeling that they were likely to be forgotten by their parent organization and perhaps passed over at promotion time or ignored when interesting positions became vacant. Many were reluctant to go into the countryside where living conditions were far below the Bangkok level and where the pleasures of the city did not exist. Nevertheless, many officials have gone out and rendered fine services, but the problem of getting officials into the field still plagues the government.

As other RTG agencies have continued to expand both in responsibility and in geography, the role of the National Security Command (NSC) diminished, though by early 1974 it looked like it might be resurrected. In any case, since 1965, it has carried out some effective programs in addition to the MDUs. It assisted in the formation of the ARD program; it has been active in psychological operations, particularly in the case of Radio Station 909 in Sakon Nakhon. The station has probably been the most effective counterinsurgency psychological operation in Thailand; originally assisted by the United States Information Agency, it is now run entirely by the Thais. The NSC has set up a similar station in the South at Yala. NSC has also been active in civic action, particularly the

5. For a careful study of MDU-2, see Lee Huff, *Observations on Mobile Development Unit-2 Operations* (June 1963), Joint Thai-U.S. Military Research and Development Center (MRDC), Bangkok. (Available from the Defense Advanced Research Projects Agency, Department of Defense, Washington, D. C.)

Flying Doctor Program which takes doctors from Bangkok to remote areas for various periods of time, and has also been experimenting with cattle and hog breeding, an important program which could improve the livestock of Thailand considerably. Except in connection with the MDUs, NSC has coordinated no programs of other agencies but has carried out its several programs on its own with its own funds.

One of its important responsibilities until January, 1970, was the counterinsurgency effort in the Far South, which involved not only tactical operations but also dealing with the Malays. Under its direction, the Border Patrol Police (BPP) of Region IX constituted the only counterinsurgency suppressive force in the Far South. The BPP number only about 1,200 to 1,400 in the region, and only a few of the line platoons have officers. The platoons remain in positions in the jungle for long periods of time, and they greatly need retraining, better leadership, rest, and recreation. Although they have launched some operations against the CTO, they have not been very aggressive, partly for the reasons given above and partly because the CTO is too strong. A series of general border committees composed of officials from the Thai and Malaysian government have been operating since 1948. The present one, established in 1965, meets twice a year, once in Bangkok and once in Kuala Lumpur; it discusses strategic plans and also such matters as hot pursuit and the use of Malaysian police in Thailand. Following the resumption of the border committee meetings, a Regional Border Committee Organization (RBCO) manned by Thais and Malaysians was established in Songkhla to carry out the day-to-day operations. It has concentrated particularly on intelligence activities, engaged in planning, and carried out some psychological operations. Under existing overall agreements, the Malaysians rotate some police platoons into Thailand; they engage in joint operations with the Thai BPP, who are always in command of the joint task forces. In January, 1970, a regional office in the South of the Communist Suppression Operations Command (CSOC), which is the RTG agency responsible for coordinating the government's counterinsurgency efforts, began to function and the fate of the RBCO was then unclear, but hopefully this useful binational organization will not be lost. Since that time the RBCO has continued to exist but its effectiveness is dependent on the ebb and flow of the insurgency and the closeness of relations between the Thais and Malaysians.

Beginning with the March, 1970, General Border Committee meeting in Bangkok the Thai delegation for the first time included officials from CSOC. It appears that the NSC will continue to head the Thai delegation and will to a certain extent be responsible for policy and strategy, while CSOC will participate in the meetings and have operational responsibilities. This sharing of responsibility for the South is further reflected by the fact that General Kriangsak Chomanan, Chief-of-Staff of NSC, was made a Deputy Chief-of-Staff of CSOC with responsibilities for the South. The Far South continues to be a somewhat special case in the Thai counterinsurgency effort.

CPM IN PRACTICE: THE PROBLEM OF COORDINATION

To better coordinate these various government agencies, the RTG created by decree the Communist Suppression Operations Command (CSOC) in late 1965. The organization was based on the CPM concept of coordination: i.e., Civilian, Police, and Military. Initially CSOC was given the responsibility of combating the growing insurgency in the Northeast. More specifically, it was to support and encourage the various agencies in their counterinsurgency mission, to order and institute coordination when needed, and to carry out counterinsurgency operations when asked to or when it saw fit. Prior to October, 1973, CSOC's commander was General Praphas, who was also Commander-in-Chief of the Army. The Chief-of-Staff was General Surikij Mayalarp, who then was Chief-of-Staff of the Army. The Chief-of-Staff has civilian and police deputies and holds weekly meetings with his deputies and representatives of other agencies such as Community Development, ARD, and Public Welfare. The key office in the beginning was the Directorate of Operations headed by General Saiyud Kerdphol, who did much of the conceptualizing and planning for counterinsurgency operations as well as directing them.

During 1966 the organization took form and began to organize subordinate offices in the Northeast as well as draw up specific plans. An organization called CPM-1 was created in Mukdahan (later moved to Sakon Nakhon) to act as a coordination office in the region. It was originally commanded by a general with police and civilian deputies. CPM-1's mission was to provide for the security and control of the population, locate and destroy the CTs, and provide civic action in the villages. CPM organizations were also formed in seven provinces of the Northeast. The governor is the head of the CPM and has military and police advisors as well as civilian. The CPM-1 had army units assigned to it, while the provincial CPM's had primarily police and village security forces. Both CPM-1 and the governors also had coordinating authority but not command.

To assist with the important task of intelligence, Joint Security Centers (JCSs) were formed. These are joint agencies, jointly manned, hopefully to bridge the gap between the various operating and intelligence agencies. They are not collection agencies. The plan is for them to be recipients of all the intelligence information collected by the CPM agencies, then collate and analyze it and produce finished intelligence. They are organized on the police region basis and numbered according to the police region each is in. The first were in Korat and Udon (Police Region III and IV) and in Chiang Mai (Police Region V). Later others were established in Nakhon Phathom (Police Region VII), Nakhon Si Thammarat (Police Region VIII), and the last in Phitsanulok (Police Region

VI). Some of them have done excellent work but others have not. They have also suffered from being joint, as the individual CPM agencies do not fully trust them. Whether they are to produce strategic (long-range) or tactical (immediate) intelligence has caused some confusion; they have tended to produce the former and this has not been particularly useful to the suppression forces in the field. As has happened many times during the counterinsurgency effort, the concept is excellent but the execution has not been as good.

The Thai initial suppressive reactions to the outbreak of open insurgency in 1965–1966 were actually a lashing back at the enemy rather than a reflection of serious thinking about counterinsurgency. Air and artillery attacks as well as large sweeps were used to strike at guerrilla bands. None of these tactics accomplished much because the guerrillas were skillful in eluding the attacks. In some cases where the action was near populated areas it tended to alienate the population and consequently aided the guerrilla cause. Fortunately, the Thais soon realized that this form of attack was not productive or in keeping with their basic insurgency philosophy, and they stopped using it, though they have resumed them to some extent beginning in 1971.

By the end of 1966 the CSOC organization in Bangkok and in the field was more or less completed and a rational counterinsurgency plan had been drawn up. The plan was usually known as the 09/10 plan (after the Buddhist calendar years 2509 and 2510, i.e., 1966 and 1967). Its basic concept was location of the sensitive areas infested by armed communist bands and then to isolate the bands from the general population, who are the source of supplies and intelligence for the guerrillas—in Mao's language, to separate the fish from the water. Originally ten target areas were designated, all in the Northeast and six of them in Sakon Nakhon and Nakhon Phanom provinces. The other four were in Udon, northeast Nong Khai, northern Ubon, and northern Kalasin. The main element of the plan was the twelve-man joint security team or village protection unit in villages surrounding the target areas. The teams were composed usually of two police-men and ten or more Volunteer Defense Corps (VDC) personnel.[6] The latter were peasants but not necessarily from the village in which they were stationed. It was essentially a local self-defense team led by better-trained policemen.

The teams received approximately one month of basic training, including a few hours of civic action and psychological operations from the Royal Thai Army. Their mission was to protect the villagers from attack and intimidation by the guerrillas, to prevent guerrillas from gaining food and supplies from the village, and to provide civic action. CSOC paid the VDC personnel with its own funds. In each of the target areas, there was usually also an army unit, com-

6. A paramilitary organization established in 1954, rather like a militia to be called to duty in natural or defense emergencies.

monly a platoon but sometimes a company, and a control headquarters located in the most tactically suitable village. The control headquarters was in communication with higher headquarters and the joint security teams in the villages. The army unit was a strike force that could be used to support the joint security teams in case of danger or to attack the CTs when they were located. However, the strike forces tended to be largely reactive and to have inadequate mobility. The plan was put into full execution in January, 1967, and has expanded regularly as new sensitive areas are discovered.

In October, 1967, there was a change in organization and to a certain extent in responsibility when the RTA essentially took over CSOC operations for the Northeast. Martial law, which had theoretically been in effect throughout Thailand, was finally more fully enforced and served as the basis for the army action. Why this happened at this time is not clear, but the most plausible reason is that the army did not like having a non-army organization, CSOC, giving direct orders to army units in the field. The CSOC Directorate of Operations in Bangkok had in fact been giving all the orders to the army units in the Northeast operating in a counterinsurgency role. Army logistic support of units under CSOC had suffered from lack of clear command channels. Some observers feel that there was also a personality clash or a conflict between the Director of CSOC Operations, General Saiyud, and some of the army generals.

Some members of the American Mission in Bangkok were somewhat disturbed about the situation, inasmuch as Americans usually feel that civilian control is preferable. In any case, after the RTA took over in October, 1967, CSOC continued but gave only general directions to army headquarters in Bangkok, which then gave orders to the field units through regular army channels. In short, the army ran CSOC. CPM-1 was abolished and the Second Army set up its forward headquarters in Sakon Nakhon with essentially the same mission as CPM-1. In essence, the Second Army commander wore two hats as the army commander and the regional CSOC commander. The change did not alter the operations as much as some people thought it might; the 09/10 plan continued and if anything the army units were more active than they had been earlier. CSOC has continued to develop plans, conduct psychological operations, and carry out some civic action projects, but its military role is almost nonexistent.

When martial law was implemented in the Northeast, the First Army in Western and Central Thailand and the Third Army in the North were directed to establish forward headquarters to coordinate the communist suppression activities in their areas. In the Mid-South, the Fifth Military Circle commander was given similar responsibilities for his area. In the Far South, the National Security Command, not CSOC, was responsible for counterinsurgency activities, and no change in organization or responsibility has been made there. Thus by the end of 1967 the counterinsurgency organization had expanded to cover almost all of Thailand.

After the promulgation of the new Constitution on June 20, 1968, and the National Assembly elections in February, 1969, many of the old decrees and proclamations were considered to have questionable status. CSOC was included in this ambiguous category; consequently a law was passed that established an Office of Communist Suppression and Prevention, with essentially the same functions and responsibilities as CSOC. CSOC was terminated, though in fact there was virtually no change and CSOC was still used as the name of the new office. Field Marshal Praphas was named Director of Communist Suppression, and all the other officers remained in place. Under the new law the Ministry of the Interior designated thirty-five of the then seventy-one provinces (Thailand currently has seventy-two provinces) as areas of communist infiltration. Five regions were created, based on the same geographical areas as the existing army organization and called CSOC-1-5. The three army commanders and the Fifth Military Circle commander were designated regional directors of communist suppression and assumed overall responsibility for CSOC affairs in their region. The Fifth Military Circle encompassed both CSOC-4 and CSOC-5. The main responsibility was largely coordination, and the army commanders worked hard to bring the various elements of the government together. However, they tended to depend mostly on the army since they command its units. The governors of the thirty-five provinces were designated province directors of communist suppression. One major change brought about by the law is the CSOC take-over of counterinsurgency operations in the Far South. A new office, CSOC-4/1, has been established in Songkhla, the fifth zone under the new law, and is responsible for tactical operations against the CTO. In theory the General in charge of CSOC-4/1 reports to the Commander of the Fifth Military Circle (CSOC-4), but in fact he operates directly under Royal Thai Army headquarters in Bangkok. After the "coup" of November, 1971, the RTG made no change in this arrangement, which was still functioning in the same way in 1973, but like the rest of the Thai counterinsurgency apparatus its future is unclear in early 1974.

CPM IN SUMMARY

While the Thais have been experimenting and developing a counterinsurgency organization structure both in Bangkok and in the field, and carrying out various programs described above, they have also been working out a counterinsurgency concept or doctrine. Although the doctrine as it has evolved may not be accepted by all officials or only certain parts may be emphasized by some, there is considerable unanimity on the major points. As in the case of most doctrines, it is both a philosophy and a goal. The Thais have violated their own doctrine in the past and probably will in the future (most governments and agencies do). However, for Americans to try to understand the Thai doctrine should be useful, since it goes a long way to explain what the Thais have done and what they have not done, and why.

The Royal Thai Government doctrine of counterinsurgency, which is referred to as the CPM (Civil, Police, Military), grew out of the fact that insurgency has two aspects: (1) the determination of the communists to gain political power; and (2) the communist strategy of using legitimate socioeconomic and political grievances for their own purposes. The breadth of the communist approach led the Thais to adopt a similarly broad counter, the CPM, which includes all the major agencies of the government. There are two main approaches: the passive and the active, and the doctrine emphasizes the passive. Even before the insurgency began, Prime Minister Sarit, who headed the Thai government until 1963, recognized the danger from communism and realized that it fed on legitimate problems. Sarit took the lead in initiating developmental plans to improve the life of the rural population and reduce their grievances, especially in the Northeast. This approach is termed passive in that it is not a direct attack on the insurgent structure; it also includes information programs designed to bridge the gap between the government and the people, to explain the developmental programs, and to counter CT propaganda efforts. Although these efforts have been accelerated by the insurgency threat, most of them are part of the nation-building program. The Thais have been aware that even if they could resolve all the problems (which they cannot) a communist desire and potentiality to overthrow the government might still exist. Therefore, they have also taken the active approach, which includes intelligence efforts, local security units, and military operations to disturb and destroy the CT guerrilla bands. This part of the effort is directed against the communist apparatus, its infrastructure, and paramilitary units, and the police and military forces are primarily responsible for it.

Coordination is the second major point in the doctrine. At the highest level the cabinet plays a coordinating role, making the policy and strategic decisions, which then are normally passed down. As noted earlier, the RTG, first through the National Security Command and later through the CSOC structure, has attempted to effect operational coordination. In fact, in most cases, military operations are handled by the army command; police instructions come from the TNPD, and directives for civilian agencies come through their Bangkok headquarters. In some cases the overall instructions go from CSOC to the regional CSOC directors (the field army commanders), and then to the governors. In other cases CSOC may deal directly with the governors. For example, the execution of the 09/10 plan has been carried out through the regional director in the Northeast, while village security is the responsibility of the appropriate governors. The coordinating mechanism, though well thought out in theory, has serious difficulties that I note later.

Inherent in the Thai concept of counterinsurgency has been the belief that the communists and communism could have no real appeal for the Thais, and therefore most citizens would remain loyal to their government and to their traditions. This notion has led the RTG to several important but not entirely valid conclusions. First is the belief that no ethnic Thais are directly involved in the insurgency, that only the minority groups (the Vietnamese in the Northeast, the hill tribes in the North, and the Chinese in the South) have been seduced by communist insurgents. Although it is true that minorities are involved, several facts have been ignored: among them that very few Vietnamese are active in the overt insurgency, and that the overwhelming majority of insurgents in the Northeast are Thais. (A few RTG officials claim that Northeasterners are not really Thais, but this idea is disappearing.) Even in the North the cadres are Thais or Sino-Thais; in the West Central and Mid-South the insurgents are all Thais; in the South, however, few ethnic Thais seem to be involved. A second consequence of this belief is that RTG officials initially and until very recently discounted the insurgency in the North as not affecting the Thais and therefore as not being serious. Many officials were slow to see that the first phase of the insurgency there involved forming a base with the hill tribes and developing base areas where training could be carried out for lowland Thais. The second phase, of penetration of the ethnic Thais and the training of some of them in the mountains, began some time ago; as a result, the RTG became finally much more concerned about the situation in the North. Another consequence of the government's high degree of confidence in the loyalty of the people to it and thus their rejection of communism is that it probably still underestimates the communist ability to recruit and motivate an adequate number of Thais to lead a rural revolt. It may also reveal a misunderstanding of the CTs' skillful use of terror to gain support or acquiescence. Even the most loyal Thais must be careful when a CT threatens or uses force against him, his family, and his fields.

The emphasis in the doctrine on the passive resolution of problems and removal of grievances leads to a graduated approach to the insurgency. In the incipient or less serious phases of the insurgency civilian and police authorities have the primary responsibility: the police maintain law and order and develop intelligence on the threat; the civilians conduct information and developmental programs—which should be the major effort—to gain active support of the people and deny that support to the CTs. If the situation worsens, the armed forces are called in to support the police or take over from them. There is also a further division of responsibility following from this, in that the police are primarily responsible for law and order in populated areas, while the armed forces are responsible for trying to find and destroy guerrilla bands and bases. In practice these responsibilities are not so clear-cut. For example, Provincial Police Special Action Forces and Mobile Reserve Platoons of the BPP have been involved in some of the bloodiest operations in the North, while army units have been stationed in populated areas largely in a public-order role.

Since 1970, largely because of developments around Thailand's borders, the division of effort has changed as the army has become somewhat worried about having troops tied up in counterinsurgency operations and more concerned about its traditional role of protecting Thailand's borders. The army, although emphasizing that it has no intention of withdrawing from the counterinsurgency campaign, has gradually taken some of its units from static positions and regrouped them in larger units alerted for possible use against communist threats from Laos and Cambodia. The army continues to play a major role in the counterinsurgency effort—for example, in the division-size operations in the North in 1972—but the number of troops continuously engaged in counterinsurgency has diminished.

There has been general recognition of the problem of village defense, though there are differences of opinion about how to solve it. The army is in favor of village defense by the villagers with police assistance. This relieves the army of the responsibility, makes the guerrillas' job of recruiting and gathering supplies more difficult, and makes the CT collection of intelligence harder. The civilians and police accept the idea of village defense and their role in it; indeed, occasionally some rivalry appears about which group should be responsible. CSOC has in the past taken the lead, with the help of police and civilians, in its village protection units. In part owing to American influence, an approach was initiated by the Thais which led to serious conflicts between the Department of Local Administration and the police. Part of the trouble stemmed from a certain ambivalence about villagers defending themselves. Although most of those involved agreed that the villagers should do this, opinions differed over what kind of arms they should be given (rifles or shotguns), whether they should be paid, and, if paid, how much. In many circles, especially among the police, uneasiness developed about so many arms being given to the people, in case the guns might fall into the wrong hands or be turned against the government. The police would like to handle the matter, but they probably will not be allowed to because of lingering altercations in the past between army and police. Nevertheless, that there should be some sort of self-defense by armed villagers is generally agreed on. Some officials, however, believe the villagers should be willing to defend themselves without pay, since their homes and families are being defended. Others feel that the additional responsibilities deserve pay. So far, all schemes for village defense have included payments, and it seems likely that modest per diems or wages will continue to be included in future plans. The whole matter of village defense is most difficult to solve, yet it is critical to the counterinsurgency effort.

The army leaders seem to be very much aware that force must be used with extreme care and that if it is not so used it can be counterproductive. Army generals, including the field commanders, accept the principle that the people are the real target and that the major effort should be directed toward providing protection for them and winning them over to the government's side. In particular, the Third Army Commander in the North, General Samran, has been most active in providing information programs and civic action; he constantly reiterates that force will be used only as a last resort. He also adopted this philosophy toward the hill peoples, although carrying it out in the rugged mountainous terrain where they live is extremely difficult. The field army commanders have been warned to use their forces carefully, particularly air strikes and artillery. They have also been told to be extremely watchful about the behavior of their troops, since the people can be alienated by bad behavior. One of the senior army generals told me that the Royal Thai Army had no intention of making the same mistakes that the United States had made in Vietnam. He said, for instance, that when the Americans learned of the presence of a few Viet Cong in a village they would rush in overwhelming armed forces. He smiled as he remarked, "They rarely found the Viet Cong, tended to smash up the village, and thereby hurt and alienated the population. We are not going to do that." At one point the army was instructed not to reply to harassing fires, because this tended to make the situation worse and was likely to increase civilian casualties. However, this doctrine has not been entirely unviolated, and in the North and Northeast it has been ignored many times during the past two years. There has been increased bombing in the North as Thai frustration with the hill tribes grows, but the Thais insist that it is only against carefully identified enemy targets. The RTG has also tried to bomb CT headquarters in the Phu Phan Mountains. In general, considering the frustration of counterinsurgency campaigns against elusive guerrillas, the Thai military has shown considerable restraint, though this appears to be weakening.

The Thai doctrine recognizes the dual aspect of the insurgent threat. It has tried to avoid some of the mistakes and pitfalls of earlier counterinsurgency efforts, emphasizing the point that the support of the people is a true target for both sides, and has also tried to work out a balance between the carrot and the stick. Students of counterinsurgency are still divided over the causes of insurgency (communist plot or socioeconomic grievances) and consequently over the cures. The Thais, while appearing to lean to the theory that socioeconomic problems are the basis, are by no means blind to the communists' militant designs on Thailand. Their counterinsurgency efforts reflect the division over the causes and cures of insurgency, as well as the political and bureaucratic strains in the government.[7] How well the Thais have been doing is the subject of Chapter 5.

7. This was the official doctrine of the Thanom-Praphas government, which I believe the new government of Prime Minister Sanya Dharmasakti will continue to support, but this remains to be seen.

Chapter 5

An Assessment of the Thai Response

It is now pertinent to examine how effective the Thai counterinsurgency effort appears to be. An overall evaluation is not only difficult to piece together but also to explain in objective or quantifiable terms. Even when the active and the passive aspects of the program are examined separately, the results are not clarified entirely. There are so many variables that judgments tend to be quite subjective. Among the factors that create this situation the following would seem to be the most important:

1. The foremost reason is that insurgency mainly concerns people and their behavior; that weapons and other equipment are secondary. Since the understanding of any people's behavior lacks precision, we are handicapped in making measurable evaluations of present reactions of the rural population to certain activities of the government and even less can we predict future behavioral patterns.

2. Intelligence about insurgency situations is a difficult and time-consuming

95

ferreting-out process. The insurgents usually have little equipment and few bases, and their apparatus is a simple one that leaves few traces and can move easily and quickly. Their clandestine operations and lack of uniforms make them almost impossible to identify, and their tight discipline in their small bases and mobile headquarters creates a nearly impenetrable cloak of invisibility. Thus, the intelligence-gathering system that is usually productive in conventional wars is not very useful against insurgents and has to be modified.

3. Evaluation needs some kind of tangible measurements, and in the case of counterinsurgency there are few. In conventional warfare, the movement of a front line, the fall of key cities and hilltops, and the destruction of communication installations can give a reasonably clear picture of progress. In guerrilla warfare, however, these events are not very important and often do not happen in any case. This leads to overemphasis on a body count of casualties which often provides a misleading measurement as counts are difficult to make given the nature of guerrilla war and the lack of distinction between real insurgents on the one hand and sympathizers, impressed persons, and innocent civilians on the other.

4. In addition, nonmilitary, or, in Thai terminology, the passive factors, appear to play important roles, but these are even more difficult to assess. Most observers agree that psychological operations can contribute to successful counterinsurgency, but almost no precise techniques exist for measuring the success or failure of the various instruments used in this field, or indeed of the overall effect of all directly psychological efforts. The many and varied developmental and civic action programs have impact in certain situations, but no one knows exactly how to determine what and how much.

In short, not being able to measure the contributions of the various components of a passive counterinsurgency program thwarts assessment of the overall effort. Thus, after many years of counterinsurgency activities, an accurate and accepted assessment capability is one of the greatest weaknesses, and much more work needs to be done to strengthen it. Even though our evaluation tools are still primitive, we must make the effort to arrive at some assessments; not surprisingly these will be quite subjective.

ACTIVE SUPPRESSION

In trying to evaluate the active suppressive effort first, we should examine the major geographical regions involved separately as they differ considerably. We can judge the effort in these regions by two criteria: (1) the state of the Communist Terrorist (CT) apparatus, and (2) the behavior of the population.[1] In the Northeast, the 09/10 plan was the primary basis for the suppression effort

---

1. The number of insurgent casualties, or "body counts," I do not consider to be accurate or greatly significant in evaluating the suppressive effort.

and it involved both our criteria. The early Royal Thai Army sweeps and patrols in these areas made life somewhat more difficult for the guerrillas by keeping them on the move and depriving them of bases where they could accumulate supplies. By 1971, however, significant elements of the Thai Second Army in the Northeast had been redeployed to meet the uncertain situation in Cambodia; this resulted in a serious reduction of the suppressive forces used against the guerrillas. Very largely army dominated at least until October, 1973, the Royal Thai Government (RTG) now believes that the police and civil agencies should constitute the primary agencies for dealing with the insurgency, thus putting the emphasis largely on passive measures. The CT efforts to improve their guerrillas and move into new areas was assisted by this deployment of the army units to the Cambodian border and other places, thus affording the guerrillas the opportunity to grow. The few remaining army units and the police and paramilitary forces are probably not able to maintain the initiative against the guerrillas. In spite of the situation the expected increase in CT incidents in 1972 and 1973 did not materialize. This was partially due to Joint Training Exercise 16 (December, 1972–January, 1973) which brought troops from Bangkok into the area. It was probably the most successful army operation since the 1967 one led by the Communist Suppression Operations Command (CSOC). A platoon was dropped into the Phu Pan Mountains and destroyed a large CT base. They also interrupted CT training of village units and generally caught the CTs off guard. It is estimated that there are in early 1974 approximately 1,600 guerrillas and over 1,500 unarmed village militia in the Northeast.

The various intelligence agencies operating against the Communist Party of Thailand (CPT) structure and their village support organization have increasingly good information in Sakon Nakhon and Nakhon Phanom but are much less informed about the rest of the Northeast. They have detailed data on the village structure in those two provinces and also reasonably good information on the important meetings of communist leaders. That the suppressive forces, even before the partial withdrawal of the army units, have not acted promptly or effectively on this information is rather baffling. A few arrests have been made and a certain number of insurgents have defected, but there have been no serious moves by the Thai forces except in 1967 and 1970 against the overall party structure, which remains still virtually intact. In other words, the party apparatus and its guerrilla units have not been seriously harmed by the Thai suppressive effort and indeed seem to be improving in a quiet but steady manner. Furthermore, the CT organization and activities have expanded into new areas.

The village protection units and the police in the Northeast have been able to provide some government presence and spotty protection to selected villages, although there are too many reports of poor behavior which does not lead to sound defense or a cooperative citizenry. Village security is most difficult to achieve, because the guerrillas' intelligence operations work well and give them the initiative and ability to hit and run. Determined villagers armed and trained by the government can make the guerrilla attacks more difficult and dangerous, but they rarely can stop them. Therefore insecurity exists in some villages in the Northeast. The security problem seems more influenced by guerrilla operations than by the protective forces. The situation varies from place to place, but many people, uncertain about the outcome of the insurgency, are probably behaving accordingly and hedging their bets. This is a gain for the guerrillas, since the government needs information and support from the population. It also seems to indicate that the guerrillas have not been separated from the people—their chief source of supply and intelligence. These conclusions apply mostly in areas where guerrillas are strongest, for example Sakon Nakhon and Nakhon Phanom and a few other areas in the Northeast. They would, of course, apply less in areas where there are few or no guerrillas and only initial efforts at subversion. Thus the suppressive operations in the Northeast have had some limited successes but have really made little impact on the CTs, which slowly grow in numbers.

In the North the situation is worse in a sense, as the guerrillas were well-trained and led when the insurgency broke out in 1967. Their operations have continued to inflict serious casualties on the RTG forces. The communists have retained the initiative and adhered to traditional guerrilla tactics—ambushes, surprise village attacks, and assassinations. The response of the Thais has been largely reactive in a very limited way. It was hoped that General Samran, who took over the RTG Third Army in 1969, would provide more dynamic leadership, both in suppressive and especially in the passive measures which he had pursued quite successfully while commanding the RTG First Army. He did initiate more personal leadership, put greater emphasis on psychological operations, and attempted to coordinate all of the agencies concerned with counterinsurgency, to include provincial governors, district officials, provincial police, and the community development agencies. In 1970 General Samran began the training of hunter-killer or hunter-capture teams to operate against the communists in guerrilla fashion, but these have had only limited use and success thus far.

In January, 1972, the RTG deployed the First Division from the Bangkok area to the Phu Lom Lo region of the North in an effort to drive out or destroy the guerrillas in that area. After three months the division was withdrawn. The RTG claimed they drove the few hundred guerrillas into Laos, but this is not certain. The government forces suffered very serious losses (about 700) while known casualties on the guerrilla side were negligible. Part of Joint Training Exercise 16 in 1973 was carried out in the North in the Phu Lom Lo area, and two Marine battalions were used for the first time in counterinsurgency operations. There were casualties as in 1972 from booby traps and ambushes, but the Thais were more careful and losses were kept down (about 70). However, little was accomplished in the way of destroying CT bases or killing and capturing CTs. One of the problems for the United States after this was that our side had pressed the Thais to take division-level actions, which then turned out to have rather poor results. Consequently, the Thais will probably evaluate our advice more critically in the future.

In 1970 CSOC developed a plan for the North which seemingly suggested a strategy opposite from that used in the Northeast. In the Northeast the strategy had been to encircle; in the North it seemed best to the CSOC planners to adopt the "oil spot" strategy, as encirclement of the mountains was an impossible task. The plan was to develop strength in the villages in the valley so as to prevent guerrilla incursion into the lowlands and to provide a springboard for offensive operations at some future date. While a trial was made of the plan in Chiang Rai province in 1970, not much had been accomplished by 1974.

Meanwhile artillery and air strikes, which are largely ineffective, are the most often used weapons against the guerrillas. The Thais know the situation is serious in the North and that they have made little headway against the communists, but they seem uncertain as to what to do next. The guerrillas remain untouched and are increasing in strength, but their activities, while expanding somewhat into the valleys, are still largely in the mountains, despite the predictions of many involved in the counterinsurgency effort that they would have established themselves in the valleys by 1972 or 1973, and despite a substantial increase during 1972 of Chinese-supplied weaponry.

Intelligence efforts against the CTs were undertaken late in the North, so it is only since 1969 that some useful information has gradually become available. It is still difficult as hilltribesmen form the bulk of the guerrilla forces, the terrain is rough, and the CTs can easily cross into Laos if necessary. Few prisoners and defectors have been taken in the region, so this important source of information has not been available. The RTG has by no means blocked the development of the communist apparatus, which actually is growing stronger and expanding its areas of operation. The CTs have already begun to try to penetrate into the ethnic Thai population; this effort if successful will create increasingly serious problems in the region. By 1974, however, this effort has had only limited success, and there are even reports of unrest among the Meo on the communist side.

In summary, in the North the guerrillas have retained the initiative, have inflicted far more serious casualties than they have suffered, and have increased their strength and made limited penetrations into the valleys and ethnic Thai population. However, after six years the insurgents' progress has not borne out the most pessimistic views; on the other hand, the RTG has not been successful in its operations against the guerrillas and their infrastructure slowly grows. In early 1974 it is estimated that there are about 2,500 guerrillas plus 800 village militia, mostly unarmed.

In the West Central and Mid-South, subversive efforts, almost entirely by ethnic Thais, have been extremely limited. The RTG's First Army in the West Central area, particularly in Prachuap, Phetchaburi, and Ratchaburi provinces, has largely concentrated on civic action and psychological operations, and very rarely engaged in suppressive military operations. The 100 or so guerrillas have so far been unharmed by any RTG actions but neither has the population's behavior been affected greatly by the guerrilla activity. In the Mid-South early in 1972 General San, under the guise of training exercises, launched active army operations against the CTs with some success. Though his tactics were considered too rough by some in Bangkok, he has continued aggressive actions. Before this, the police were largely responsible for the few suppressive actions in the area. One police campaign in 1970 in Phattalung and Trang did net a few guerrillas, but this seemed not to curtail their activities or inflict any serious casualties and there were very aggressive counter-actions by the CTs. Intelligence on the party apparatus is improving but is still limited, and action against the covert party apparatus (as opposed to the guerrillas) by the police has been almost nil. The Village Security Units in the Mid-South have performed rather poorly; they have not provided protection for the villagers and have often been sources of supply for the CTs. The situation in the Mid-South seems to be deteriorating as the RTG has been having little or no impact on the CT apparatus. However, the insurgents are moving quite slowly as in the other areas; their guerrilla strength is estimated to be about 400 in early 1974.

In the Far South, because of the inadequate number of police and their generally poor training and leadership, few really successful operations have been executed; there have, however, been few disasters. Thanks to the intelligence generated by the Regional Border Committee Organization (RBCO) in Songkhla, a number of Communist Terrorist Organization (CTO) camps have been located, but by the time the land forces arrived the CTO had fled, leaving few documents or materiel behind. Sweeps by combined Thai-Malaysian search forces have netted very little. Although the intelligence is reasonably good about the infrastructure, little or no action has been taken against it. Practically no damage has been inflicted on the highly disciplined and well-equipped CTO apparatus which is expanding and growing stronger even while some of it moves back to Malaysia. The population in certain districts, notably Betong, Sadao, Na Thawi, and Waeng, are strongly pro-CTO. Betong is largely Chinese and the other districts are Thai-Muslim areas. The RTG, because of the CTO's declared objective (a return to Malaysia), its distance from Bangkok, and probably because of the ethnic composition of the area, has not made a great effort against the CTO and indeed seems to have followed to a large extent a live-and-let-live policy. The beginning of the CTO return to Malaysia in 1971 reinforced this approach. That the Thais cannot concentrate on all the areas of insurgency at once—and that this one probably comes last—is understandable. On the other hand, their Malaysian neighbors are very much concerned about the situation in the Far South and have constantly urged the Thais to greater efforts; but the RTG has undertaken few suppressive operations against the CTO. In 1973 there were about 2,000 CTO guerrillas in southern Thailand.

PASSIVE APPROACH

The RTG's passive approach, which must be based on a successful suppression effort, should have as its ultimate objective the creation of a behavioral pattern favorable to the government through redressing the people's grievances and providing needed services. However, the objective has seldom been expressed in such a way. More often, intermediate objectives or accomplishments have been emphasized, largely because they were easier to observe, measure, and report. For example, most agencies have programs with goals for building "X" miles of road, "X" number of schools and health centers, etc. Often these intermediate goals are the only ones stated, and the real objective—the impact on the people and their behavior—is completely ignored. One would assume that intermediate objectives for rural programs from a counterinsurgency point of view should include increased income, better education and health services, and better communications between towns and villages. Such programs tend to foster favorable behavior, but could be thwarted by persuasive enemy action, such as force. Also, passive measures do not always lead to good will or favorable behavior if the services or programs provided are less than people expected or are poorly administered. The popular response to such programs has varied and depends on many complex factors often incompletely known to the government and susceptible to major change by the actions of the CTs. Each local situation should be studied separately and in detail, which I have of course not had the facilities to do; for this reason only a brief and very tentative evaluation of the Thai passive approach can be made here.

Most of the passive effort has been in the Northeast, though since 1968 efforts have been extended to the North. Accelerated Rural Development (ARD), Community Development (CD), and the Mobile Development Units (MDUs) are now active in parts of most of the northern provinces, but accomplishments are limited and it is too early to evaluate higher objectives. In the other areas of the insurgency—West Central, Mid-South, and Far South—the RTG has made very, very limited efforts, though the MDUs and CD have been active for some years in both parts of the South. Therefore, our review concerns itself primarily with the efforts in the Northeast, where small passive programs began in 1962. The largest effort has been road building. The Highway Department provides the major highway system, based primarily on economic needs and occasionally on strategic needs. ARD, CD, the MDUs, and the Royal Thai Army concentrate on the feeder and local road-building effort. A few thousand kilometers of such roads have been built; these have primarily and directly affected the lives of some of the people in remote rural areas, although the indirect effects on some 200,000 town and city people also are important. Hopefully, a two-way flow over the new roads will better the lot of the villagers by permitting them to get to town to market their produce, and by allowing officials to visit the villages to help the people and to explain government plans and programs. In a sense, however, roads are neutral and people's attitudes are affected not so much by having the roads as by the new experiences that the roads make possible. If the villagers profit from access to town and official visits are made to the villages, and both factors are a contribution to rural well-being and security, the roads may be regarded as an asset. If, on the other hand, trips to town merely whet villagers' appetites for goods they cannot afford and officials do not take the trouble to visit the villages, or, when they do visit are ill-mannered, uncooperative, or corrupt, the government's road-building effort will have failed in its desired impact on popular attitudes and behavior. In either case, the contribution of roads to the counterinsurgency effort is difficult to evaluate and also depends to a great extent on the security situation.

In general, however, the roads appear to have been an asset. The people seem to be pleased with the greater freedom of movement that allows them to get a share of some modern goods that they want, and to have contacts with government officials, although in some cases the contacts have been less than satisfactory. The RTG is trying to resolve problems arising from the behavior of some police and other officials, but many difficulties in this regard need to be corrected, especially in view of the openings that they provide for communist propaganda.

The material benefits from roads and other developmental programs are observable and generally desirable. I can remember flying over the Northeast region in 1961 and viewing thatched roofed houses in all the villages. Ten years later the glimmer of corrugated steel roofing can be seen in all sections of the Northeast, even in remote villages. This along with the prevalence of motorbikes and transistor radios is clear evidence that some extra money is reaching the villagers and that even the so-called remote villages are no longer so remote.

The roads have also allowed follow-on programs to be carried out, such as provision of more schools, health stations, marketing facilities, and other benefits of modern life. The roads extend access for the Mobile Information Teams that include officials who visit the people to explain government plans and activities directly to them. Where the CT presence has not been strong and the

Thai officials' behavior has been proper, these developments should help retain the loyalty of the people.

Emphasis on development of the Northeast's rural areas has led to a series of programs designed to assist the farmers, whose most fundamental problem—floods in the wet season and drought in the dry season—began to be addressed seriously only in the past few years. The Korat Plateau is so level that most large-scale dams, with a few exceptions, can be built only in the higher ground on the edge of the region. The RTG, using long-term loan funds from several foreign sources, has completed construction or is in the process of building thirteen of these on the rim of the Plateau. The dams will store water for large irrigation projects, will help in flood control, and some will also provide hydroelectric power. Of more immediate interest to farmers is the initially USOM-assisted ARD water program, which includes construction of small local storage reservoirs and construction of the needed irrigation canals, which will permit village irrigation projects and provide water for livestock. Another aspect of this water program is construction of both shallow and deep wells and the supplying of the necessary pumps.

Drinking water is a serious problem in the region as most of the Plateau has underlying salt deposits which necessitate very deep drilling of wells in order to reach water that is not brackish. Surface water tends to be contaminated because of its multi-use by animals and human beings. USOM is aiding the RTG by helping with the drilling costs, providing purification units and assisting in the education of the people on the subject of potable water.

The RTG, with USOM assistance, has a number of projects aimed at increasing the farmers' income. It has encouraged and assisted various clubs and district cooperatives which can consolidate and strengthen farmers' financial management, improve marketing capabilities, and improve the farmers' ability to borrow money from participating banks at government-sponsored low interest rates for fertilizer, pesticides, water pumps, etc. The RTG is also providing assistance in improving livestock breeds and veterinarian services, increasing the production of cattle and poultry and encouraging diversification of crops and better land usage. It has expanded agricultural demonstration centers and its agricultural education extension program. These programs are responsive to the high priorities stated by Thai villagers in the Northeast. While progress is clearly being made, the problem is to keep up with the villagers' expectations.

Both the RTG Department of Agriculture and ARD have backed the formation of clubs for rural youth. The agricultural clubs resemble U. S. 4-H Clubs; the ARD clubs encourage development of leadership, sports and recreation, and vocational training. The programs have been small, but they could offer a useful counter to insurgent appeals to restless youths. This sort of social effort is particularly important but has too often been neglected.

To help meet the general need for modern medical services the RTG Department of Health has maintained three levels of health centers, ranging from hospitals in large towns to small dispensaries and midwife centers in villages. These are supplemented by the Mobile Medical Teams who come, mainly from Bangkok, for a few months of duty in the rural health centers. A notable health program for malaria eradication began in the 1950s. With assistance from USOM and the World Health Organization the incidence of malaria in Thailand has been radically reduced. Health services on a continuing basis still rank high among village needs.

The Royal Thai Government, with aid from USOM, the United Nations, and other foreign sources, has put much effort into improving and expanding its schools at all levels. Vocational training in junior and senior high schools has been especially stressed. ARD has a program of Mobile Trade Training Units that visit rural areas to teach villagers such trades as barbering, carpentry, and dressmaking, which may provide some cash income and occupation during the dry season when farm duties are light.

Given the average 3 percent annual population increase, the RTG has had difficulties in constructing enough new elementary schools and finding teachers for the ever-increasing numbers of children. Because of low salaries and the isolation of some of the schools, teaching has not been a popular profession. In mid-1969, for example, 12,000 new teachers were needed but only 8,000 were available. The importance of education is recognized, but the competition for funds in a developing nation is heavy.

As might be expected, development projects have been most numerous in areas where the threat from insurgents has been most obvious but also tend to be located in the vicinity of district towns rather than in the more remote villages of such an area. Many remote villages still have had little or no evidence of the government's desire to better their lot. To the extent that developmental efforts do forestall or counter insurgent efforts, such villages are the real vulnerable spots.

The RTG has, on the whole, shown relatively little interest in psychological operations, and accomplishments in this regard have come about largely because the United States took the initiative in pushing this type of program. The Thais have, however, taken an increasing interest in Mobile Information Teams (MITs) which were started with United States Information Service (USIS) assistance in 1962 and which are now conducted by Thai district officials. The typical MIT consists of the district officer or one of his deputies, local representatives of ministries or departments (e.g., Health, Community Development, Agriculture), and a Modular Auditory-Visual Unit (MAVU). The teams go out for one to four days, visit one or more villages, make speeches and talk with the villagers, give some token services such as dispensing medicine, and show movies that relate to government activities, or narrate an anti-communist story. A village is likely to be visited by an MIT no more than three or four times a year, some only once and some not at all.

In the earlier years when official visits to villages were very rare, the MITs served to get officials out to see rural conditions first-hand and brought information to the villagers on government plans and policies, which they received from no other source. Furthermore, the movies were a miracle to villagers who had never seen any before. A 1971 survey, however, suggested that the MITs, as they had been conducted, might have outlived their usefulness. Only the villages most seldom visited and the older villagers who are confined to their village showed that an MIT visit had any real impact. Most villagers stated that they relied on the headman and their radios as sources of information about government activities and the outside world. They said the MIT visits tended to be perfunctory, that the officials were interested only in seeing whether regulations were being obeyed and not in bringing relevant services to the villagers, and that there was little or no follow-up action to meet village needs. Even the movies were no longer a rarity to the many villages that were visited by traveling commercial outfits or whose inhabitants could by that time go occasionally to the district town. The study suggested, however, that a well-organized and planned MIT visit, which brought services aimed specifically at the real needs of a specific village to reinforce its message of the government's concern for its people, might still be a useful way of extending government influence, especially if effective follow-up actions are carried out.

The RTG's psyops pamphlets and posters are distributed widely to schools, to village headmen, and to other official representatives, but what their impact has been is difficult to evaluate. Since functional literacy in the rural areas is rather low, possibly nothing but the simplest wording gets across. It is perhaps significant that no one interviewed in the above-mentioned MIT survey cited these materials as chief sources of information about the government and its officials. The publications may, however, be a principal source for the headmen and schoolteachers, who pass the word along to the villagers.

The radio is probably the most effective medium for reaching a large audience in Thailand. A survey made in 1969 indicated that some 67 percent of rural households and 87 percent of urban households in the Northeast had a radio.[2] No doubt the percentages have continued to increase, just as they did markedly after a survey in 1964. The 1969 survey also showed that Station 909 near Sakon Nakhon city was listened to more frequently and was preferred to all the other stations reaching the area. This noncommercial station, established with American assistance, is operated by the National Security Command and pre-

2. Business Research Limited, *Northeast Radio Media Survey 1969*, prepared for Research Office, United States Information Service, Bangkok, 1969.

sents programs that support the government's security and development efforts in the Northeast. Among program suppliers have been the RTG Second Army, the Department of Public Relations, and the Communist Suppression Operations Command (CSOC). The station has also regularly broadcast Ministry of Education programs for the schools. Perhaps one reason for the station's popularity is that some of its programs are in the Northeast Thai dialect; others use the sing-song style of delivery (*mohlam*) traditional in Northeast Thai storytelling. A popular feature of the station are the recordings made by its field teams on village self-help projects, items about government projects in remote villages, and interviews with insurgent defectors. Villagers are encouraged to report intelligence on the insurgency to the station and many have done so. Defectors have indicated that 909 broadcasts influenced their decision to desert the insurgent movement. The popularity of the station is further attested by the thousands of letters it receives and the even larger numbers of people who visit it.

At Lampang, in the North, the Department of Public Information has operated a radio station that broadcasts in the major hill-tribe languages and is programed especially to reach the hill-tribe audience of the North. The station was slow in getting under way but is now increasing its operating time and scope. However, getting any reliable data on its impact on the hill-tribe people is most difficult.

To discover the effects of RTG counterinsurgency efforts and to gain some feeling for the effects on the youth of rural Thailand of communist propaganda that exploits government weaknesses, a study was made in the Northeast by a Thai professor and some of his graduate students between late 1967 and March 1969.[3] The study tended to confirm that Thai youth were basically loyal but apolitical in outlook. It also revealed that the youth had a critical attitude toward the general situation in the Northeast. Three primary sources of youth dissatisfaction in the area were defined.

1. A majority of the youth felt that economic conditions were deteriorating and that the villagers were themselves unable to rectify the situation. They saw the government as the only source of help but were not very happy with its development projects because of procrastination, termination of some before full completion, and mishandling of some of the funds. They were particularly upset over alleged corruption. Thus the situation was frustrating for the youths.

2. The lack of security—the government's failure to protect life and property—was also a source of complaint. Where there were no insurgents, many young villagers felt threatened by robbers and bandits; in the insurgent areas

3. The study, sponsored by the Military Research and Development Center (MRDC), a joint Thai-U.S. research agency, was carried on primarily in Ubon province. It is an old study but reflects serious differences between the views of the rural population and the government about the CTs. I suspect that these differences still exist today and that the findings of this study are still instructive and useful.

they feared the CTs. Again the government was blamed for the situation and criticized for its inadequate performance.

3. Unjust or oppressive treatment by the authorities was alleged. The injustice complaint included too rigid enforcement of laws that the villagers felt to be unfair. Two in particular bothered them—prohibition of making "home brew" and the restrictions on cutting teak wood. Besides the restrictions on freedom, the villagers felt that enforcement of the rules created an unfair and oppressive economic burden. The complaints about oppressive treatment included numerous charges about corrupt officials who insisted on "tea money" (payments more than an official fee, or bribes before a motorcycle license or a permit to cut a tree would be granted). These complaints are serious sources of dissatisfaction among some of the residents of the Northeast that the RTG must try to cope with. The pace of the coping is slow and the communists' propaganda takes pains to make the pace seem even slower and less efficient than it is.

Very significantly, the study also revealed that many young villagers have an image of the CTs quite different from the one propagated by the government. The following views of the CTs were found.

1. The communists are Northeastern villagers like themselves. These communists are the enemies of the RTG and the U.S. but not of the people.

2. Life under communism is tolerable and probably very similar to the present regime.

3. Villagers join the communists in the hills because CTs are successful in convincing them that they are the friends of villagers and are dedicated in the fight for national independence and the improvement of villagers' general well-being.

4. The present pacification and rehabilitation programs are not adequate to win over the hearts of the CT returnees. To be successful (according to these youths) a much more energetic RTG development effort is required. The authorities must take a more friendly and more egalitarian attitude toward villagers, and effective measures must be taken to punish or eliminate corrupt and oppressive officials.

The study indicated a need for better education of the rural people about the way their government functions, and the role they can play in influencing its decisions. Obviously, two-way channels of communication must be expanded so that the people and the government can understand each other better. Ways of "people" involvement must be found, not only for solid economic growth but for effective counterinsurgency. (The study also suggested that the RTG might well review its propaganda themes to ensure that the youth will find them credible and effective.)

I should point out that the study, at least parts of it, was based on information now several years old. Since then, the RTG has made progress in expanding its presence in the Northeast and in increasing at least some of the services that the people desire. That the communists have not made greater progress in winning the people to their cause, despite strenuous efforts, indicates that traditional forces are still strong in the countryside, that the people in an overall sense are not acutely unhappy and that the communist appeals and performance do not impress them greatly. The communists' limited progress also suggests that communist doctrine and violence have not had as great or widespread effect as the insurgents hoped. Nevertheless, that a number of young Thais voiced serious dissatisfaction with their lives and with the government's performance give the communists some very powerful weapons. Recent developments suggest that the communists are improving their appeals to and impact on the youth and making greater progress than in the earlier years of the insurgency.

CHANGES AFFECTING THAI VULNERABILITY
TO COMMUNISM

For some time changes have been going on in Thailand that could have a very serious impact on the stability and security of the country and which have weakened Thai values and society and made the Thais more vulnerable to outside influences, including communism. In the first place, although Thailand has enjoyed prosperity since World War II, socioeconomic problems have been looming on the horizon that will be a severe test to the RTG.

All of this would come at a time when there are increased demands on the Thai budget, both for additional development programs and for increased security forces because of the insurgency. The possible net reduction of American economic input due to the redeployment of U.S. forces from Southeast Asia could not have come at a worse time as far as the Thais are concerned. The government, which over the years has demonstrated a considerable capability for adapting to change both from within and from without, may be extremely hard pressed to satisfy the increasing demands and aspirations of the people.

The introduction of mass media into Thailand has already made this task considerably more difficult. Advertising for new clothes, transistor radios, motorbikes, and other modern items whets the appetites of both the urban people and the rural people. Movies and television, which are spreading out into the rural areas of Thailand, raise expectations, as do the masses of printed materials. The mass media, even without any direct political intent, tend to raise expectations far beyond what it is possible for a government and its society to satisfy as promptly as demanded. Communist propaganda techniques and means, with precise political objectives, may be able to make this situation even more unmanageable.

Many Thais have become increasingly worried about the growing, major impact of modern (and particularly Western) attitudes and desires. In the past the government had been able to control to a large degree the influx of ideas and notions from the "outside"; opportunities for education of Thais abroad were carefully selected, as was the role of foreigners inside Thailand. This slow injection of alien ideas permitted the Thais to modify and adapt so as to evolve a Thai way of modernization; the gradual approach also allowed many of the traditional values and beliefs to remain strong. The government, unless it went to an extreme like that adopted by the Burmese government,[4] simply could not shut out modernization, nor did it really wish to. The RTG's very pressing problem is how to preserve the best of the past and introduce the best of the new, without bringing about violent social upheaval and political chaos.

The case of the young and well-educated bureaucrats who have recently been staffing the middle levels of government illustrates the problem. They feel, and are, underpaid and are increasingly worried about their futures. Many are also dissatisfied with the traditional Thai way of doing things—the personalized and loose organization which is the opposite of what most modern administrative and technical societies require. These young people are disturbed about the corruption and favoritism in the government. Unlike the majority of Thais, they are impatient for changes in government and society in general and also for ways to improve their own lot. They have not made the great break with the past that the communists have, but they could be on the way. Some are at the crossroads: do they join freely the ruling elite whom they see as imperfect, or do they make a break and try to change the system, probably at a considerable loss of prestige and future promotions? One real test for Thailand is whether adequate improvements in government and personal opportunities for the able young men can be made in time. However, the change in the Thai government which occurred in October, 1973, as a result of the students' dissatisfaction, may provide greater opportunities for able young people and a chance to modify the old system.

Thus there is ferment and change within Thai society in political, economic, and social spheres. These new stresses make it uncertain whether the cultural traditions of pragmatism and apoliticality can continue to insulate the vast

4. The Burmese government, under General (now a civilian) Ne Win, shut off Burma from the rest of the world in the early 1960s and attempted to develop an independent socialist system aimed at making the country self-sufficient. As a result of lack of contact with the outside world, Burma has been almost static, if not decaying. In 1969 tourists were once again permitted to visit Burma for short periods in order to help the country's economic situation. In 1973 Ne Win opened Burma to even greater international contacts, and it seems likely that this trend will continue.

majority of Thais from the increasing communist effort to develop and exploit disruptive factors so as first to break down the society and the government, and then take them over.

In early 1974 the Royal Thai Government is still not devoting enough time and attention to the insurgency or applying with sufficient effectiveness the resources they already have. As noted earlier, there are several reasons for this. First, the government is somewhat accustomed to a certain amount of dissidence and some disorder in the more remote parts of the kingdom. Not enough officials recognize that the communist-inspired insurgency differs from other forms of opposition, that it is a centrally organized effort based on an accepted doctrine, and that it has some rather potent outside support. Furthermore, the belief in the basic loyalty of the Thai people as a brake to expansion of the insurgency and the conviction that the insurgency is primarily a minority problem tends to breed some amount of complacency that will probably not be justified in the future, given the communist techniques and the changing society in Thailand.

As in many countries, there has been a tendency for most high and aspiring officials to concentrate their attention on the capital city, since it is the symbol and source of power and wealth which they seek. Bangkok surpasses all other cities in Thailand in population, wealth, prestige, and power. Many officials try to avoid being assigned to the provinces because such posts do not further their careers. Happily, this is slowly changing. Officials have recently been rotated, and service in the countryside is becoming more acceptable and no longer considered "exile to Siberia." The fun-loving Thais also like Bangkok because it provides many pleasures that are harder to find in the provinces. However, as many provincial cities have grown, they have expanded their social capabilities. Nevertheless, officials tend to want to be in Bangkok, and this has hurt the counterinsurgency effort in the remote areas. Happily, there is some evidence that attitudes are changing. High commodity prices in the world market are resulting in a great enrichment of the provinces, while Bangkok is reeling from the effects of the energy crisis. New wealth is giving farmers influence and greater respect, as became evident from the participation of some of them in the Constitutional Convention called by the King in late 1973.

Many external problems have competed with the insurgency for the attention of the government. The Royal Thai Government is worried about the continued violence and precarious cease-fire in Vietnam and is still very much concerned about the situation in Laos and Cambodia. It fears that the communists operating in these countries may be developing a serious threat to Thailand and much attention is given to the problem of coping with these possible external threats. Laos and Cambodia, parts of which Thailand has claimed in the past, present even more serious worries to the Thais as they have acted as buffers between the

Thais and the Vietnamese, the two dominant groups of mainland Southeast Asia. The concern of the Thais has led them to pull away army forces needed for internal counterinsurgency operations in order to protect the border areas of Thailand and has diverted the attention of top government leadership from the insurgency in Thailand to what is happening in the neighboring countries.

The RTG is also worried about the effect of its relationship with the United States, especially in the light of this continuous communist activity. U.S. aid levels, both economic and military, have recently been drastically reduced and will be lowered further in 1974. The question of U.S. use of Thai air bases is central to the problem. At first under the Nixon Doctrine there was a gradual withdrawal of American military men stationed in Thailand, but in 1972 this trend was reversed, and in early 1973 the U.S. used more Thai air bases than ever before. However, during the summer and fall of 1973 negotiations on a reduction of U.S. forces in Thailand were held between representatives of the two governments, and by late 1973 some of these forces had already been withdrawn. The U.S. has also headquartered its military command for Southeast Asia in Thailand after moving it from Saigon when the Vietnam peace agreement was put into effect. The RTG, though seeming to waver at times, appears to want the U.S. presence in Thailand to continue but not to increase. Many RTG leaders have said that the Thais need the U.S. protection and that the presence of the American military in Thailand does not invite increased communist attacks. On the other hand, former Foreign Minister Thanat Khoman has argued that the American presence does invite communist attacks and does not aid the security of Thailand. Some Thai intellectuals argue that removal of the bases will also remove the barriers to further dialogue and accommodation with North Vietnam and the People's Republic of China. Though Chinese Premier Chou En-lai, who is more concerned with Russian threats to his country, has certainly not encouraged this view; rather he has encouraged the Thais to keep the bases, obviously to check Soviet designs in Southeast Asia. Clearly the Thais are going through an agonizing debate over what is best for their country in these troublesome and changing times. No one can predict the outcome with any certainty, but the Thais are clearly moving toward greater flexibility in their foreign policy, which has been their tradition.

Although these problems are real and require attention, recent American experience suggests that if the home base is not reasonably content and does not support a foreign policy, then that policy is in jeopardy. Americans reinforced the Thai tendency to put highest priority on foreign affairs by requesting Thai assistance in the Indochina conflict. This suited United States policy as well as Thai, but was it really best for the Thais? Few governments can handle more than one or two top-priority items at a time. In the case of Thailand, the situation put the insurgency at a rather low priority—appropriate in the sense of its earlier threat, but as I have noted, although the progress of the communist insurgents has been slow, it has also been steady. The longer effective counter-measures are put off the more expensive and difficult they become. The communists have in fact been aided more by the threat they pose in all Southeast Asia, than by direct aid, as they have diverted the Thai government's attention from its own internal cancer.

Given these problems, it is not difficult to see that the top RTG officials are worried and busy men. Unfortunately, in light of the other problems noted above, the concern about the insurgency has not been growing as fast as the insurgency itself, even though the growth is quite slow—an overall 11 percent in 1972, for example. Many people thought that with a new government in power after the student-instigated upheaval of October, 1973, the RTG would increase its concern for the insurgency, but at least at one level the exact opposite occurred. Prime Minister Sanya, in a formal listing of his new government's fourteen priorities, did not mention the insurgency. The new government not unjustly feels that it has far more important matters to deal with, but ones that ultimately are related to the insurgency. Cleaning up the government, restoring its credibility, after so many years in which the nation had been led by increasingly disrespected men, after all is more important than dealing directly with the CTs. Only a coherent, effective, and fair government, in the long run, can truly solve the grave problems, including insurgency, in the provinces.

Yet it is difficult to be sanguine about the government's prospects for mounting an effective campaign. Counterinsurgency, in the view of the increasingly influential intellectual community in Bangkok, is closely associated, ironically, with the deposed government of Thanom and Praphas. There is genuine ambivalence reflected in the government's attitude. "Communist suppression activities in this country have ground to a halt as a result of the 'indecisive attitude' of the Sanya Dharmasakti Government," a Thai journalist wrote after an interview with CSOC's General Saiyud Kerdphol.

Meantime the men who survived the 1973 coup are jockeying for position in the new order and trying to pick up the counterinsurgency pieces in a manner suitable to their interests. There are essentially four positions advanced by different groups about the fate of the counterinsurgency effort. Preeminent among them is the position advocated by Air Marshal Dawee, the present Minister of Defense, and several prominent army generals, who want CSOC brought under the National Security Command, as had originally been proposed ten years earlier. Another position, strongly supported by many of the civilians working in the counterinsurgency effort, is for CSOC to be strengthened and placed directly under the Prime Minister's office, as ARD had once been, in order to guarantee attention at the top. A third group wants to integrate, in effect, all CPM functions into CSOC, including the ARD and MDU programs. A final group wants CSOC's functions returned to the respective line agencies from which its parts had originally been extracted. It is no secret that this group simply does not feel that the insurgency is a real threat, and their solution is designed in accordance with that perception.

The solution, probably a temporary one, that has been arrived at in January, 1974, is not a bad one, at least on paper. CSOC as a unit has been saved and moved from its position under the army to the Prime Minister's office, but with the Minister of Defense (presently Air Marshal Dawee) in charge at the top. Whether this will result in a more concerted effort against the CTs is not clear at the time of this writing, though by its very nature and increasing threat the insurgency requires precisely that.

Chapter 6

United States Government Apparatus

As early as 1961 some members of the American Mission in Bangkok, including Ambassador Kenneth T. Young, had seen evidence that led them to predict a communist-inspired insurgency in Thailand within a few years. Some of this evidence appeared in the findings in that year of the Southeast Asia Treaty Organization (SEATO) Expert Study Group on Countersubversion. In Washington members of the new Kennedy Administration began to take a fresh look at the dangers of communist-led movements in developing countries and to call for assessments of the internal security problems of threatened areas, including Thailand. There was, however, to be no unanimity within the Mission in Bangkok on the imminence of the threat, as this chapter chronicles, and some officials thought the possibility of an impending insurgency was nonsense. The Mission did, however, go to work on a plan of action for Thailand, which was issued in late 1962, and which remains the basic reference for American counterinsurgency efforts.

There is, unfortunately, always a lag between new realities and the perception of them. While the Mission paper was being prepared in 1962 the view that American assistance in the economic and social fields could be phased out within a few years was gaining ground—a perception based on realities of several years earlier; it was to take much time to reverse the perception so as to make apparent the seriousness of the threat. Ambassador Graham Martin, who arrived in Bangkok in late 1963, rapidly developed a sense of urgency about combatting the incipient insurgency and began the arduous task of trying to "turn the ship around," so that additional aid could be received from the United States.

The goal of the 1962 plan had been to focus American efforts and marshal American resources so as to stimulate the Thais to greater activity both to prevent the predicted overt insurgency and, should it actually break out, to defeat it. More specifically the plan called for measures to be undertaken by the Royal Thai Government (RTG), with American assistance as needed, to gain the allegiance of the people, improve the intelligence process, enhance the welfare of the people, and develop both the active and passive counterinsurgency capabilities of the RTG. The Ambassador rightly believed that preventive measures were preferable to corrective ones and urged the Thais to make greater efforts in the rural areas. The Northeast was given the highest priority. In 1962 the Thais (as noted earlier) had begun the Community Development and Mobile Development Unit programs. These were, however, still very small, and there was no energetic government-wide campaign to prevent the incipient insurgency from escalating or to minimize the alleged governmental deficiencies upon which it fed. Even the Provincial Police training program that the Mission had been urging since 1957 was not really in action until the autumn of 1962.

Thus by late 1963, Ambassador Martin felt that top priorities should be given to training and reequipping first the Provincial Police and then the Border Patrol Police for building roads to and along the Lao border, and for the establishment of the Accelerated Rural Development (ARD) program. Even though the insurgent threat seemed to be somewhat less menacing early in 1964, Martin continued to urge the Thais to take more preventive action. He also fought for increased aid from Washington to encourage and help the Thais. When terrorist incidents in the Northeast increased during late 1964 and 1965, he intensified his efforts.

In January, 1966, when armed insurgents were clearly operating in the Northeast and the RTG had shown appreciation of the situation by establishing the Communist Suppression Operations Command (CSOC), Martin enlisted all of the Mission elements in a crash counterinsurgency program to get things moving as fast as possible. Initial steps were to hasten progress of the programs already under consideration or under way, and to try to speed up the arrival of commodities and equipment already on order. High priority was also placed on initiating programming of additional equipment, especially helicopters for the proposed Police Air Division, needed for combatting the insurgents in a highly visible, quick-response fashion.

The problem of consensus continued to intrude. Some Mission members, for example, became increasingly concerned about providing security from insurgent attacks to villagers. Martin on the other hand, eager to get action of *any* kind, started on this problem, supported the initiation of several pilot projects in separate areas in the hope that experience might show which was best for general adoption. With his backing, People's Assistance Teams (PATs), somewhat similar to those developed in Vietnam, were started in Sakon Nakhon to help improve the people's welfare, demonstrate the government's interest, collect intelligence, and provide security to the villagers. Martin also supported the Census Aspiration program for collecting intelligence and approved two other varieties of village protection units sponsored by CSOC and by the Department of Local Administration (DOLA) in the Thai Ministry of the Interior.

The Mission elements under Martin's urging focused their efforts more directly on counterinsurgency. The support of the U.S. Operations Mission (USOM), the name of the Agency for International Development (AID) organization in Thailand, particularly of ARD and the Police programs, was increased. Not only were Military Assistance Program (MAP) funds increased but additional emphasis was placed on counterinsurgency training programs and civic action. Martin also succeeded in getting the U.S. Operations Mission and the U.S. Military Assistance Command, Thailand (MACTHAI) to provide gasoline and oil to the Thai police and military so that they would have additional funds to pay per diem to their forces in counterinsurgency operations. (Unfortunately the shortage of per diem funds has never been solved, despite this massive attempt to help.) Efforts at training Thais in intelligence were increased. The U.S. Information Service (USIS) began to expand and establish new branch offices which had the mission of assisting provincial officials in psychological operations designed to counter Communist Terrorist (CT) propaganda and activities. The Advanced Projects Research Agency (ARPA) shifted its emphasis to research bearing directly on counterinsurgency problems.

Martin's concern about the situation in Thailand and the need for greater action on the part of the RTG was reinforced by his belief that American aid to Vietnam in the early stages had been too tardy and too little. More prompt attention to the re-emerging insurgency would, he felt, probably have stemmed it. As it was, in 1965–1966 in Vietnam, failure in the earlier phases was leading to a massive commitment of American manpower and resources. He was determined not to repeat this mistake in Thailand.

Presentation of his case to the Washington agency headquarters won some supporters but doubt still lingered in some official circles as to whether the insurgency in Thailand was in fact as serious a threat as it was represented to be. In the spring of 1966 a joint team of representatives from the State Department, Defense Department, and CIA, visiting Thailand to investigate the situation, unanimously agreed with the Ambassador that the insurgency was growing and that American efforts to help the Thais should be increased and accelerated. Their report to Washington supported and reinforced Martin's position on the insurgency as well as his desire to improve the coordination of the United States counterinsurgency assistance effort.

In this chapter we are, overall, dealing with the difficulties that ensued from the lack of consensus within the American community as to the seriousness of the insurgency and as to the way it should be handled, at a time when the insurgency itself was rapidly increasing its momentum. To do this we examine the specific roles and functions of the American hierarchies involved in the American effort—the Ambassador, the civilian sector, and the military sector. The emerging need for more effective coordination within the American community, through a reshaping of the Mission's internal organization, and between the American and Thai communities, becomes the focus of Chapter 7.

COUNTERINSURGENCY ROLES IN THE AMERICAN DIPLOMATIC MISSION

The Ambassador and the Embassy

The Ambassador is Chief of the Diplomatic Mission which is composed of several civilian and military elements. He is the personal representative of the President of the United States in carrying out the Chief Executive's foreign affairs role vis-à-vis Thailand. In a letter dated December 9, 1969, President Nixon spelled out the responsibilities and authority of all American Ambassadors with the intent of trying to "improve and tighten the processes of foreign policy implementation abroad."[1] The key paragraph of the letter stated:

> As Chief of the United States Diplomatic Mission, you have full responsibility to direct and coordinate the activities and operations of all of its elements. You will exercise this mandate not only by providing policy leadership and guidance, but also by assuring positive program direction to the end that all United States Activities in Thailand are relevant to current realities, are efficiently and economically administered, and are effectively inter-related so that they will make a maximum contribution to United States interests in that country as well as to our regional and international objectives.

Later in the letter the President seemed to except, in certain circumstances, the military from these provisions, though he exhorted the military to keep the Ambassador informed and to work together with him. Since the military in

1. President Kennedy had issued a similar letter in 1961.

Thailand are the most numerous and the most independent-minded American element, this ambiguity may be a serious weakness in the system intended to assure the unity of American efforts. The President wrote:

> I will reserve for myself, as Commander-in-Chief, direct authority over the military chain of command to United States military forces under the command of a United States area military commander, and over such other military activities as I elect, as Commander-in-Chief, to conduct through military channels.

> However, I will expect you and the military commanders concerned to maintain close relations with each other, to keep each other currently informed on matters of mutual interest and in general to cooperate in carrying out our national policy. If differences of view not capable of resolution in the field should arise, I will expect you to keep me informed through the Secretary of State.

Nevertheless, the President was apparently seeking to have a tightly coordinated and well-led and directed American effort in Thailand and other countries where the United States has a large and diversified Mission. The interpretations and implementation of such presidential letters are, of course, up to the various agency heads and to the individual Ambassador. The interpretations have varied considerably in Thailand at various times.

With the best will in the world, it is difficult for an Ambassador to orchestrate the activities of the diverse agencies in his Mission. The contradiction in the Nixon letter is compounded by practical administrative problems. Each of the Mission elements has its own institutional loyalties, each of the parent agencies in Washington has its own goals and interests, and its own private channels of communication, as well as a congressional constituency to serve. Even when a Mission can speak with a single voice from the field, there is no single listener in Washington. Instead, there is a mixed audience which can respond only after a sometimes lengthy process of negotiation and compromise. A further complication is that Mission elements tend to build up client relationships with the various agencies of the foreign host government; in time, this symbiotic relationship can become very strong indeed. And, of course, separate program definitions and budgetary processes in Washington, which are largely outside ambassadorial control, contribute to this diverging of views and goals. In this connection, it should be pointed out that, although the Ambassador can provide leadership and impetus, most of the direct control of resources and manpower resides in the agencies represented in the Mission, particularly in USOM and MACTHAI.

An Ambassador, in addition to his duties as Chief of Mission, of course also heads the Embassy staff that carries out the many detailed diplomatic responsibilities. Bangkok Embassy personnel in early 1974 number about 101, making it one of the largest American Embassies in the world. Additionally, in Thailand the Embassy staff acts as the Ambassador's coordinating staff and is involved in a multitude of nondiplomatic activities. Besides the usual political, economic, and consular sections, the Bangkok Embassy has three other main sections. The Politico-Military Section works with the American and Thai military on the various problems arising out of the large U.S. military presence and military assistance. It also deals with the Thais on regional security matters, such as the Southeast Asia Treaty Organization (SEATO), and negotiated the agreements for Thai military forces when they were in Vietnam. A Regional Economic Development office, financed separately by the Agency for International Development (AID), is an adjunct of the Embassy and is responsible for planning and implementation of Mekong River basin development. And in 1966 the section of the Special Assistant for Counterinsurgency (SA/CI), in 1974 called the Development and Security Section, was established. This section will be discussed separately in Chapter 7.

The Civilian Sector

Most of the U.S. funds allocated for Thailand have been channeled through the Military Assistance Program (MAP) and the Agency for International Development (AID). The three major categories of assistance include: provision of commodities and equipment not available in Thailand; technical and other advice from U.S. official personnel and contractors; and training of Thais in many varied fields in Thailand, the United States, and other countries. Of the U.S. funds expended for Thailand, by far the largest proportion has gone for commodities and equipment. A monetary basis is not, however, the best criterion for the relative value to Thailand of the assistance given in these three categories. For example, in common with other developing countries, Thailand has suffered from a shortage of technically trained specialists; therefore, much of the effort of U.S. official personnel and contractors has been devoted to helping the Thais develop their own expertise in many fields through training programs and has had a high value, for outweighing the monetary investment involved. There is no doubt that this has contributed greatly to the counterinsurgency effort, both directly and indirectly.

The largest civilian agency is the AID mission which was established in Thailand in 1954. Officially known as the United States Operations Mission (USOM) in Bangkok, in early 1974 it numbers about 179 U.S. staff members and some contractor personnel. It is responsible for planning U.S. economic aid to Thailand and for ensuring the delivery of equipment and supplies and their proper maintenance and use, according to agreed program objectives. It also provides a number of advisors, not only in the fields of economic development in general, but also in agriculture, health, public administration, education, community development, and police affairs. Most of the advisors are located in

Bangkok, though many have been stationed off and on in the provinces to assist Thai local officials in the rural areas. The largest number of advisors are associated with Accelerated Rural Development (ARD) and Thai police programs. USOM also assists the RTG by contracting for additional advisors in technical fields, such as agriculture and education. It finances training programs and assists in providing educational opportunities for Thai professionals and technicians, in Thailand, in the United States, and in other countries. The largest numbers of participants in these programs are in the fields of agriculture, education, health, and public administration. Particularly under the ARD program, USOM personnel and contractors have trained many Thais in technical skills ranging from office management to mechanical equipment maintenance and truck driving. As rapidly as possible the training task has been turned over to the Thais themselves. Many of USOM's efforts have been directed toward assisting the Thais' counterinsurgency efforts, though many of the programs contribute at least equally to nation-building. From the early 1960s, USOM has put major emphasis on improving the security and economic status of the rural population in the Northeast and more recently also in the North.

The greatest part of USOM's effort has been devoted to ARD and to the police programs (as reviewed in Chapter 5). Equipment for road construction and village improvements have been the major items of expense in the ARD program. In the police programs, commodity emphasis has been on uniforms, weapons, vehicles, radios, and aircraft for the Police Air Division. The Village Radio System, originally supported by MAP and later USOM-assisted, was proposed by Secretary of Defense Robert S. McNamara in 1962. USOM has provided radios for a growing network in security-sensitive areas. The system establishes direct communications between the kamnans in the tambons[2] and district officers and provides a means for rapid reporting of insurgent incidents as well as a channel for administrative messages.

Since 1965 USOM has provided commodities and advisory assistance to the Border Patrol Police (BPP) in the Remote Area Security (RAS) program. This is an expansion of the earlier efforts by the BPP to gain the friendship of the border inhabitants including the hill people of the North and thus to increase intelligence from these sources. Operation of schools as well as medical and agricultural assistance, already part of the BPP activities, were included in RAS and small BPP development teams for village work were added. Village development under the program has also been assisted by a group of Thai specialists under an American contracting company that surveys popular needs and makes recommendations for BPP developmental work. In 1966, under the RAS program, U.S. Seabee teams were brought in to train and work with the BPP in

2. A tambon is a cluster of villages, and the kamnan is its chief who is elected by the village chiefs.

small engineering projects. The Seabees turned out to be more doers than trainers, and because of the U.S. policy of not actively participating in counterinsurgency activities, the last elements of the group were phased out early in 1969.

The United States Information Service (USIS) in Thailand operates as the field element of the United States Information Agency (USIA). USIS is small compared to USOM and the U.S. military component in Thailand, but is large by USIA standards. In 1973 it numbered about 26 U.S. personnel. USIS carries out its usual information and cultural activities—such as libraries, films, pamphlets, and cultural performances, in order to inform the Thais about the United States. It administers the State Department's leadership grants for Thais who show promise of leadership talents to visit the United States to improve their understanding of America as well as to learn more about their particular fields of interest. USIS also became directly involved in the RTG's counterinsurgency effort, because the information and psychological approaches seemed weak. Therefore, additional USIS field offices were established—eleven at one time— which aided and encouraged provincial-level authorities in psychological operations. An advisor was also provided to CSOC on psychological operations. USIS supported the development and production of many of the counterinsurgency-oriented publications distributed in Thailand, and prepared radio programs and films on subjects pertinent to counterinsurgency. As mentioned in Chapter 4, it gave advice and assistance in technical operation and programming of the highly effective Radio Station 909 near the city of Sakon Nakhon in the Northeast from 1967, when 909 went into operation, until mid-1969 when the Thai National Security Command took over the station. USIS also provided the equipment (jeeps and projectors) for the Mobile Information Teams (MITs), most of the materials (films and publications), and usually the motivation to get them into the villages. When these teams began to visit remote villages in 1961, their early reports were among the first indication that an incipient insurgency might be developing in the Northeast and the North. USIS also worked at the Bangkok level to help the Thais develop coordinated and effective psychological operations. In 1969, the decision was made to phase out USIS counterinsurgency activities and revert to the more normal USIS role. This has gone on gradually. The number of posts in the field has been reduced from a high of eleven to only three in 1973. USIS participation in the counterinsurgency psychological effort has gradually lessened while arrangements for the Thais to take over those efforts has been getting into gear. By 1973 USIS had reverted almost entirely to its primary role of informing the Thais about the United States and now no longer participates directly in the counterinsurgency propaganda effort.

The Military Sector

The United States military structure in Thailand is quite complicated, largely because of the Indochina war. Since 1950 a military advisory group—called the Joint United States Military Advisory Group (JUSMAG)—has been concerned with military assistance and a training and advisory effort. It includes separate Army, Navy, and Air Force sections, which deal directly with the corresponding Thai services. In 1962 the Military Assistance Command-Thailand (MACTHAI) was established, under the Military Assistance Command-Vietnam (MACV), to provide operational combat assistance for Thailand should the need arise in the context of communist aggression in Vietnam and Laos. In 1956 the Command was separated from MACV, and the JUSMAG and MACTHAI were combined, though not merged. The Commander of MACTHAI is also the Chief of JUS-MAG. The resulting structure is still complicated; therefore, I shall use the term MACTHAI to include the JUSMAG and its original responsibilities. In any case, the combination gives one commander the responsibility for all military planning—unilateral and bilateral (i.e., with the Thais)—as well as military assistance and advisory and training functions. In addition, he has operational control of a U.S. Army Special Forces company, supervises many small attached units, and is concerned with base tenancy, status of forces, and the multitude of issues associated with the large American military presence in Thailand.

The Commander of MACTHAI is in a difficult position, since he reports both to the Ambassador and to the Commander-in-Chief, Pacific (CINCPAC), who is located in Hawaii. Which of these officials has the primary responsibility has not always been clear to him. He also must consider his position and future career in his own service.[3] President Nixon's letter to the Ambassador (cited earlier) was not very helpful in this regard, since one could argue from it that the COMUS-MACTHAI (Commander, U.S. Military Assistance Command, Thailand) is responsible to CINCPAC, but as Chief of JUSMAG is responsible primarily to the Ambassador for policy guidance. In practice, this has not been a major problem, given the desire on all sides to make the situation work. However, these multiple relationships are inherently difficult, and the United States would do well to try to improve and simplify its overseas command arrangements, particularly for situations of low-level involvement.

The J-3 (Operations) staff has been the focal point within MACTHAI for all matters relating to counterinsurgency. The staff is backed up in the counterinsurgency field by representatives from other MACTHAI elements that work together with J-3 representatives as a plans and analysis center concentrating on

3. The CINCPAC has always been a naval officer, while the last two Commanders of MACTHAI have been Air Force officers. However, Army personnel compose the majority of the MACTHAI staff.

counterinsurgency problems. J-4 (Logistics) deals with military aid equipment and is particularly concerned with assisting the Thais to develop integrated helicopter repair services and improved single-manager concepts for the Thai Army, Air Force, and Police. Representatives of J-5 (Plans) sit with Thai military officers on the bilateral committees and subcommittees such as Planning and Training.

MACTHAI provides advisors to Thai military offices and units both in Bangkok and in the field. Each of the three Thai field armies, First, Second, and Third, has a senior United States Army advisor, who commands subordinate advisors at division and regimental level. The advisors are responsible for evaluating the use of United States-supplied equipment, advising on and observing training exercises, and giving general advice on planning, tactics, and other military matters. They are strictly forbidden to participate in combat in Thailand. Americans are also advisors at schools, headquarters, specialized offices, and technical centers. The Navy and Air Force sections of MACTHAI have advisors with the appropriate Thai units, schools, and headquarters. Air Force advisors in the field are concerned with helicopter, tactical fighter, and other Thai Air Force units, not only with respect to combat planning and tactics, but also on airlift and reconnaissance. From the three services, about 100 military advisors have been in the field, the remainder in Bangkok. MACTHAI has a strength of 550 in early 1974.

The United States has supplied the Thai armed forces with rifles, crew-served weapons, artillery, jet airplanes, helicopters, naval vessels, and other military equipment. Most of the equipment is standard for regular armed services, but much of it can be used in both conventional and counter-guerrilla warfare. Emphasis has been placed on modernization of equipment and providing means for fast reaction. Although the equipment has a dual purpose and the amounts provided take this into consideration, the training and advisory effort has tried to balance emphasis on the tactics and techniques of conventional and counterinsurgency warfare. A principal justification for military aid in the past few years has been the counterinsurgency needs of the Thai armed forces; however, conventional war contingency planning of the Thai force structure has tended to restrict the Thai military counterinsurgency capabilities. Preparation of the annually revised Military Assistance Program and joint Thai-U.S. inspection of the performance of units receiving MAP supplies requires a substantial continuing effort from military advisors as well as from the MACTHAI staff.

Training of Thai armed forces in counterinsurgency by United States elements began in the early 1960s, at first by Mobile Training Teams (MTTs), and then, from April, 1967, by a company of U.S. Army Special Forces. The objective from the beginning was to train Thai officers and NCOs to serve as trainers of their own forces. Since Thai army recruits serve a maximum of two years, the training task goes on and on. In addition to giving a variety of courses to all elements of the armed forces, including especially Thai Special Forces, the U.S. Special Forces have also participated in counterinsurgency training for Provincial Police, Border Patrol Police, and other police elements. MTTs in the country for brief tours of duty from other U.S. military elements have given specialized instruction, for example, to helicopter pilots and mechanics. A U.S. Army Psychological Operations company, specially tailored for the task, advised, trained, and assisted Thai units engaged in psychological operations. As of early 1974, all these efforts have been phased out.

The United States military have also participated in on-the-job training, through which Thais have been instructed in techniques such as maintenance, radio operation and repair, electronics, etc. American personnel have conducted English-language courses at many military installations to enable Thais to read instruction manuals and directions accompanying equipment of U.S. origin and to assist them in getting the most out of opportunities for study in the United States. Much of this on-the-job training is a spin-off from the presence of U.S. Air Force units, but it has made an important contribution to upgrading scarce Thai technical know-how.

From 1961 to 1972 the Advanced Research Projects Agency (ARPA) of the Department of Defense had a field unit in Bangkok. It was initiated as part of Project AGILE, which was concerned with research on remote area conflict. The unit was established for a variety of reasons: to facilitate United States research in tropical environments and so make the research more realistic; to help develop the Thai counterinsurgency capabilities; and to encourage and strengthen development of a Thai military research and development effort. The ARPA field unit (called ARPA Research and Development Center—Thailand) was part of the joint U.S.-Thai Military Research and Development Center (MRDC). The Thai part of the Center, which was established at the same time as the ARPA field unit and is still in existence, is commanded by a Thai general officer, and reports to the Directorate of Research and Education under the Chief of Staff of the Thai Supreme Command. At times Australian and United Kingdom military specialists have assisted and advised MRDC. The Director of the ARPA field unit, like the Commander of MACTHAI, worked under overlapping lines of command. He reported to the Ambassador, coordinated with the Commander of MACTHAI and CINCPAC, and was ultimately under the control of ARPA officials in Washington. Initiation of projects required approval from both the U.S. Mission in Bangkok and the Thai Supreme Command.

Some joint work was done in the Center, but to a very large extent the work was done by Americans, some of whom were military and civilian personnel assigned to ARPA, but most of whom were U.S. contractor personnel who at one time numbered nearly 200. In the very late 1960s increasing emphasis was put on training Thais as researchers with the objective of phasing ARPA out. On-the-job training was conducted and selected Thais were sent for schooling in the United States. Increasingly the Thais have developed the capability to do their own research. Whether they undertake to do an adequate amount is another question.

Early ARPA studies were primarily related to ground mobility and radio communications under tropical conditions but also sought to improve individual combat rations, clothing, and equipment for the Thai soldier. Only a few early studies related to counterinsurgency. For example, one in 1965 on village security was a pioneer approach to that vital aspect of counterinsurgency. In 1966–1967, however, the whole ARPA effort in Thailand was reoriented toward research primarily relevant to counterinsurgency, and the ARPA field unit was informally recognized as the research arm of the United States Mission regarding internal security problems. Though much of its work was controversial, under the Rural Security Systems Program, ARPA studied border control, village security, insurgent psychological operations, ethnic groups of North Thailand, and a host of other counterinsurgency-related subjects. Working with its Thai counterpart, it compiled much-needed data, and tested various equipment for the Thai armed forces. An Electronics Laboratory started in 1963 is now operated by a Thai staff; an Aerial Reconnaissance Laboratory with a specially-equipped plane which participates in counterinsurgency operations is now also run by the Thais.

Because of the increased Thai capability and in keeping with the spirit of the Nixon Doctrine, the ARPA field unit was rapidly phased down in 1971 and was closed down completely in December, 1972.

The other major United States military elements in Thailand have had only a marginal role in support of the counterinsurgency effort. The 7/13th Air Force, with headquarters at the air base in Udorn, was a hybrid which reported to 13th Air Force at Clark Air Force Base in the Philippines for logistic support and administration, and to 7th Air Force in Saigon for tactical direction. In 1973, with the formation of the U.S. Support and Advisory Group (USSAG) at Nakhon Phanom, the 7/13th Air Force ceased to exist. It had conducted air operations outside Thailand as there are no U.S. air operations within Thailand. The 7/13th had civic action teams in the field in the Northeast, which played some counterinsurgency role, but these were phased out in 1969. U.S. Army Support Thailand (SUPTHAI) is not considered a separate component of the Mission, but at present has about 4,000 men. It is subordinate to MACTHAI and to Army Pacific Command in Hawaii and is essentially an Army logistic command which controls the United States engineer units in Thailand and supervises the contractors who have built the Thai airfields and associated facilities as well as strategic roads and the port of Sattahip. It is phasing down as the construction is completed and very little new building is planned. SUPTHAI has undertaken some civic action but this has been reduced in keeping with the United States policy of no direct United States operations in Thailand. The bases and facilities of the USSAG and SUPTHAI could be targets for guerrilla attacks and so they are important in base defense planning which, on the American side, is considered to fall within the counterinsurgency context. Outside of civic action and base defense these military organizations are not concerned with counterinsurgency and play no role in the United States support of the Thai counterinsurgency effort.

As a result of the peace agreement in Vietnam, the United States has moved all its military forces out of that country. In order to keep a presence and a headquarters in the region, the United States asked and the Thais agreed that a small headquarters, the U.S. Support and Advisory Group (USSAG), be established at Nakhon Phanom air base in Northeast Thailand, which replaced the 7/13th Air Force organization. This headquarters, perhaps temporary, takes the place of MACV in Saigon and directs all U.S. air operations which might in the future be undertaken in Indochina.

Things might have continued as described for some time, save for a very unfortunate incident in January, 1974, which has tended to poison U.S.-Thai relations and has cast considerable doubt on the future of U.S. organizations in Thailand.

It is perhaps inevitable, given the sensitivities involved, that the end of the long period of Thai-American intimacy would be precipitated by an incident involving our cooperation in the insurgency area. In a period in which the leadership of the American Embassy was changing, and as fundamental changes were occurring in the Thai government itself, a CIA agent operating out of Nakhon Phanom sent a spurious letter to several Thai newspapers and to the Prime Minister, purporting to be from a CT, and offering a cease-fire in exchange for a recognition of "liberated areas." Unbelievably, the agent allowed the inexcusable letter to be posted by an office boy, who registered the letter, allowing its true source to be traced. The purpose of the letter was at least twofold. Perhaps such a letter would sow confusion among the CTs. It would also advertise, in effect, the fact that "liberated areas" existed, and spur the RTG into more effective counterinsurgency actions. Of course, it did the precise opposite.

The uproar that has resulted, while entirely understandable, hardly has aided the understanding of what is needed to solve the insurgency problem. The conclusion being inferred by some educated Thais is that the CIA is itself the cause of the insurgency and is sustaining the rebellion in order that Thailand will continue to need American help to combat it—giving us a trade-off for continued use of the Thai air bases. Other Thais just see the incident as American meddling in Thai internal affairs—a procedure which should never have occurred.

The whole incident provides eloquent testimony to the importance of effective coordination in such situations, and even more pertinent, to the importance of working *with* governments, not over their heads or behind their backs. It is a principal thesis of this book that no government can settle an insurgency for another country, and that if the Thais are able to resolve their problems, it will be almost entirely because of their own efforts. To that end, and to keep our team from involving itself in any untoward way with the insurgency, while I was in Thailand I had written the very explicit counterinsurgency guidelines, which are described in detail in Chapter 7, about what U.S. counterinsurgency assistance was appropriate in Thailand, including certain individual actions. The 1974 incident violated both the letter and spirit of those guidelines, and places in grave jeopardy even the efforts of those Thais convinced of the seriousness of the insurgency. It is inappropriate and wrong in any event that the U.S. should appear to be more concerned with a Thai problem than the Thais are themselves; we can try through our many associations and long history of close ties with them to help them see how grave the threat is, and can help them work out appropriate Thai solutions to them. But for us to resort to the kind of meddling witnessed in this incident in order to trick them into believing that the problem is more serious than they believe it to be is the nadir of what has been at times a very fruitful association.

In order to avoid such incidents Ambassador Martin had years before seen the need for a closely coordinated, centrally directed, U.S. effort to help the Thais in their struggle against the CTs. He did establish a special office in the Embassy to undertake this difficult mission, and the next chapter discusses this effort.

Chapter 7

Special Assistant for Counterinsurgency

The problem of coordination within any but very small organizations is always one of the most difficult to solve. Once solved, the problem of permitting innovation within the existing bureaucratic structures must be tackled, particularly in fast-moving situations like an insurgency. These two problems became increasingly important for the American Embassy as U.S. involvement in Southeast Asia grew in the 1960s. As early as 1964 Ambassador Graham Martin created within the Embassy the post of Counselor for Operations which included, among other duties, the job of trying to coordinate United States aid to Thailand. During 1965–1966 the number of Thai counterinsurgency programs assisted by the United States proliferated, as did the number of Royal Thai Government (RTG) agencies involved. In turn, counterpart relations among those agencies and Mission members grew more complex, and the number of U.S. Mission personnel also increased. Furthermore, the Ambassador was more and more obliged to devote a large part of his time to matters involving the influx of American military based in Thailand for operations related to the Indochina war. Informal methods of procedure appropriate to a small Mission in a quiet country were at that point obviously inadequate for the situation in Thailand.

Ambassador Martin's appreciation of the necessity for improved coordination of the American counterinsurgency assistance effort was reinforced further by lessons he had learned from the United States experience in Vietnam. He was convinced that the U.S. effort there had been greatly overmilitarized at the expense of political, economic, and psychological factors, and so, in consequence, had been the approach to counterinsurgency taken by the Vietnamese Government. Overmilitarization was another way of saying that there had been inadequate civilian management at the top so that the military had been allowed (or forced by "necessity," as they saw it) to go their own way. Martin also noted, correctly, that, in any case, the efforts of the United States to aid the Government of Vietnam had not only been poorly coordinated but also on many occasions had been in actual conflict with each other. Interagency squabbles were well known, and President Diem and his successors had sometimes used these conflicts to their own advantage. In these matters also Martin was determined to avoid such mistakes.

By the summer of 1966, Martin, in furtherance of his single-manager method of procedure, was ready to appoint one man as Special Assistant for Counterinsurgency (SA/CI), to act for him in all counterinsurgency matters. The man he chose was Peer de Silva, who had been Special Assistant to the U.S. Ambassador in Vietnam and who shared wholeheartedly Martin's judgments about the American experience there. The staff provided for De Silva ultimately numbered ten men, brought in from the civilian and military advisory and assistance agencies and from other concerned elements within the Mission.

Martin's letter to the heads of the Mission components announcing the new post and De Silva's appointment spelled out the terms of reference as follows:

In Thailand, our common concern and joint effort in supporting and assisting our Thai colleagues in dealing with their insurgency problem has assumed such proportions and complexities that I have sought specific assistance in helping me carry out this aspect of the Presidentially assigned responsibility in the manner I think necessary. It is for this purpose that Mr. de Silva has joined my staff and that the post of SA/CI has been created. I shall expect him to discharge this overall coordinating and regulating task covering all U. S. activities, military and civil, which are directly related to the problem of insurgency in Thailand . . . . Mr. de Silva will be acting for me and in my name in dealing with you on matters of the CI field, and it is to him that you should in the first instance address yourselves on matters requiring coordination on the American side, or concerning the relevance of new concepts or proposals . . . . He . . . will, in my behalf, make decisions as may be necessary in the face of conflicting priorities or in conflicting claims on resources

. . . . Such decisions as he does make, however, or such requirements as he may levy on you, you may assume to have originated with me.

Martin added, however, that De Silva would consult with him "on matters involving U.S. Diplomatic Mission policy." He pointed out that "you each of course have a standing right of direct access to me on any matter which you think should be brought to my attention." "I would anticipate," he added, "that, in the CI field, this would occur infrequently."

In an introductory paragraph, Martin stated, "All of you know that I am the personal representative of the President. Also, you are all aware that the President has specifically charged me with the responsibility and duty of the direction and control of all U.S. elements in Thailand as Chief of the United States Diplomatic Mission." This set forth clearly Martin's belief that as Ambassador he was empowered to be the single manager of the Mission, but a part of that authority he was now delegating to De Silva. However, exactly what amount of this authority he was delegating, or indeed possessed to delegate, was a matter of subsequent testing. "Coordinating" was perhaps clear enough but exactly what "regulating" implied was less certain. There was also the question as to what U.S. activities should be considered to be directly related to the problem of insurgency in Thailand. These were matters which had to be worked out piece by piece as time went on.

There was also the question of staffing. Being composed of people from various agencies but none from the Foreign Service made SA/CI something of a stepchild within the Embassy. Furthermore, there were overlapping responsibilities among some of the Embassy sections. The Mission Coordinator was to have responsibility for coordinating civilian and military aid, while the Economic Section of the Embassy had responsibility for some of the economic aid, and the POMIL (Politico-Military) Section coordinated military aid. The SA/CI mission was to coordinate all aspects of aid related to counterinsurgency, but exactly what this included had never been spelled out very precisely. The size of the Embassy had grown steadily in response to the increasing United States activities in Thailand, and no one had recently surveyed the Embassy staff to see how it functioned and whether it was organized in the best possible manner.

DE SILVA DEFINES HIS TASK

Peer de Silva took office in November, 1966. He promptly set about clarifying for the Mission members what he conceived the new position to entail and the basic problems regarding counterinsurgency that he believed must be tackled first. His task, he stated, included: (1) evaluation of the applicability of counterinsurgency programs to the Thai counterinsurgency effort; (2) coordination of all United States-supported counterinsurgency programs and elimination of contradictions among them; (3) special attention to programs with impact at the village level; (4) regulation of liaison between U.S. Mission elements and their Thai counterparts; (5) establishment of a counterinsurgency information center at the Embassy; and (6) responsibility for reports on the progress of United States-assisted and other Thai counterinsurgency programs to the Ambassador and on his behalf to the relevant agencies in Washington.

De Silva specified the most important basic problems to be tackled to buttress the counterinsurgency effort as (1) prevention of insurgency reinforcement from sources outside Thailand; (2) creation and maintenance of Thai armed security elements, including a quick reaction capability and an aggressive intelligence system; and (3) the identification, harassment, and neutralization of the insurgents' clandestine organization. Even more important, and an aspect of counterinsurgency least well understood by Americans and Thais alike, was, he felt, the necessity for a continuing and constantly developing effort by the RTG at the village, and even the household, level to make the rural population and the lower governmental echelons mutually and willingly responsive to each other through political approaches and civic action. These were the broad lines (with special emphasis on the last mentioned) along which De Silva worked during his fifteen months as SA/CI.

The Tuesday Group

De Silva began at once to establish mechanisms for increased control over the counterinsurgency-support aspects of the Mission's work. With Martin's approval, he instituted the so-called "Tuesday Group" meetings—weekly sessions attended by agency heads and their key staff personnel and Embassy officials concerned with counterinsurgency matters. (These were the first intra-agency meetings held during Martin's ambassadorship.) Since De Silva had announced at the outset that decisions he made in the meetings would be binding whether top officials were present or not, the principal officers usually attended regularly. A report on current insurgency activities was a regular feature, but otherwise no agendas were prepared; De Silva presided and for the most part determined the matters to be presented. This procedure enabled him to pass on and acquire information expeditiously and to state and explain policies to those most concerned. It also was intended to ensure that key Mission personnel kept in close touch with what was going on in their departments, since any member might be called on for a report on any aspect of the programs and problems within his jurisdiction. The subjects taken up in the meetings ran the gamut of counterinsurgency concerns, some of them recurrent week after week: Thai military operations, psychological operations, air base defense, village security forces, ARD, the police programs, and the insurgency situations in the various regions of Thailand.

Detailed minutes of the Tuesday Group meetings were kept and distributed not only among the Group members but also to relevant agencies in Washington. The minutes served both as an informal means of reporting and of airing problems, disagreements, and policy definition. In short, they provided De Silva with one of his few means for leverage on Mission personnel.

Committees were frequently appointed by De Silva from the Tuesday Group, usually ad hoc and to collect and consolidate information rather than to formulate policies. In some cases, however, as in the matter of air base defense with which the Mission was especially concerned since insurgent attacks could possibly be launched from the perimeter around the bases, the committees prepared detailed proposals to be submitted to De Silva and then to the Thais. Committees also might be called on for progress reports during the Group meetings.

THE COUNTERINSURGENCY SUPPORT MANAGEMENT CENTER

From the time De Silva took office as SA/CI he worked for the formation of a Counterinsurgency Support Management Center (CSMC) within the Embassy. He also hoped that the Thais would eventually inaugurate a similar facility. He saw the Center as a recipient of data on all counterinsurgency-oriented programs, such as locations, staff, funding and expenditures, and accomplishments, for compilation and easy retrieval through automatic data processing. It would be a management tool that would reveal overlaps, gaps, successes, and failures, and the need for further development in elements of the total counterinsurgency effort. It would also keep the Mission abreast of what was going on and how well objectives were being reached in all insurgent-threatened regions.

For lack of funds, the Center got under way slowly, but by the time of De Silva's departure it had progressed to the completion of a well-equipped briefing and information display facility in the Embassy building. Whether the plans for collection of detailed information on all phases of counterinsurgency programs would materialize was, however, problematical, considering the evident reluctance of the Mission elements to provide the necessary money and manpower to collect and analyze the inputs. This was in fact never done, and the room that was to have housed the Center was used for displays of special information and statistics and for briefings and meetings. The semifailure of the idea was partly due to lack of personnel but also due to the inability to obtain the proper data. In turn, this was partially due to the inadequate data-gathering capabilities of the

Thais, but even more basically to the uncertainty and disagreement about what data were required.

By 1967 a large percentage of funds from both the Agency for International Development (AID) and the Military Assistance Program (MAP) was allotted to programs having more or less direct bearing on counterinsurgency. Given the small SA/CI staff and De Silva's own conscientious determination to keep his fingers on all that was happening in the counterinsurgency field, the SA/CI office earned the reputation for being something of a bottleneck. Nevertheless, under De Silva coordination on a day-to-day basis decidedly improved, and incidents of uncoordinated agency actions were kept to a minimum.

Conflicts of course did arise. The SA/CI office had no Embassy-provided funds of its own to administer. Control over budgets and personnel involved in United States-assisted counterinsurgency programs remained with the Mission agencies, particularly the Military Assistance Command, Thailand (MACTHAI) and the United States Operations Mission (USOM). Over these matters even the Ambassador could do no more than exert his personal influence, usually through review of annual AID and Military Assistance Program (MAP) submissions to Washington; De Silva as his representative had even more limited powers. On a few occasions when De Silva tried to require the adherence of Mission agencies to his counterinsurgency policies and doctrines, he was largely unable to impose his will. Insofar as these policies affected agency programs and the use of agency manpower and resources, the agency heads were adamant in maintaining their ultimate personal responsibility to make decisions.[1] For such cases there were no solutions except to attempt to work out the answers to counterinsurgency problems together with as much amicability as could be mustered.

The task of serving as center for liaison with the Thais on counterinsurgency matters was both onerous and sensitive. All contacts by U.S. personnel in Bangkok with the RTG on counterinsurgency matters, including official visits upcountry, were expected to be made or cleared by SA/CI. All papers dealing with counterinsurgency crossed his desk, and his was the final decision as to whether the subject lay within his domain. The purposes of these controls were, of course, to avoid burdening Thai officials with unnecessary visitors and to obviate the danger that preliminary discussions or correspondence with the Thais might be mistaken for official American promises or endorsements. De Silva became the liaison with General Saiyud, Director of Operations at the RTG's Communist Suppression Operations Command (CSOC), and an officer from the United States Information Service (USIS) was assigned to the staff of SA/CI and made liaison with CSOC on psychological operations. These arrangements, in

---

1. It is true that agency heads did have legal responsibilities to their agencies which conflicted with Martin's view of the Ambassador's role. These conflicts and contradictions still exist.

accord with Martin's determination to prevent in Thailand the over-militarization that had occurred in Vietnam, excluded MACTHAI from direct liaison with CSOC headquarters, and not until January, 1967, was an American military officer permitted the post of liaison with CPM-1 (later Second Army Forward).

The requirement to channel all contacts with the Thais on insurgency matters through SA/CI caused some resentment in MACTHAI. For while the principle of civilian control of the military is both implicit and explicit in U.S. constitutional law and has been followed throughout our history, this idea is meaningless in present-day Thailand. The military, particularly the Royal Thai Army, domi-nates the present RTG as we have seen. Furthermore, the military men of Thailand and the United States have certain things in common and often can communicate with each other better than with civilians. Some American military men in Thailand, therefore, found it particularly galling to have American civilians trying to tell them when and about what they could talk with their Thai military friends. In fact, of course, the American military had broad contacts with the Thais, discussed military matters with them, and were unable to totally separate counterinsurgency matters from the more conventional military ones.

However, De Silva made the most of his CSOC liaison assignment to bring home to the Thais his convictions that successful counterinsurgency involved not only suppression operations but also, and more importantly, civil actions and psychological operations that would win the villagers to the government's side and make them willing to defend themselves against the insurgents. Active participation in the CSOC CPMs by the civil authorities and police was, he believed, the essential element in CSOC operations. General Saiyud proved sympathetic to De Silva's views, and the two met weekly until the take-over in October, 1967, of CSOC operations in the Northeast by the Thai Second Army. De Silva also held frequent meetings with Dr. Chamnan, Director General of the Department of Local Administration and head of the CSOC Civil Affairs staff, who at that time was even more important as the unofficial right-hand man of Field Marshal Praphas, then Commander of CSOC and Commander-in-Chief of the Royal Thai Army. These continued until April, 1967, when Dr. Chamnan turned his Civil Affairs staff over to a less directly concerned civil official and concentrated on other duties. However, De Silva continued to see these men frequently and other Thai officials until he left Thailand in February, 1968.

An early victory for De Silva's viewpoints occurred late in 1966 when the Thai so-called "Dry Season Plan" for countering the insurgency in the Northeast was converted from a plan for military sweeps into the 09/10 Plan mentioned in Chapter 4, which provided for local forces to remain in the villages around target areas to give continuing security.

In pursuit of his goal of improving intelligence on the insurgency De Silva took every opportunity to press for emphasis on securing information about the nature and extent of the infrastructure that the insurgents were presumably seeking to establish in the villages. He himself believed that village supporters of the insurgents were primarily kinsfolk and friends of the jungle-band members, but, knowing from Vietnam how essential to Viet Cong success was the establishment of local organizations along communist lines (political, youth, women's, and farmers' groups), he was anxious that such organizational developments in Thailand be nipped in the bud. Numbers of overt incidents, which Thai and American intelligence collectors were concentrating on compiling, represented, he maintained, only surface manifestations and were no true indication of the strength of the insurgent movement.

The principal aim of counterinsurgency should be, De Silva reiterated to the Thais and to the Mission members, denial to the insurgents of village supporters without whom the jungle soldiers could not continue to operate. The prime essentials to achieve this goal were some visibly effective degree of physical security for the villagers and prompt and effective response by local authorities to rural needs in health, education, agricultural assistance, etc. Again drawing on his experience in Vietnam, De Silva believed that the People's Assistance Team (PAT) concept offered the best means for village-level efforts. Such a team, recruited from the village in which it was to serve and given high motivation through specialized training, would provide armed protection, assist the villagers to better their living conditions, and buttress their allegiance to the RTG.

Under De Silva's impetus the Mission in the spring of 1967 began to expend a major effort on assisting the Thais to consolidate the existing varieties of village defense forces into one Village Security Force (VSF) that might number several thousand members and to provide them with motivational training such as the PATs received. This effort continued to absorb much of the time and energy of many Mission staff members in Bangkok, as well as De Silva throughout 1967. The VSF concept included the expectation that the teams would have support in civic projects from district and provincial officials and quick-response security assistance, from police or army, when needed. The idea was in a sense a natural outgrowth of the pilot programs for village defense which had been started in 1966 with the object of discovering which technique was the most effective. Thai and American committees, at two levels, were established. They met frequently, sometimes separately and sometimes together, to hammer out such details as location of the training sites, areas for initial recruitment and deployment, the question of whether the teams should be paid full-time or part-time salaries, and how the expenses were to be divided between the United States and Thai governments. However, in their zeal for the program some members of the Mission had failed to perceive the realities of the delicate balance of political power in Thailand. Beneath the surface of agreement lay the strong opposition of the Police Department to the formation of a new paramilitary force not under their control. Other departments also had reservations because some aspects of this broad village program seemed to impinge on their domains. These differences surfaced after De Silva's departure and led the Mission to withdraw U.S. support for the program until the Thais worked out their conflicts. They never really agreed on this program but slowly worked out another village development and security scheme which included the police and other agencies under the general direction of the Department of Local Administration. This program has a training center in Prachuap Khiri Khan province and has become operational in several provinces.

Early in 1967 De Silva had stated his belief that this would be "the year of decision" during which either the RTG would start winning the counterinsurgency struggle or the insurgents would succeed in getting the village supporters organized. As events turned out, apparently nothing so decisive developed. The RTG increased its emphasis on civil aspects of counterinsurgency and seemed to be increasing its strength in the Northeast as the Second Army assumed responsibility for and control of operations there; meanwhile, there was no specific evidence that the insurgents were having widespread success in improving their organization and basic strength in that region, though they were trying hard. Late in the year, the unforeseen outbreak of overt armed attacks in the North demonstrated clearly that the insurgency was by no means on the decline but indeed was spreading, and that the counterinsurgency effort must continue with even greater impetus.

Leonard Unger replaced Martin as Ambassador in November, 1967, and the new leadership brought changes. For example, Unger was less insistent than Martin on the single-manager concept and tended to rely on meetings and the Mission Council—a biweekly meeting of top officials chaired by the Ambassador. De Silva elected to leave in February, 1968, for a long-postponed operation for eye injuries received when the American Embassy in Saigon was bombed.

In retrospect, De Silva felt that his successor should be buttressed by a higher rank within the Mission, but that the job of SA/CI should be, as he had accepted it, temporary even though the need for such a post in Thailand might continue for several years. Although he would certainly have liked a larger staff, De Silva himself apparently did not complain, considering the manifold duties which the SA/CI office was required to perform. In the judgment of the then Commander of MACTHAI, De Silva had tackled the most difficult job in the Mission with fewer staff and resources than were allotted to any other Mission element. Furthermore, he had undertaken a job for which there were no precedents and had worked with American officials to whom precedents and established procedures were extremely important and all of whom had their own programs, jurisdictions, and points of view to protect. It was De Silva's proudest estimate of the achievement of United States aid to Thailand in coping with the insurgency during his incumbency that, harking back to Vietnam as contrast, this had been managed without crushing the political and social structure of the host country.

After De Silva's departure, there was no SA/CI for nearly two months. This was an extremely difficult period for the SA/CI staff, because De Silva had provided strong leadership, and after he had gone little leadership was available. The SA/CI staff members were naturally uneasy in this situation but tried to function as they believed they were authorized to do.

THE NEW SA/CI

These were the conditions which I found when I arrived in April, 1968, to succeed De Silva as SA/CI. Thanks to his recommendation I had been given the personal rank of Minister by President Johnson, but I soon found, to no great surprise, that rank and title did not solve conflicting views about responsibilities. On my first night in Thailand I was greeted with a proposal that the SA/CI office be divided into two parts: the SA/CI himself, supported by his secretary, would be concerned mainly with policy and the "big picture"; the SA/CI staff would be under the Mission Coordinator, a Foreign Service officer already working in the Bangkok Embassy, who had the rank of Counselor, and would do the actual coordination and program review heretofore carried out by the SA/CI and his staff. The struggle to prevent this proposed division, along with restoration of staff morale and my own preservation of the role and responsibilities that I had been offered when I took the position, took up most of my time and effort during my first six to eight weeks in Thailand, but the problems were eventually settled reasonably well. I was then able to get down to the real job of organizing and coordinating the American attempts to help the Thais in their counterinsurgency effort.

Part of the resolution of the differences about the nature of my job involved taking the Mission Coordinator, William N. Stokes (who had kept the position in its non-counterinsurgency aspect), as my deputy. A clear delineation between the Office of Mission Coordination and SA/CI was never made, but we arrived at a workable arrangement during the two years I held the job; at times, however, the circumstances were very trying. At least the State Department was beginning to contribute to the SA/CI office, and later another junior Foreign Service Officer was added to my staff. (I was, of course, from the State Department, but not a true-blue, classical Foreign Service Officer.) The State Department should obviously have contributed the core staff of the SA/CI office, since it was one of the main tools of the Ambassador in his role as chief of the U.S. Mission in Thailand. Since my departure the State Department has dominated the office but largely because the other agencies have withdrawn their personnel, and the office is now composed of only a few Foreign Service officers.

Because of the variety of jobs and the turnover of personnel, I did not create well-defined positions in the office but tried to adapt the jobs to the personnel who were provided me vis-à-vis the tasks at hand. For example, some officers were fine staff men but not good coordinators in dealing with other agencies. Those who dealt with people well and were good leaders I made chairmen of the ad hoc and permanent committees. The good staff officers wrote cables and reports and did other paper work; such general duties were important and had to be done properly. The flexible organization meant that each officer had several responsibilities, but these were not necessarily passed on to the next representative from his agency. At one time the officer from International Security Affairs in the Office of the Secretary of Defense (OSD/ISA) acted as my office manager. The next year it was the representative from the Advanced Research Projects Agency in the Office of the Secretary of Defense (OSD/ARPA). One officer, for example, had responsibility for keeping up with the insurgency in the South, was chairman of the air base defense committee, and was liaison with MACTHAI, while another officer, who was liaison with the Southeast Asia Treaty Organization (SEATO) on insurgency matters, kept up with and wrote special memos and studies on the insurgency in the North. Sometimes the agency representative was liaison with his parent unit, sometimes not. I varied it as I saw fit, but always tried to maintain a structural approach to the overall counterinsurgency problem on a combined functional, program, and regional basis. The job descriptions were thus written for the individual and not vice versa. They were all reviewed and often revised when new officers replaced old ones. I think the system worked quite well, but it was sometimes confusing to traditional bureaucrats, as well as being demanding on the individuals concerned, who often faced a conflict between their immediate assignments and the expectations of their parent agencies.

As has been mentioned, De Silva had initiated the Tuesday Group (or the United States Mission's Coordinating Counterinsurgency Group) which became his primary tool for overall coordination. The various agency heads were the principals, and each brought key staff members. Thus about twenty-five to thirty persons usually attended. The weekly meetings were not viewed by De Silva as instruments for decision-making but rather as opportunities for enunciating and elaborating on his own decisions, although additional matters could be brought up by himself or by agency heads.

I continued this procedure but modified it as I went along. The forum was extremely useful as a means for learning about the insurgency and counterinsurgency and for getting acquainted with the agency heads. It was also useful as a gathering at which I as chairman could perform a visible role as coordinator and establisher of policy. However, for my own personal style, such a large meeting was not the best vehicle for carrying out my goals. The size of the group and the presence of staff members, while generally educative for those attending, made it difficult to get the principals to discuss controversial issues frankly and openly and, more importantly, to compromise and agree on solutions. My style, to a large extent dictated by the situation in Bangkok, involved trying to get consensus (though admittedly along the lines I wanted) rather than to issue decrees, and for this I needed a different type of forum.

Executive Sessions of the Tuesday Group

Some months after my arrival I began to hold what I called "executive sessions" of the Tuesday Group, in my office and attended by the agency heads only. The sessions were conducted in an informal, relaxed manner over coffee and usually with no written agenda. The group was thus able to discuss a wide variety of issues privately and directly without fear of reports circulating that one or another had given in or failed to get his way. I was extremely fortunate at that time in having an able and cooperative group of agency heads, and although each was a strong personality, and of course oriented to his own agency, they were all able during these meetings to think largely as officials of the United States Government even though they brought their own backgrounds to bear on the problems.

The smallness and congeniality of the group led me to explore ways of building on that base. I decided to take the group overnight to the MACTHAI recreation facility at Pattaya, a beach resort on the eastern shore of the Gulf of Siam. This location allowed us privacy for discussion and also opportunities for sports and relaxation. The first experiment was successful and was repeated at irregular intervals until I left Bangkok in May, 1970. The expeditions were sometimes laughingly referred to as "Tanham's pajama parties." The schedule was to leave Bangkok by helicopter late in the afternoon, have an hour or so of recreation followed by drinks and dinner, and then some serious, or sometimes not so serious, conversation. We spent the night at Pattaya and returned to our offices in Bangkok after breakfast. All told we missed four or five hours in the office, but I think we all agreed it was worth it, since we were all getting better acquainted in a relaxed way and this resulted in a free and frank flow of information and the development of a team spirit.

Encouraged by the "pajama party," I inaugurated two-and-three-day trips for the group to various regions of Thailand. Since these were unfortunately more difficult to arrange for busy men, they were not undertaken very frequently and usually some of the group were not free to go. The trips had several purposes in addition to strengthening the cohesion of the Tuesday Group. One was to demonstrate to the American officials serving in the field that the Mission in Bangkok had a coordinating mechanism and a coordinated outlook that was striving to solve the numerous and complex problems involved in aiding the Thai counterinsurgency effort. This was especially important, since (as is described later) I had inaugurated regional coordinating organizations and I wanted to show them that there was solidarity at the top. Also, as I had learned in Vietnam, it was useful for senior officials to see the countryside and listen to briefings by officials in the field together. This not only tended to result in closer agreement but avoided the tendency of officials who had made trips individually to come back with markedly differing impressions. Another result that I hoped might come from the group trips was that the Thais, whose strongpoint is certainly not formal coordination, would see that the Americans were also grappling with that problem and were apparently making some headway.

I continued De Silva's procedure of establishing interagency ad hoc groups as well as more or less permanent interagency standing committees. One of the first of the ad hoc groups in June, 1968, was under the chairmanship of Lamar Prosser of my staff, whose task was to gather as much information as possible about the situation in the North and to make recommendations for action to counter the increasing insurgent threat in that region. The group produced a fine paper with some good recommendations which became the basis for numerous discussions with the Thais. The group also stimulated ARPA's production of a handbook on the Meo, the hilltribesmen in the North who were providing most insurgent recruits and about whom little was known in the Thai government, or for that matter, elsewhere.

As time went on, I found myself increasingly concerned about the efficacy of the U.S. training programs for the Thais. I asked Colonel (now Major General) John Cleland of my staff to make a systematic review of the counterinsurgency training programs of all U.S. agencies—MACTHAI, USOM, USIS, and ARPA. The results seemed to indicate that many trainees were not being used properly or as productively as we had hoped, and indeed the training programs themselves did not have a high priority in the American or Thai scheme of things. We summarized the findings of this review and sent it to Washington. There was no policy-level response of any sort to this rather depressing information, thus revealing Washington's lack of effective concern for the real core of counterinsurgency effort—developing human resources. This attitude of course had existed in the case of Vietnam and is one of the tragedies of our whole counterinsurgency effort. The study had some interesting by-products and showed that the problem was broader than just training. For example, of approximately one hundred Thais sent to the U.S. for advanced agricultural training, the Thais assigned only about ten to the provinces where this training could be best used. The rest were ensconced in Bangkok. This sad example demonstrated that without proper personnel management practices the much-needed but limited skilled personnel among the Thais were not most effectively utilized.

Standing Committees

In addition to the ad hoc groups, there were standing committees on air operations, base defense, and psychological operations (psyops). The air operations committee, chaired at first by John Eisenhour and later by Jerry Milsted, both of my staff, tried to assure that U.S. policies would be uniform, particularly between MACTHAI and USOM, on helicopters and aircraft given to the Thais. The base defense group, originally set up by De Silva with Lamar Prosser as chairman (later chaired by Colonel John Cleland), continued its excellent work on developing policies and procedures for the defense of U.S.-occupied bases and for working with the Thais to explore a coordinated effort. There was also a Mission Psyops Committee (MPC) chaired by G. Lewis Schmidt, Director of USIS. This area of counterinsurgency, which affected almost every U.S. agency, was important because it was new for the Thais and had also been somewhat neglected by the U.S. Government. The committee decided how aid from the civilian as well as military agencies would be used, how liaison would be conducted with the Thais; it also established general policies regarding our overall psyops support efforts for the Thais. In almost all cases these committees were able to resolve their differences and make the appropriate decisions. In the few cases when this was not so, I made the decisions and assured that they would be carried out. An important function of the committees was to bring directly concerned staff officers of various agencies face-to-face so that they could exchange information and proposals within their peer group, as well as establish relationships leading to private collaboration. In other words, the committees were another mechanism for trying to get the Americans to work together as a team.

PROBLEMS—PROGRESS—PROBLEMS

Neither the Tuesday Group nor the various coordinating committees resolved all problems. Agencies remained somewhat jealous of their prerogatives and indeed were sometimes compelled to operate independently because of legislative decrees as well as agency regulations laid down by Washington. These differences also meant that coordination among American officials was a problem by no means confined to Bangkok. Before my arrival, the Embassy had held one or two meetings in the regions in an attempt to get the regional officials from all the U.S. agencies together. I decided to build on the Embassy experiment. Ambassador Unger was enthusiastic about regional coordination and, after we had done the staff work, he appointed as regional coordinators the Consuls in the Northeast and the North and later the Consul in the South when that consulate was established in 1969.

This move seemed sound on paper, but some serious problems were involved. In the first place, the Consuls were middle-grade Foreign Service Officers and sometimes junior in rank to many of the officials of other agencies, particularly of USOM and MACTHAI. Although the coordinating mission was not a command line, it put junior people in the position of chairing meetings and acting as coordinators of their seniors. Another more difficult problem arose over command lines within the agencies. The military had a senior representative in each region, but USOM and USIS were organized along provincial lines with direct lines to Bangkok and had no officer with regional responsibilities. These latter agencies complained that all senior provincial representatives were equal, were primarily acquainted with their province and not with the region, and did not have the authority or the facilities to coordinate with the other provincial advisors. Finally, however, the agencies were prevailed on to provide a representative for the meetings that the Consuls held at irregular intervals and served as chairmen. These meetings were intended to fill at a lower echelon the same role as the Bangkok Tuesday Group. Their success in large measure depended on the ability and personality of the Consul and the willingness of the agency representatives in the field to cooperate. In practice, although most of the field officials wanted to participate, they were torn between this desire and the opposition, often explicit, of some of their agency heads to the procedure.

In an effort to bolster the Consuls, strengthen this coordinating mechanism, and get acquainted with the officials in the countryside, I initiated quarterly regional meetings, one a month in rotation in the three regions. All U.S. officials in the region were invited, not just those attending the Consul's meetings. I attended with three or four people from Bangkok, but the Consuls continued as chairmen. Additional purposes were to let the officials know each other and the various agency programs better and to provide me with a succinct briefing on (1) the status of the insurgency as seen from the field, (2) the Thai efforts countering it, and (3) the effectiveness of the American assistance effort. Most of this was presented formally, but in an informal seminar at the end of the meeting one subject, say village security and development, could be thoroughly thrashed out. I encouraged the regional representatives to bring any complaints or grievances to my attention and to make suggestions about how we in Bangkok could help. In turn I explained to them the United States counterinsurgency policies as presented in Embassy guidelines and the reasons for them. I also exposed the regional people to some of the difficulties we in Bangkok encountered, mainly to give them a feeling that they were not alone in facing problems.

As the regional meetings slowly developed into useful forums, I decided on the somewhat novel move of inviting U.S. Ambassador William Sullivan in Vientiane, Laos, and his successor, Ambassador G. McMurtrie Godley, to send representatives to them. This seemed desirable because some aid was coming to the Thai insurgents from the western part of Laos that adjoins the North and Northeastern regions of Thailand, and the situation in the border areas was thus of considerable interest to us. The response from the Embassy in Vientiane was enthusiastic. Four or five representatives from the various agencies in Laos usually attended, gave a short summation of current conditions on their side of the border, and shared with their colleagues in Thailand their own experience in counterinsurgency. That the American role in Laos was very active and the American role in Thailand was passive sometimes caused difficulties, but on the whole the exchange of views and information at the working level seemed very worthwhile to both Embassies. Later I invited Ambassador Jack W. Lydman in Malaysia to send a representative to our regional meeting in the South. Since there were only about a dozen Americans in that region of Thailand, I had at first been hesitant to invite Embassy representation at such a small meeting, but Ambassador Lydman eagerly agreed. Thus the regional meetings became also to some extent inter-Embassy—a kind of regular exchange that was unusual, if not unique. When I first arrived in Thailand I had been struck by the vertical reporting to Washington and the general lack of close contact among the American Embassies in the area. These regional meetings in Thailand, therefore, also served to help with this broader problem.

To further the working relationship among neighboring Embassies, to see how the situation looked from their viewpoint, and to broaden my own view of border problems, I made a number of trips to the countries surrounding Thailand. The Thais have a close working relationship with Malaysia through the joint Border Committee and the Regional Border Committee Organization in Songkhla. I visited the border areas with Thai officers and accompanied them on visits to the Malaysian police training center at Ipoh and on missions to Kuala Lumpur. The Thai-Burmese Border Committee had usually been inactive, and my visit to Burma was on a unilateral basis, but it was extremely profitable in instructing me on the Burma situation. Also, since Laos was important from the Thai point of view, because of its close association with the insurgency, I frequently visited that country to see the border regions and to hold discussions with the Americans in Vientiane. All the visits were extremely worthwhile, not only because they were instructive to me but also because they brought the American Embassies somewhat closer together.

THE POLICY PAPER

Concurrently with the development of these coordinating mechanisms I began an attempt in the summer of 1968 to codify American policy and to provide specific guidance for our counterinsurgency assistance effort. When I arrived in Thailand, no written statement on Mission counterinsurgency objectives or written guidance for advisors on various situations existed. After I had been trapped several times among conflicting views on what American policy or practice actually was, I became convinced that written policy instructions were indeed necessary, even without guidance from Washington.

While this might seem to be a simple and obvious process, I was told it would be impossible because of the conflicting views within the Mission. However, I appointed an interagency ad hoc group to try to draw up such a paper. In a first draft I had my staff, under the leadership of Lieutenant Colonel (now Colonel) George K. Osborn, USA, incorporate the ideas I had gleaned from Mission practice and documents along with other ideas I particularly wished to emphasize. We tried to define U.S. objectives in Thailand and then outline our policy as precisely as possible. I felt very strongly, for example, that Americans should not participate directly in the counterinsurgency effort. Although this had always supposedly been American policy in Thailand, some participation had nevertheless crept in; for example, U.S. Air Force and Army personnel were at that time directly engaged in civic action in the Northeast. Also, I wished to emphasize the importance of training the Thais and of developing Thai human resources, in contrast to what I had long felt was too great concentration on arms and equipment. We developed a slogan for this effort—"train the trainers." The resultant "guidelines" also spelled out specific U.S. Mission policy on the role of Americans in the defense of the Thai air bases on which they were tenants and on the limitations of American civic action (the primary exception being permission for American action only around these air bases), and on the coordinating role of the Consuls. While there was no intent to outline a counterinsurgency doctrine, the paper also included many ideas about it.

The general tenor of the guidelines may be gathered from a very brief summary provided in late 1969 to the Subcommittee on U.S. Security Agreements and Commitments Abroad of the U.S. Senate Foreign Relations Committee:

U.S. Mission Counterinsurgency Policy Guidelines—Thailand

The Kingdom of Thailand is confronted with a Communist-inspired and directed insurgency whose objective is the overthrow of the Royal Thai Government (RTG) and its replacement by a Communist regime. The RTG has undertaken a comprehensive response to this threat. Its counterinsurgency (CI) efforts include four broad categories of activities: economic and political development, information and psychological operations, intelligence, and protection and suppression.

Thailand and the United States agree that the purpose of U.S. assistance should be to help the RTG improve its capability to conduct such a comprehensive CI effort using Thai resources, manpower and leadership. Therefore, U.S. assistance to Thailand takes the form of economic and military assistance programs, training, and advice designed to assist in the development of their capability to counter Communist insurgency on their own. This policy stems from the mutual recognition that only the Thai can deal effectively with their internal security problem.

If the U.S. is to achieve its basic objectives of helping the RTG to develop its capacity for effective CI performance, U.S. personnel must not assume responsibility for taking action which the Thai could take for themselves. Direct action by U.S. personnel to facilitate a particular CI task in the long run impedes the development of RTG capabilities. Those U.S. agencies and personnel who formulate and supervise U.S. programs supporting Thai CI efforts, or who engage in advising or training activities should always act within the context of this general guidance.

Accordingly, all personnel engaged in formulating and implementing U.S. training programs should work toward the primary objective of training Thai instructors to train Thai. Direct training is an exception to policy; any exception must be approved by the Embassy. Existing programs that involve U.S. personnel in direct training of Thai will be redirected to training Thai trainers in accordance with timetables to be approved by the Embassy.

U.S. military may provide assistance for civic action projects sponsored by an element of the RTG in the vicinity of Thai bases where U.S. forces are stationed when authorized by prior approval of SA/CI.

The actions of U.S. advisors and all other U.S. personnel in Thailand are governed by the U.S. and RTG policy that suppression operations are a Thai responsibility. The following injunctions grow out of this policy:

1. There will be no direct support of Thai combat operations by U.S. military or civilian personnel;

2. No U.S. personnel will approach by air, land, or water the immediate areas in which Thai combat operations are taking place;

3. U.S. personnel are to avoid actions and situations which could give the appearance of involvement in RTG Communist terrorist suppression operations;

4. In no case will U.S. advisors accompany units below battalion headquarters or their equivalent on military or police operations.

Authority and responsibility for formulation of U.S. Mission counterinsurgency policy and for coordination of U.S. Mission support for RTG counterinsurgency activities is exercised on behalf of the Ambassador by the Special Assistant for Counterinsurgency (SA/CI). Major additions to U.S. support activities or programs, or significant modifications of their content, require prior approval by SA/CI. All reports by U.S. Mission elements to higher echelons involving the insurgency or counterinsurgency activities are coordinated with the Ambassador's Special Assistant.

The paper was sent to the various agencies for comments, and many suggestions and a few criticisms were received. A revised version went through the same procedure. Agreement was reached on most points, but I made the decisions on remaining differences. Ambassador Unger then approved the paper and issued it as official guidance for all United States personnel in Thailand concerned with helping the Thais in their counterinsurgency effort.

However, once the paper was completed, the difficult job remained of explaining it and the reasoning behind it and of gaining the active agreement and support of all those participating in American efforts to help Thailand. Having tried the philosophy of no direct U.S. participation in Vietnam in 1964, I was not surprised by the initial opposition it aroused in some Americans in Thailand. Many of these were activists who had been in Vietnam where we were "doing the job"; others simply didn't see why we didn't do it, when "we could do it quicker and better." Furthermore, intermittent pressure from Washington for quick results did not always make it easier to keep in mind the long-term goal of enhancing Thai capabilities. With the support of the agency heads, however, we made considerable progress toward convincing the doubters and enforcing the policy. The Tuesday Group and the regional meetings were particularly helpful in this effort.

The 1962 plan and the subsequent statement of guidelines served as a basis for evaluation and reporting of the counterinsurgency situation and the progress of U.S.-supported counterinsurgency programs in Thailand. Contributions of pertinent information from the agencies concerned were requested by my office and reviewed and evaluated by my staff. A U.S. Mission report containing statistics, narrative description, and evaluation was produced in different formats at periodic intervals and served a vitally important informative function within the Mission as well as in higher headquarters in Hawaii (Pacific Command) and in Washington. While this reporting function was not without its competitors in the channels of other agencies, the comprehensiveness and quality of the SA/CI product was widely appreciated as a basis for executive appraisal and decision-making. Middleton A. Martin, detailed from the Office of the Secretary of Defense, International Security Affairs (OSD/ISA), played a key role in developing SA/CI reporting as a source of information and sound judgment on the Thailand insurgency situation.

Implementing the Guidelines

In the light of the policy guidelines, I asked the Deputy Commander of the 7/13th Air Force to draw up a plan for withdrawal of all United States Air Force civic action personnel scattered throughout the Northeast beyond the immediate proximity of U.S.-tenanted bases. His staff responded with a good plan for withdrawal in one year. I approved it and its execution was completed by early 1970. In this I received the full support from the Air Force even though some of them pointed out that the policy violated their own Air Force doctrine. The Thais did not fill all the vacancies left by the Americans, but they did somewhat increase their civic action efforts as a result of this action. In any case, the policy that Americans should not do the job for the Thais was clearly enforced and demonstrated.

Another instance of policy enforcement was an agreement involving USOM and MACTHAI in support of the Thai National Police Department. Here both the policy on limitations of civic action and the emphasis on training were issues.

The Thai police requested the Public Safety Division of USOM to arrange for U.S. Special Forces to train police in counterinsurgency operations. I agreed that USOM and MACTHAI should provide this support, but I laid down several conditions. First, it must be clearly stated that the U.S. Special Forces would train only Thai police instructors, who in turn would instruct the police trainees. Second, I insisted that half the U.S. Special Forces were to be withdrawn from the program after the first year and the remaining half phased back at the end of the second year. Third, I insisted on restricting the travel of the Special Forces and prohibited them from going into areas obviously or suspected to be dangerous in which the Thais might carry out training exercises. This informal agreement was drawn up in writing, accepted by the three parties concerned, and approved by me. Unfortunately, the program was slow to get started; thus the timing of the withdrawal became somewhat confused and was necessarily extended. I enforced the agreement while I was in Thailand and can happily report that, since my departure, the Special Forces phased out according to the plan.

Do It Yourselfism for the Thais

One incident illustrates how easy it would be for dependence on the Americans to develop in a local crisis.[2] In December, 1968, one of the first Thai helicopters was shot down by the insurgents in the difficult mountainous area of the Tri-Province or Phu Lom Lo area. The Thais quickly asked for U.S. assistance in repairing the chopper and the Commander of MACTHAI dutifully asked for an exception to our policy of no direct assistance and no entrance to a dangerous area. I asked why the Thai mechanics who had been recently well-trained in the United States could not repair the chopper. The answer I received was only the argument that the Thais might be slower and were less experienced than the Americans. I pointed out that I was even more reluctant to allow Americans into the area if the need for haste was based on the high level of danger in the area. Two days later the chopper was still unrepaired, but no further damage had been inflicted, so I was asked to approve the dispatch of a Jolly Green (USAF) chopper which could lift the disabled Thai chopper out of the danger area. I refused as the same reasons held, but there was a broad hint from MACTHAI that I would be responsible to Washington if the Thai chopper was destroyed. I accepted this, but countered by urging that the Thais try again. They did and succeeded beautifully. They put a fifty-gallon drum in the chopper, jerry-rigged a fuel line, and flew it out themselves. All concerned (and not least the Thais) were terribly pleased. They showed us and, even more important, themselves what they could really do. We could, of course, have done it for them, but think

2. See "Watch on the Mekong" by Arnold Abrams, *Far Eastern Economic Review*, May 14, 1970, for an independent report on this incident.

what they would have missed in satisfaction. (Of course, the chopper might have been destroyed, so think what I missed!)

The guidelines paper clarified a number of issues and made much more specific the policy guidance provided to U.S. personnel in Thailand. To the best of my knowledge it was enforced. However, it had at least one major weakness and some lesser shortcomings. Not then and not in the early 1970s has there been a U.S. agency-wide concept of revolutionary warfare, counterinsurgency doctrine, and strategy. Several agencies, particularly the U.S. Army, have made laudable attempts to fill this gap, but of necessity one agency cannot do it alone. Therefore, the paper could not spell out authoritative U.S. doctrine on counterinsurgency itself as contrasted with the U.S. role in helping the Thais, though in general terms the main ingredients of a counterinsurgency doctrine were at least enumerated for Thailand. This major defect thus prohibited any establishment of priorities for counterinsurgency assistance, made the coordination problem more difficult, and did not inspire the Thais with confidence that we, as a government, knew what we were doing. And I suspect at this writing that the strong conflicting feelings in the U.S. in general and Washington in particular about Vietnam and insurgency in general suggest that a doctrine is still much needed but will not soon be developed.

THE MAIN OBJECTIVE OF SA/CI

While most of my time and energy was devoted to better organization and coordination of the U.S. effort, the real objective of all this was to provide the best possible help to the Thai counterinsurgency effort and put them on their own feet so that the Americans could leave as soon as possible. The various agencies of the Mission had their contacts with appropriate Thai government offices—the U.S. military with the Thai Ministry of Defense; USOM with the Ministries of Economic Development, Health, Education, and Interior, as well as other offices such as Accelerated Rural Development (ARD)—, but SA/CI was the U.S. liaison with the Communist Suppression Operations Command (CSOC), and we had dealings with all the Thai offices working on the counterinsurgency effort. I personally developed close working relationships with officers in CSOC, the Army, National Security Command, Police, Department of Local Administration (DOLA), ARD, and Community Development (CD), as well as with many provincial officials. I found that a low profile and small meetings seemed most successful with the Thais. Lunches, usually with just one official, led, I believe, to a good exchange of ideas, enjoyment, and eventually in some cases to close friendships.

Inasmuch as I do not speak Thai, language was somewhat of a problem, particularly in the countryside, although many Thais speak excellent English.

There were a few misunderstandings due to language difficulties but they were usually, when discovered, quickly clarified. The Thais are proud and intelligent people and therefore not always easily receptive to American advice, even when it was tendered in the most diplomatic manner. I must say that, on occasion, I found it a little embarrassing and even presumptuous to try to tell the Thais what to do in certain circumstances. Another problem was the rather complicated and not fully understood Thai political structure and *modus operandi*. Americans were often remiss in not learning about and trying to understand the Thai political structure, and especially the importance of personal relationships in all aspects of Thai life. I was unable to get the Mission to make a concentrated and unified effort on this matter. As suggested earlier, the Thais generally do things unobtrusively; thus, for outsiders to detect when a decision has been made may be difficult. Furthermore, a number of Thais saw clearly that we had made some mistakes in Vietnam—mistakes they did not wish to have repeated in their country. I remember a Thai general telling me that they were not going to send battalions into a village searching for a couple of communists and likely alienating all of the villagers in the process. To sensitive Americans the situation of advisor and advisee, giver and receiver, is a delicate one, and the Thailand situation was no exception; nevertheless, the various relationships worked out surprisingly well. I think the Thais did learn some useful things from us, but I know that they were also exposed to some pretty bad ideas. I also know that we learned some useful things from them.

For a variety of reasons I decided that I would leave after a little over two years. This was reluctantly done, as I had developed a great attachment for Thailand. I had made some lasting friendships among its people and had also made a start toward understanding the Thai way of life. I felt that I had also developed a policy and mechanism for U.S. counterinsurgency assistance to Thailand which I wanted to see prosper. However, I felt that I had done all I could under the circumstances, and so I left Thailand in May, 1970. The increasing loss of interest in counterinsurgency in Washington was reflected in the future of the SA/CI office. Its name was changed to the Development and Security Section and was headed by my former deputy, William Stokes, who had the rank of Counselor, not Minister. The chairmanship of the Tuesday Group was transferred to the Deputy Chief of Mission and eventually the Ambassador took over the group and used it as a vehicle for discussing all the problems of the Mission, not just counterinsurgency. Stokes formed a low-level working committee for operations and continued much of the work we had already begun in SA/CI. However, the office has shrunk in size and influence, and the experiment of strong American coordination is essentially finished.

Chapter 8

Some Reflections

This last chapter is composed of some personal reflections on the general subject of insurgency and counterinsurgency in Southeast Asia based on study and direct involvement in counterinsurgency efforts in that area.[1] I have also included some observations on the United States role in assisting certain countries in their counterinsurgency efforts. I have attempted to present a balanced view of a now controversial activity that is almost entirely ignored in Washington though it continues in most countries in Southeast Asia.

VIEWS ON COUNTERINSURGENCY

I start with a simple assertion but one I believe to be very important. In dealing with insurgency and counterinsurgency, especially in their early stages, *people*

1. Considerable portions of this chapter were published in my article, "Some Lessons Learned in Southeast Asia," in the Fall 1972 issue of *Orbis,* published by the Foreign Policy Research Institute in association with the Fletcher School of Law and Diplomacy. I wish to thank the editor for permission to use those parts in this chapter.

are more important than *things*. The communists know this well, having learned
it at least partly from necessity. Starting with nothing but people, they concentrate on recruiting, training, and developing capable cadres, thus forming an
effective organization. Only after this basic instrument, composed entirely of
people, is well under way do they introduce things, such as explosives and guns.
But their primary emphasis remains on improving the quality and intensifying
the revolutionary fervor of members and new recruits, and enhancing the
collective capabilities of the organization. Once the organizational machine is
formed by developing good cadres and a disciplined organization, the communist
leadership has a flexible tool for the varying demands of insurgency. On the
non-communist side, usually the government of a threatened country that is
engaged in counterinsurgency operations, the tendency has been to stress weapons and other material aspects and to neglect the human resources required to
do the job. (This tendency has unfortunately been encouraged by the nature of
American aid.) Once the insurgent threat has been recognized, the first reaction
has been to seek better arms and equipment, rather than to launch an intensive
effort to improve the quality of government officials, especially military personnel and police. And from then on, the demand for more and more weapons and
equipment usually becomes more persistent. When things go wrong, it is alleged
that the weapons were not modern enough or too few—rarely that the men were
not well enough led or trained or motivated.

I am not saying that material things are unimportant, but I am saying that the
human element must receive first priority. In the more successful counterinsurgency campaigns, this has always been the case. For example, when Magsaysay
took over as Defense Minister in the Philippines in 1950, the government's
campaign against an insurgency, the communist-led Huks, was going very badly.
The Army, geared to conventional military operations and prone to pillaging,
was feared and disliked by the people as much as the Huks were. I would argue
that the key factor in Magsaysay's successful campaign was not his laudable and
much-mentioned resettlement plan, but his reform of the Army. He removed
corrupt and inefficient officers, and he insisted that all military personnel deal
justly and properly with the people and take part in constructive actions. He also
instituted more imaginative military operations against the Huks. As these
changes became evident, not only through Magsaysay's statements but also (and
more importantly) through the behavior of the troops, the course of the conflict
itself changed. By providing better security and treatment of the people, the
Army received more intelligence from the people, which enabled it to begin
eliminating the Huks—a cycle that continued to the final victory. Under Magsaysay there was no profusion of helicopters or any influx of the latest rifles—only
more effective people. The Philippines were not scarred by incredible tonnages

of firepower; the brain and the scalpel, not the sledgehammer, solved the problem.

One can argue, of course, that there are few Magsaysays, and that all situations are different. But the other successful major counterinsurgency effort, in Malaya, also was distinguished by its emphasis on the importance, at all levels, of imaginative leadership and trained and dedicated personnel. Special Branch (police intelligence) and the constabulary were as carefully selected, trained, and disciplined as were the soldiers, perhaps even more so. I remember hearing of a Malay soldier who nearly burst his eardrums diving for his rifle in deep water because he was too proud or perhaps afraid to report it lost. Such training and discipline, though perhaps carried too far in that case, are the foundation for successful counterinsurgency, yet all too often have been missing. One has never heard of such behavior in Vietnam where supplies are so abundant.

There is really no gainsaying that the development of needed human resources can have only positive benefits, while overconcentration on weapons and other inanimate objects entails serious and often unnecessary costs and drawbacks. If an effective intelligence system is developed in the initial stages of an insurgency, the movement can possibly be stopped very early. In any case, the costs to the government of such a system are small, and few weapons and little equipment are required. A certain number of weapons and so on will be needed for constabulary or rural police forces, but, no matter what the stage or size of the insurgency, these are necessary elements and the cost of equipping them is relatively low, especially since the enemy often (though, as Vietnam shows, not always) has inferior arms and equipment and the more difficult logistic system. A government that places too much stress on weapons and equipment in counterinsurgency operations is apt to overtax its logistic and administrative capabilities, and indeed to overburden its troops. It is also likely to depend too much on means that are less effective and more expensive—for example, air reconnaisance rather than foot patrol, loudspeakers in the place of person-to-person information operations. Worse still, having an abundance of sophisticated weapons and ammunition may tempt the government side to use the firepower too liberally and incautiously, thereby adding to civilian casualties and creating hostility between the troops and the populace. The ill feelings are bad enough in themselves, but, in a practical sense, they contribute to drying up the intelligence information and other active popular support needed by the government to bring an end to the violence.

Though some may argue otherwise, men and objects usually are in competition with each other in counterinsurgent warfare. In the less developed countries, the skilled and educated are the scarcest resource. The more of this scarce resource that must be used to operate sophisticated equipment, the less of it is available for the fundamental processes and problems of government and counterinsurgency. It is patently absurd, for example, to have excellent helicopter pilots to ferry troops to the battle scene, but to lack the aggressive, trained infantry lieutenants and noncommissioned officers needed to lead the troops after they have landed—yet this happened many times. An indirect drawback of highly sophisticated weapons and equipment is that they tend to dazzle and unduly absorb the attention of the leaders of threatened nations again to the neglect of the basic problems. Further, since such paraphernalia is very expensive, it either creates a strong dependence on the donor (most often the United States) or consumes entirely too much of the indigenous country's budget.

This is not to say that threatened nations should refrain from using material that will help them conduct a difficult struggle for existence. But they should also concentrate on developing human resources, weigh carefully all the costs of acquiring sophisticated weapons and equipment, and, above all, remember that weapons and equipment are the tools of men, not vice versa.

I believe our recent experiences in counterinsurgency have shown that wars of national liberation are a form of total conflict—total with respect to both goal and means. As the communists themselves have said very clearly, the ultimate objective of such wars of liberation is to overthrow existing political and economic regimes and establish communist governments and societies in their place. In other words, the goal involves full political power and a complete reorganization of society and the economy. We need not go into either the morality or desirability of that objective or evaluate its ultimate feasibility to admit that it is the broadest possible goal, which to those who pursue it merits the total commitment of their efforts and means.

Most of us today are reasonably familiar with the writings of Mao and other communist ideologists, and know that they conceive of the revolutionary struggle as one that orchestrates all the means, including the use of force, and, furthermore, that they allow for changes in the relative emphasis on the different means. Thus, they regard recruiting, organizing, and propaganda work as the key functions in the initial stages of an insurgency. Once the organization has been formed and overt action begins, violence and terror can be introduced, and preparations made for more aggressive military actions. And in the latter stages of insurgency and the rush toward victory, the emphasis is on military means that are almost conventional. Such socioeconomic measures as are undertaken tend to be small and local during most of the conflict, but of course, revolutionary changes are promised for the future. Political activity and propaganda, however, both local and international, are always highest priority.[2]

2. At times it seems that propaganda aimed at the world is the primary weapon of the communists. Indeed it seems that the war in Vietnam was to a large extent a Hanoi-Washington psychological struggle rather than a military war in Indochina. This is a form of conflict I have often called "war over the heads of the combatants."

Though the relative emphasis on the different means may change, the totality of the effort is maintained. Within each of the primary means itself, there may be shifts of tactics and strategy. For example, the effort in the political sphere at one time may be toward a coalition government as the means to the goal, while at other times the chosen instrument to that end may be a national uprising— more a political weapon than military. In military action, the stress at times will be on regular military operations, and at other times on guerrilla and terrorist activities. Terror, though not often mentioned openly as a weapon by the communists, is actually a very important and integral part of their strategy and is rarely employed without a purpose. There are times when the communists will use terror to mask their own weakness, by letting it create the impression that their movement is stronger and larger than it really is. They also use it to demonstrate the impotence of the threatened government, to intimidate teachers and officials, and to subdue the population—in short, to strengthen the insurgency while weakening the government and, if not winning the support of the people, at least neutralizing them.

Once we recognize that communist insurgents employ all known means of warfare—political, economic, and military—and their variants, the lesson to be gained from this insight is that counterinsurgency must be a fully integrated effort, in which every program or action must be related to others. For example, let us assume that an intelligence service has a sensitive operation going in a village but that the military believes the village should be attacked, which would mean destroying the intelligence effort. Some one, or some small group, should be able to determine which action is the more important, and have the authority to make the decision and enforce it. Military and police actions, intelligence, and socioeconomic actions must be planned and executed to reinforce, and not hinder, each other. Wherever this lesson has been practiced, the results have usually been good. In the Malayan Emergency, Field Marshal Templar, using the Briggs Plan as a basis for action, orchestrated his efforts and waged the campaign against the communists successfully.[3] Similarly, Magsaysay in the Philippines was able to suppress the Huks by assuming full integrating powers and providing enlightened leadership. In most other counterinsurgency campaigns, this unity of command has been less perfect, with large committees or vague coordinating mechanisms expected to solve the bureaucratic and political problems of centralized control. Such approaches may work with strong leadership, as was the case with Templar in Malaya, but where the committee system or loose coordination extends all the way to the top and lacks firm control and direction, it will not work.

3. Lt. General Sir Harold Briggs was Director of Operations reporting directly to the High Commissioner of Malaya from April, 1950, to November, 1951, and devised this successful plan. In February, 1952, General Sir Gerald Templar was appointed both High Commissioner and Director of Operations.

Another important characteristic of communist insurgency is its evolutionary nature, yet this obvious point is usually ignored in counterinsurgency doctrine and operations. Mao, in his three-stage theory, and later Giap have allowed for steps backward when necessary and have taught that adversity strengthens the will and improves the effort. Yet Americans have neglected to take full account of the implications that the evolutionary and flexible nature of insurgency has for counterinsurgent planning, and tend instead to discuss and approach the problems posed by insurgent warfare as though they were static, as unchanging as the conventional warfare in Europe in World War II. There, the two sides lined up their troops, artillery, and air power and slugged it out across the Continent, the major problem for each being how best to pierce the enemy's front line so as to get to the soft rear, and either encircle the combat forces or cause them to withdraw rapidly. From the Normandy landings to the final battles in Germany, this was the objective as pursued, with some variations, by the Americans, the British, and the Russians. The reverse was true for the Germans in 1940.

Unlike conventional war, insurgencies have no formal beginnings, continuing conventional characteristics, or formal measuring devices of success. The origins of most insurgencies are shrouded in mystery and silence.

As we have seen in the case of Thailand (despite the misguided belief of some that the insurgency there emerged full-blown in 1965 and mainly in response to U.S. air attacks on Vietnam), a closer look reveals the slow, painstaking, and often frustrated efforts to develop an insurgent apparatus. The Communist Party Congresses of 1956 and 1961 proclaimed wars of national liberation as the proper method, but we know little of the insurgent leadership and its actions, though we do know about some of the communists' activities. These included recruiting and propagandizing in the villages, taking some Thais and hill tribes to Vietnam and China for training, and infusing very small amounts of money and material into parts of the country. Even as late as 1963 and 1964, this embryonic organization could hardly have served as the target of conventional military operations. It should, however, have been the object of intensive Royal Thai Government intelligence operations designed to identify and, where appropriate, arrest the leaders. At the same time, efforts ought to have been made (and a few were actually begun) to deal with the very real socioeconomic problems in Northeast Thailand, which the communists were using to camouflage their real aim of seizing political power.

By mid-1965 the rising number of hostile incidents showed the insurgents had organized guerrilla bands and acquired small bases from which to support them. That greater resources and force were needed to deal with the insurgents should have been clear. Bands of forty to fifty guerrillas could not be handled by the Thai police at that time. Army units, skillfully led, were required, but the units that were in fact used proved to rely mainly on conventional sweeps and artillery and air power, and the Thais soon realized that these methods were not the answer.

It was that context which led the Thai government to organize the Communist Suppression Operations Command (CSOC), an admirably-conceived organization composed of representatives from most of the agencies concerned in integrating the Thai counterinsurgency effort. But because of the delicate balance of political power in Bangkok, the conflicts within the Thai bureaucracy, and the nature of CSOC itself, it has not provided the needed leadership, for it does not exercise real command, nor does it carry out integrated planning. General Saiyud Kerdphol, CSOC's Director of Operations, said before the 1973 coup that "CSOC needs more authority. . . . CSOC needs the support of the national leadership. . . . At the moment, no one body is really making the decisions in this field."[4] One doubts that the Thai counterinsurgency effort will really succeed in halting the expansion of the insurgency until an organization, or a single man, is given adequate authority and resources to make a concerted drive against it, but as of early 1974 this seems unlikely to happen.

As now organized, the lags between the identification of problems and their solutions is intolerably long. After the Thai counterinsurgency effort got under way in the jungles in the late 1960s, for example, the communist terrorists began putting more effort into the villages, as they were unwilling to confront the army. "CSOC learned this," General Saiyud went on, "and tried to convince the authorities that, in 1970, we must come back to the villages because the communists already had some villages under their control. It took one year to convince the authorities."

Virtually the same pattern may now be repeating itself. With the cease-fire in Vietnam the communists may well deemphasize anew the military side of their operations, concentrating instead on political "education" in the countryside. This seems to be happening to an extent in the Northeast but not in the North. This might well have the effect of lulling many Thais into believing that their counterinsurgency efforts have succeeded—and there might well be some officials willing to take credit but who know better; that's human nature.

This brief review of the origins of the Thai insurgency and of the government's counterinsurgency efforts suggest at least three further lessons for counterinsurgency. The first is that it is best to respond to an insurgent threat early and effectively, at a time when the communists are still weak and small in number and it may be possible to stop them entirely, whereas, if their organization is allowed to develop, not only will they become stronger, but their means of fighting the government will grow beyond the mere talk about force to the use of force and terror, and finally to conventional war. There is a tendency in

4. Quoted in "Changing Tune," by David Jenkins, *Far Eastern Economic Review,* 19 March 1973.

certain places to dismiss a few communist organizers or guerrillas as constituting no threat, but doing so is to ignore the evolutionary nature of insurgency. The earlier the counterinsurgent effort is begun, the easier, less expensive, and less bloody it will be. This has seemed to be an especially hard lesson to apply, because insurgent activity in its earliest phase commands little attention of top officials; therefore its potential seriousness is not readily apparent.

Second, we must recognize that the response to insurgency may need to vary from place to place and from one time to another; not only the instruments of counterinsurgency (such as the choice between military and police) but also the plans and actions must be constantly adjusted to the changing nature of the struggle. A program looks good and works well at one time but may be of little relevance a year or two later. Thus, in trying to prevent the spread of insurgency at a given time, concentration on village development units designed to help villagers solve their socioeconomic problems may be useful—possibly, though not necessarily, as part of a larger effort involving intelligence and police activities as well. If, however, the insurgency grows in spite of these efforts and the communists are able to terrorize and intimidate the population, the earlier programs aimed at providing wells, new schools, better sanitation facilities, and the like cease to be the most persuasive counterinsurgency measures for the peasant who primarily wants protection and security for himself and his family. Education, pure water, and sanitation become secondary to the preservation of life itself, and no amount of government propaganda will convince the peasant otherwise. At this stage, the means of ensuring protection must be devised and made visible, and this remains one of the most perplexing and difficult problems for a government to solve. However, once counterinsurgency efforts have been successful and have made the guerrilla elements less threatening, a return to productive socioeconomic measures and a reduction in the security forces may be possible and desirable. Hence the importance of a counterinsurgency doctrine and command organization that are flexible enough to respond to the constantly changing nature of the struggle.

Third, and even more important than flexibility, which is a reactive, defensive capability, it is essential that a good counterinsurgency organization have a strategic plan if it is to defeat the insurgents. Although in the early stages the insurgents may have the initiative and make it difficult for the government to go on the offensive, this goal must nevertheless be kept clearly in mind. In Malaya the Briggs Plan was formulated in spite of the fact and during the time that the CTs (Chinese Terrorists) had the initiative. It laid out two immediate objectives: depriving the guerrillas of supplies provided from the villages, and severing contact between the guerrillas and the communist cells in the villages. After the British developed their human resources, obtained unified leadership under Templar, and were able to execute their strategy, the nature of the campaign changed and the CTs were put on the defensive. It took all three elements to make counterinsurgency work, but the plan gave cohesion and direction to the effort.

THE UNITED STATES AND COUNTERINSURGENCY

As noted in Chapter 7, the Office of the Special Assistant for Counterinsurgency was established in the American Embassy to help the Thais combat the communist-inspired insurgency which had the major characteristics described above. While it was important for the Thais to have a command or coordinating organization to meet the communist threat, it was also important for the United States Government to have a coordinating mechanism for its various agencies helping the Thais. As we have seen, there was MACTHAI, USOM, USIS, ARPA, and Headquarters 7/13th Air Force on the American side, all of which were more or less involved in assisting the Thais. But there was no accepted U.S. counterinsurgency doctrine which could have served to focus the efforts of these American agencies. Furthermore, although the State Department's Country Director for Thailand chairs an interagency committee in Washington, neither the Country Director nor the committee has any real authority. Their meetings are merely discussions of problems and a means of keeping each other informed. While such discussions are useful, they do not develop any decision-making capability or provide strong guidance and direction to the U.S. agencies in the field. The higher-level coordinating mechanisms in Washington, such as the National Security Council, provide only the most general guidance. This suggests that coordination and agreed policy guidance of some enduring nature from Washington is unlikely to be available to officials in the field. This situation was recognized by Ambassador Martin when he established the Office of SA/CI.

Most observers would agree that the State Department, as the agency responsible for overall American foreign policy, should perform the policy formulation and coordination role, but it seldom has done so in recent years. There are a number of reasons for this.

1. The Department appears to recruit and train bright young men to be polite negotiators, writers of reports and cables, and diplomatic party goers. With the possible exception of some personnel for Vietnam, seldom have I detected any attempt on the part of the Department to develop and train executive managers and leaders who could make decisions and insure their execution.[5]

2. The Department itself has to an increasing extent been overshadowed, if not dominated, by the Defense Department and the CIA in overseas operations. Both of these agencies have been run by action-oriented leaders and have

5. In mid-1973 a new effort was initiated to develop more capable managers and administrators, but it is too early to evaluate the results so far.

developed resources for operating in foreign countries. More recently the foreign-policy role of the National Security Council has grown tremendously and now completely overshadows the State Department. Thus the oldest executive department of the U.S. Government, and originally designated as the primary adviser to the President in the formulation and execution of foreign policy, is now not able to exercise the necessary leadership in Washington and often not in the field. Whether the new Secretary of State, Henry Kissinger, is able to change this remains to be seen, though personal diplomacy seems to be his inclination, and this does not bode well for the State Department's future role.

3. The Department has few if any resources which enable it to lead and manage U.S. missions in the field. For example, its communications and transportation facilities within a foreign country have been and are very limited. Since it has no transportation facilities except for a few Embassy cars, it is obliged to use commercial transportation in Thailand, which is reasonably good but does not reach all parts of the country. All of the other U.S. agencies in Thailand either have aircraft of their own or rent them. At one time I proposed that I be given $20,000 a year for the rental of aircraft so that I might have some independence, but this idea was ignored. While this dependence on other agencies for communications, transportation, and other assistance was not crucial, it certainly did not contribute to strong independent Embassy leadership. Operating capability is particularly important in counterinsurgency situations but does not apply in more normal diplomatic situations. It can be seen, therefore, that although State should have the leadership role in foreign policy, there are important factors, both external and internal, working against its exercise of the role in an active situation.

THE U.S. COUNTERINSURGENCY EFFORT IN THAILAND

All of the U.S. agencies operating in Thailand are independent, though theoretically under the general and insufficiently defined supervision of the Ambassador. A strong officer, such as Ambassador Martin, could make the system work to an extent, but even he had some difficulties with the various agencies, especially the military. Their independence in the field is reinforced by their independence in Washington. Furthermore, Congress appropriates money for which the agencies are responsible, and this is independent, to a large extent, of the wishes of the Ambassador. Various Congressional committees oversee the work of the separate agencies, but except for the Appropriations Committees, which are understaffed and lack the time to do a thorough job, there is no overview of the U.S. overseas effort. An agency has its separate communications with Washington and often uses special channels—for example, sending private messages to its agency headquarters in Washington without distributing copies to the other agencies or the Ambassador as is the normal procedure for regular messages. This technique permits an agency head to disagree with the Ambassador or anyone else in the Mission and to carry the disputes to Washington. While the system has its useful side, it is not conducive to a unified effort. Each agency has its own personnel and promotion system and though the Ambassador may have some influence on the careers of the top agency heads, it is not pronounced. The military and the CIA are strongly independent, partially because of their position in Washington, but also because their personnel are aggressive and action-oriented. They have plentiful operational resources and, especially in the case of the military, the largest number of personnel.

The Office of the SA/CI was set up as a possible way of achieving some coordination in the field, and did not attempt to direct or manage the total U.S. effort to assist the Thais. The authority of the office emanated from the Ambassador. Ambassador Martin and Ambassador Unger have both stated that the SA/CI spoke for them on counterinsurgency matters. Inasmuch as the Ambassador's power is very generally defined by the President so was his delegation to the SA/CI. I interpreted my mission as including the establishment and enforcement of counterinsurgency policy, coordination of various agencies' efforts to avoid duplication or contradictory efforts, and taking the initiative in formulating policies and procedures where there had been none—for example, restriction on movements of U.S. advisors, the insurgency in the North, and training. It seemed to me that, except in general policy matters, ordering the agency heads to do or not to do certain things was not possible. I felt, however, that there was enough good will and concern for U.S. Government positions and interests that I could, by the various means described earlier, develop a consensus and agreement on most matters. Persuasion and quiet leadership offered the best roads to success.

When I departed in May, 1970, the Office of SA/CI had been in existence nearly four years. Thus, if anyone had asked what we had achieved, I would have considered the question reasonable. What would have been my first answer then has not changed with the lapse of time: that a U.S. policy on counterinsurgency for Thailand had been written, staffed, and promulgated, a breakthrough in itself. Furthermore, I made it clear that the policy was not just a piece of paper. It would be the basis for our actions in Thailand, and I made strenuous efforts to ensure that it was enforced. I knew that there were some violations, some of which I discovered and stopped, some of which I discovered too late, and some which I am sure I did not learn about.[6] On the whole, the American team did rally around, and by the time I left I felt that we had the beginnings of a coordinated counterinsurgency support effort in Thailand.

6. When one Special Forces officer, assigned by the U.S. Army to Thailand, seemed to have violated the policy of noninvolvement, his superior officer rebuked him and hinted he might be sent home in a classic remark. The superior officer said: "You've got one foot on the airplane and the other on a banana peel."

Some achievements resulting from this effort were quite important. First, the policy of Americans not doing the job for the Thais, though expressed for a long time in Thailand, had finally been clearly enunciated in the official counterinsurgency policy paper and constantly enforced as far as possible. This meant that American military advisors would not go on combat missions or into dangerous areas, that civic action was the responsibility of the Thais and not of the Americans, that the U.S. would train the Thai trainers, not the trainees, and in general that the Thais would be forced to do the job themselves. This was no mean achievement. (It happened to coincide with, and actually preceded, the Nixon Doctrine promulgated at Guam in 1969 and certainly was in keeping with the prevailing attitude in America.) It also meant that there was some coordination and a reduction of conflicting U.S. programs. For example, USOM stopped petroleum support for the Thais for one year, thus throwing an additional burden on the Thai budget. MACTHAI intended to do the same for the military forces, but this was postponed to lessen the impact on the Thai budget in one year. It did not, however, wipe away all the independent actions and programs of the various agencies. It did not stop the use of separate and special channels to Washington, it did not result in a unified policy or effort, and it did not set as good an example to the Thais as I would have liked, but it was progress.

Second, the Tuesday Group, its meetings and trips, the coordinating role of the Consuls, and the quarterly regional meetings, plus the ad hoc and standing committees on various subjects were all planned to bring about greater adherence to the policy and improve the coordinating effort. None of these factors worked perfectly; much still remained to be done at the time of my departure. An additional effort (unusual, if not unique) was our attempt at coordination with the Embassies in neighboring countries. As mentioned earlier, the American Embassy in Laos sent representatives who participated in quarterly regional meetings in the North and Northeast, and the American Embassy in Malaysia participated to a lesser extent in the South. Most of the participants felt that the meetings were extremely helpful, that they provided a forum for discussion, exchange of ideas and information at the working level.

Third, it was one example at least when the State Department through Ambassador Unger and the SA/CI took the lead and the initiative in a very positive way. As noted earlier, the SA/CI not only took the initiative in the policy and coordinating role, but also approved all reporting on counterinsurgency to Washington, reviewed counterinsurgency programs of the various agencies, and briefed visitors on the overall insurgency situation and the U.S. assistance to the Thais.

How could the whole program have been improved? Given the uncoordinated situation in Washington and the somewhat ambiguous power of the Ambassador at the time, it is hard to see how much more could have been done. Clearly it would have been better to have more power—not so much that it would have been used frequently, but to have in the background for use at critical junctures. Some have suggested that the SA/CI should have had some funds at his own disposal. Certainly, in some instances, some would have been useful, particularly when I was unable to get other agencies to fund small projects which the Thais really seemed to need and want. However, I rather liked the idea of not having any money, inasmuch as no one could then suggest that I was buying what the U.S. wanted the Thais to do. In other words, it seemed sounder to be able to discuss ideas and plant suggestions and let the Thais accept and modify or reject as they saw fit without fear of losing U.S. funds. I often felt that the Thais, and other recipients of U.S. aid, initiated programs and did things either to get the funds or to please the Americans and thereby receive future funds. In summary, some funds at my own disposal and discreetly used might have been useful, but I doubt that they would have made a major difference. Other observers suggested that a larger staff would have made SA/CI more effective. To an extent that is true. It was difficult for the SA/CI staff to keep up with the activities of some of the other agencies, all of which were larger and had a multitude of programs. On the other hand, SA/CI was not intended to be an operating agency and the very fine staff I had was able to be knowledgeable about the more important things and to accomplish the major staffing efforts required. I am still convinced that the small group of first-rate people properly motivated and led were quite adequate for the job.

In summary, I believe that, given the present situation in the U.S. government, major improvements in our coordination of overseas activities are unlikely. To overhaul the existing system would call for improvements such as an effective coordinating mechanism in Washington, a clear delegation of authority to the Ambassador, and the subordination by Congress and the Executive Branch of other government agencies to the control and recommendations of the Ambassador. None of these improvements seem likely because of the nature of our bureaucracy. However, because of the present public attitude in the U.S., which seems to favor a lessening of our overseas activities and commitments and a generally more passive role abroad for the U.S., the State Department may be best suited for this new subdued posture.

The experiment of coordinating the U.S. counterinsurgency effort in Thailand is essentially over, at least for the time being. This does not mean that the SA/CI effort was in vain; certain important accomplishments resulted, and the effort demonstrated that much could be done even under familiar bureaucratic conditions. Most important, the U.S. so far has not become inextricably involved in Thai insurgency (as it was in Vietnam), and SA/CI can take some credit for this.

COUNTERINSURGENCY AND AMERICAN
ATTITUDES AND POLICY

The above reflections on my specific personal experiences in Thailand and other parts of Southeast Asia inevitably lead me to express some more general thoughts about the role of the United States overseas. For instance, many Americans may be surprised to learn that the United States actually has only a limited influence on foreign governments, even those that need assistance from us in coping with insurgency. Oddly enough, not only do most overseas government leaders think that they know their countries better than we do, but also, especially in the case of those plagued by insurgency, they still concentrate more on their personal politics or pressing domestic issues than on problems of counterinsurgency. A country that is newly independent is likely to be especially proud and therefore inclined to resent being told what to do and how to do it. In the case of Thailand, the pride includes its long history of independence, entailing many memories of older events and local sentiments, which seem to loom as large (or larger) than present-day happenings. For example, when I was calling on a high Thai official in late spring 1968, I asked him how he thought things were going in Paris—meaning the Vietnam peace talks. To my utter bewilderment, he chuckled and said over and over, "Serves them right." When I finally asked him what he meant, he replied: "Serves the French right that they are having those troubles and riots in Paris. They took away, you know, part of my country." What rankled my host had happened about one hundred years earlier, when the French incorporated into Indochina some provinces that the Thais firmly considered theirs. Yet at the time of our conversation Thai troops were fighting in Vietnam and the government was actually very concerned about the Paris peace talks. Americans tend to ignore the regional history of other countries and the local feelings that stem from it, which are often far more powerful as motivation factors than our thousands-of-miles-away view of a situation. This failure robs our advice and actions of some of their meaning and sometimes makes them entirely irrelevant to a host country.

Another tendency of Americans, because they themselves are usually in a hurry, is to fear that, if a foreign government does not act instantly, a catastrophe will result. Again, we fail to consider that many countries move at a much slower tempo. Especially in Southeast Asia, the American idea of progress and the necessity to rush into action is a novel concept—and one that sometimes leaves the Southeast Asians rather amused. We also seem to forget that the insurgents themselves are Asians. Although the communists have developed some interesting motivational techniques, the protracted warfare they are practicing is well suited to the Asian temperament.

Too often, American ignorance of the values and interests of the people in a given overseas country, as well as our impatience with their ways, alienates the people, even though superficial evidence may not show this clearly. Foreign governments may go through the motions of doing what we wish as a matter of courtesy, or out of a desire for aid, or because they are simply tired of listening to our advice. Unless they believe what we are saying, however, they will not really act effectively, and this is one of the hardest lessons for us to accept.

Incidentally, through the same misreading of the extent of our influence abroad, Washington has often made the mistake of asking its foreign missions to get better results and exert a stronger influence than they are in fact able to do. The missions, in turn, eager to please Washington and earn good efficiency ratings for themselves and their own agencies, tend to exaggerate what they have accomplished with the host governments. This may often be no more than the usual reaction of the public servant trying to do his job in the manner expected of him. In some cases, however, officials have deliberately sent glowing reports to Washington, knowing that it does not reflect the true situation or, worse, have actually suppressed bad news and failures. Though humanly understandable, such action can mislead the decision-makers in Washington, with possible serious consequences. Washington should be more aware of this danger and become more realistic in its demands on the missions and also in its view of U.S. influence abroad. Sometimes a mission deserves high grades even when it is not able to accomplish all that Washington wishes.[7]

Another observation derives from a related failing—our tendency to shape other nations in our own image, i.e. to do what we think is best and in the way we think best. Thus, the most glowing reports about the behavior of a foreign government usually dwell on its having accepted the American way of doing things. Not long ago, for example, an American colonel told me how pleased he was that the particular army to which he was an advisor had, after careful consideration, designed a course for its Special Forces that was exactly like the one at Ft. Bragg. His manner indicated that he thought I might view this as a happy surprise. I was, however, not surprised. Officers from that country's army had been sent to Ft. Bragg for training; some of its general officers had visited Ft. Bragg; copies of the Ft. Bragg curriculum had been generously distributed to their army; and U.S. Special Forces were serving as advisors to it. Some of the officers had visited the British Jungle Warfare School at Jahore near Singapore, but few had been exposed to any other army in the world. Yet with full allowance for the fact that Ft. Bragg has a first-class training center, one may wonder whether a carbon copy of it is exactly the right thing for soldiers of a

7. To avoid this in Vietnam, I informed my subordinates in the provinces that they were rated on their performance as advisors, not on how things went in the province, thus trying to avoid overly optimistic reporting on their part. See my book *War Without Guns: American Civilians in Rural Vietnam*, Praeger Publishers, Inc., New York, 1966.

less developed country at this time. Training in celestial navigation at night, compass patrols, and the use and maintenance of sophisticated weapons, for example, are not the most urgent needs of armies that must cope with training peasants in the fundamentals of guerrilla warfare. Less gadgetry and more training in effective patrolling, marksmanship, and ambushes would seem more appropriate.

Nor is the situation very different in the civilian sector, where, again, we tend to give top marks to the country that adopts our ideas and institutions, and level criticism (and occasionally the threat of reduced U.S. aid) at the one that opts for any other system. Yet what is best for one of the most advanced countries of the twentieth century may not always be best for a developing country, if for no other reason than that it is too expensive. In any case, every such country should have the privilege of shopping around for ideas and of adapting modern ideas to its own culture. Perhaps more than anything else, this insistence that other countries adopt our ways is the cause of ill will abroad, even though the feeling is not always expressed for fear of losing American aid. Our attitudes have often generated lack of respect, and sometimes cynicism. For example, when I was talking with a Thai official about the European advisors whom the Thai government had hired at the turn of the century, I expressed my opinion that it had been a good system and had served Thailand well. He agreed, but said that it was no longer needed, because Thailand had trained many of its own people to do the jobs the advisors had formerly done. When I asked him why in that case they were using U.S. advisors, he smiled and then replied that these were "free" and that a lot of "aid" came with them.

This takes me back to my earlier criticism of the tendency of governments to stress material things such as weapons and equipment over the importance of developing human resources. My own government, I am afraid, must share in the blame for this error in emphasis. The bulk of the aid money as well as of the time and energy of U.S. officials is devoted to weapons and equipment. True, U.S. agencies have many good training programs, and some excellent examples can be cited. (In Thailand, the helicopter programs for both military and police provided for the training of pilots and mechanics in such a way that the personnel had completed their training by the time the "choppers" arrived in the country.) But the development of human resources more often takes second place to the acquisition of objects. While training is receiving a little attention, other aspects of human development are being neglected. Personnel management, including the assignment of trained personnel, is one of them. It has been found in Thailand, for example, that 90 percent of those with advanced agricultural training and education are assigned to capital cities, while only 10 percent are in the provinces, where their skills are directly applicable and needed. Admittedly, an inadequate personnel management system is not the only reason for this imbalance. But it serves to reinforce the lesson that the United States must stress the importance of the human resource; indeed, this seems to be a cardinal point of the Nixon Doctrine, but in fact not much has actually changed. Our material resources could be used as an enticement, or even as a means of influence, by which to prevail on recipient countries to improve the quality and increase the number of their trained manpower, but they seldom are. In fact the reverse is usually the case.

A related failing of the United States is forcing too many new programs on the often limited government apparatus of a developing country, especially those which emerged from colonial status less than a generation ago. However, many of them can manage their own countries well enough as long as they do not face an insurrection. But insurgency produces extra burdens, and its demands can easily overwhelm a developing civil service and political structure. In addition to overloading the system, hastily conceived counterinsurgency programs can exacerbate personal and bureaucratic rivalries to the detriment of the counterinsurgency effort. Too often, Americans coming in full of ideas and anxious to please Washington with their initiatives tend to dream up too many new programs. Instead, I believe that one of the first objectives should be to ensure the basic ability of the host government to continue functioning. Once this is done, programs may be added with due deliberation. Counterinsurgency may require some new programs, but the first step should be to improve such ongoing ones as the indigenous intelligence service, the police, and certain other public services. It is not very dramatic, and it probably does not earn the mission officials many kudos in Washington, but if official Washington could be one of the subjects of the learning process, the mission officials might eventually achieve more kudos.

A final lesson is that we must learn to recognize what is most important. One reason for our concentration on material things and on programs is that their results seem more readily measurable. We try to keep records on the maintenance, operational condition, and the number of days or hours used for a variety of American equipment. For example, we can state with a fair degree of accuracy how many helicopters, both police and military, are operational on a given day and how many are down for maintenance. We can tell the number of hours an American-provided helicopter flew in one month, how the hours were spent, whether the helicopters were ferrying VIPs or dropping supplies to beleaguered soldiers; but it is more difficult to obtain answers to the question of what the helicopters actually contributed to the campaign, or how a given program affected the behavior of the population or influenced the insurgents. Yet it is essential that we go beyond the statistics on the uses of equipment, the number of trainees, and the tons of fertilizer spread, and make a greater effort to evaluate the impact of programs and other important parts of our assistance.

Admittedly these are the hard questions, but they are crucial and deserve most careful attention.

Indeed, the overwhelming lesson of our last ten to fifteen years' experience in Southeast Asia is that the U.S. must think through its objectives clearly and for the long range. These objectives must be examined objectively and critically in the light of U.S. capabilities, our allies' capabilities, and any opposition or enemy capabilities. There must be continuing evaluation to determine whether our efforts are contributing to the objectives. This is essential regardless of the nature of the activity abroad.

Glossary

AID	Agency for International Development, U.S. Department of State
ARD	Accelerated Rural Development
ARPA	Advanced Research Projects Agency, U.S. Department of Defense
ASEAN	Association of Southeast Nations
BPP	Border Patrol Police
CD	Community Development
CI	Counterinsurgency
CPM	Civilian, Police, Military (Thai counterinsurgency doctrine)
CPT	Communist Party of Thailand
CSMC	Counterinsurgency Support Management Center, U.S. Embassy
CSOC	Communist Suppression Operations Command
CT	Communist Terrorist
CTO	Communist Terrorist Organization
DCM	Deputy Chief of Mission, U.S. Embassy
DOLA	Department of Local Administration, Thai Ministry of Interior
ISA	International Security Affairs, U.S. Department of Defense
JSC	Joint Security Center
JUSMAG	Joint United States Military Advisory Group
MACTHAI	U.S. Military Assistance Command, Thailand
MACV	U.S. Military Assistance Command, Vietnam
MAP	U.S. Military Assistance Program
MAVU	Modular Auditory-Visual Unit
MCYL	Malaysian Communist Youth League
MDU	Mobile Development Units
MIT	Mobile Information Team
MPC	U.S. Mission Psychological Operations Committee
MRDC	Joint Thai-U.S. Military Research and Development Center

MTT	Mobile Training Team
NIPSO	National Information Psychological Operations Organization
NSC	National Security Command
PAT	People's Assistance Team
RBCO	Regional Border Committee Organization
RTA	Royal Thai Army
RTG	Royal Thai Government
SA/CI	U.S. Special Assistant for Counterinsurgency
SEATO	Southeast Asia Treaty Organization
TNPD	Thai National Police Department
USIS	U.S. Information Service
USOM	U.S. Operations Mission
USSAG	U.S. Support and Advisory Group
VPU	Village Protection Unit
VSF	Village Security Force

Index

Accelerated Rural Development (ARD), 74-75, 101-102, 103, 121
Agriculture, 5, 6; government assistance to, 103; hill tribe farming and crops, 7-8; rice, 5, 6, 8, 12, 38; rubber, 8, 9, 38
Air bases: defense of, 133, 142, 145; influence on economy, 6; insurgent attacks on, 43; U.S. use of, 12, 21-22, 111, 128
Association of Southeast Asian Nations (ASEAN), 24

Bangkok, 3, 4, 5, 6, 12, 15, 30, 34, 39, 41, 42, 76, 81, 84, 110, 121, 124, 125, 142, 143
Bhumibol Adulyadej (Rama IX), His Majesty, 4, 13, 14, 16, 17, 18, 110. *See also* Royal Family
Border Patrol Police (BPP): counterinsurgency role of, 66-67, 80, 84, 91; with hill tribes, 79-80; organization of, 78-79; Remote Area Security Program, 121; schools, 8; strength of, 78-79. *See also* Counterinsurgency; Police
Buddhism: as class-leveling institution, 39; differences from communism, 38; influence of, 14, 36
Burma, 5, 7, 8, 12, 32, 40, 62, 109, 144

Cambodia, 5, 6, 12, 20, 91, 97, 110
Central Thailand, 12. *See also* West Central Thailand
Chakri Dynasty, 4, 15; King Chulalongkorn (Rama V), 4; King Mongkut (Rama IV), 4. *See also* Bhumibol Adulyadej (Rama IX); Coups; Royal Family
Chao Phya River, 5, 6, 12

Chin Peng, 11, 54, 65
China, 7, 31, 32, 33, 34, 42, 44, 48, 59, 69,
  111, 156
Chinese Communist Party, 28, 33, 41, 43,
  44
Civic action: by Border Patrol Police, 8, 79;
  by National Security Command, 83-84; by
  Royal Thai Army, 92, 100; U.S. participation in, 117, 126, 127, 145, 147
Communism: anti-colonial movement, 27-
  28; Bandung Conference, 33; beginnings
  of, 27-31; Comintern Congress, 28; Communist Youth League, 32; concentration
  on minorities, 29, 32; Far East Bureau,
  28, 29; fronts of, 33, 35; importance of
  people, 151-152; indifference to, 29, 31;
  organization for, 37; slow development of,
  35-41; suppression of, 30, 31, 32, 33, 40;
  tactical mistakes of, 40-41; use of terror,
  155; wars of national liberation, 154-155,
  156. See also Communist Party of Thailand; Chinese Communist Party; Insurgency
Communist Party of Thailand (CPT): anti-
  Japanese movement, 31; Central Committee of, 5, 49; Congress of, 31, 32, 34, 156;
  former names of, 30; "hero-martyrs" of,
  34; image of, 55; influence on, 44; leadership of, 12, 42-43; Maoist control of, 32,
  34, 35; organization of, 42-43, 97; origins
  of, 28-31; political indoctrination for, 34;
  training for insurgency, 34. See also Communism; Communist Terrorists; Insurgency
Communist Suppression Operations Command (CSOC): army influence over, 87;
  counterinsurgency plans of, 86-87, 99,
  135; creation of, 51, 85; organization of,
  85-87; Psychological Operations Division
  of, 76-77, 122, 134; reorganization of, 88;
  role of, 112-113; in South, role of, 84-85,
  88; village security, 117; weaknesses of,
  157. See also Counterinsurgency; Royal
  Thai Government
Communist Terrorists (CTs): beginnings of,
  48-50; defections from, 54, 106; image of,
  107; recruitment for, 49-50, 56; rehabilitation of, 77; retrenchment of, 55;
  strength of, 51, 57, 62, 63, 65, 97, 100.
  See also Communist Party of Thailand;
  Insurgency
Communist Terrorist Organization (CTO):
  growth of, 100-101; influence of, 11; objectives of, 66; organization of, 63-64,

65-66; strength of, 66, 68, 84, 101. See
  also Far South Thailand; Insurgency
Community Development, Department of,
  73-74, 101-102, 116
Constitutions, 15, 16, 17, 18, 88, 100
Counterinsurgency: assessment of active,
  96-101; assessment of passive, 101-108;
  competition of men and machines, 153-
  154; difficulties of assessment, 95-96;
  dilemmas of, 72; doctrine of, 72-93; integrated effort, 155; lessons learned, 157-
  159; other successful efforts, 152-153;
  reorganization of, 112-113; summary of,
  156-157; village security, 91-92, 97-98,
  100, 117, 126, 132, 136-137. See also
  Communist Suppression Operations Command; Royal Thai Government; U.S. Mission; U.S. Special Assistant for Counterinsurgency
Coups, 4, 15, 17, 18, 19, 30, 31, 33, 112
Crime, 9, 10-11

Dawee Chullasyapa, 18, 112, 113
Democracy, 15, 16, 37
De Silva, Peer, 130-138, 139, 142
Divisive elements, 12-13

Far South Thailand: counterinsurgency
  problems of, 100-101; economy of, 9;
  neglect of, 11; racial problems in, 10;
  Thai-Malaysian border committees, 84;
  Thai-Malaysian police actions, 66; Thai-
  Malaysian relations, 10, 101, 144. See also
  Agriculture; Communist Terrorist Organization; Geography; Resources
Foreign policy: accommodation with China,
  23-24; current dilemmas of, 25; during
  Korean War, 21; outside influence on,
  21-22; reappraisal of, 23-25, 111; regional
  cooperation, 24; relationship with U.S.,
  20-25, 127-128; traditional, 20-25; during
  Vietnam War, 21-23; during World War II,
  20
Free Thai Movement, 20, 31

Geography, 4-5; Central, 12; East, 11-12;
  Far South, 9; Mid-South, 8; North, 6-7;
  Northeast, 5; West, 12

Hill tribes: communist appeals to, 12, 59;
  communist training of, 58, 156; friction
  with Thais, 7-8; government policies for,
  8, 76; insurgency role of, 57; major groupings of, 7; number of, 7; organization of,

7; police programs for, 121; radio station for, 106; rebellion of, 58. *See also* Agriculture; North Thailand
Ho Chi Minh, 29, 32, 35

Insurgency: anti-Americanism, 43; Chinese role in, 47-48; decision to launch, 41-42, 43-44; incidents, 51, 69, 156; involvement of Thais, 90, 100; progress of, 68-69, 108, 112; strength, 69; summary of, 156-157; tactics of, 50-51, 52, 55, 60, 63, 64-65, 67; training for, 48; village support of, 49. *See also* Communist Terrorists; Communist Terrorist Organization; Far South Thailand; Mid-South Thailand; North Thailand; Northeast Thailand; West Central Thailand
Intellectuals, 36, 39, 111, 112

Joint Security Centers (JCSs), 77, 85-86

Kriangsak Chomanan, 84
Kris Sivara, 17, 18

Labor, 13
Laos, 5, 6, 7, 21, 32, 34, 48, 57, 58, 59, 61, 62, 91, 98, 99, 110, 123, 144, 162
Lenin, Vladimir I., 27
Local Administration, Department of, 74, 75-76, 117, 137

Malayan Emergency, 48, 155
Malaysia, 5, 10, 11, 32, 40, 63, 66, 67, 68, 100-101, 144, 162
Malaysian Communist Party, 65
Malaysian Communist Youth League, 66
Martin, Graham, 44, 116, 117-119, 128, 129-131, 135, 137, 159, 160, 161
Mekong River, 5, 6, 7, 61, 120
Mid-South Thailand: beginning of insurgency, 64; counterinsurgency problems, 100; economy of, 9; growth of insurgency, 65; insurgent incidents, 64; insurgent strongholds, 63; neglect of, 9, 11. *See also* Agriculture; Communist Terrorist Organization; Geography; Resources
Military Research and Development Center (MRDC), 125
Minorities: Chinese, 9, 41; exploitation by communists, 12, 29; insurgency role of, 48, 90; in Northeast Thailand, 5; Sino-Thais, 13, 42, 44, 59, 90. *See also* Hill tribes; Muslims
Mobile Development Units (MDUs), 82-83, 101-102, 116

Mobile Information Teams (MITs), 77, 102, 104, 122
Mobile Medical Teams, 104
Modernization, 4, 14, 109
Modular Audio-Visual Units (MAVUs), 77, 104-105
Muslims, 9; differences from Thais, 10; exploitation by communists, 12, 67, 68; government attitude toward, 9; separatist movement by, 10, 65; solution to problems, 11

Nai Amphur Academy, 76
National Information Psychological Operations Organization (NIPSO), 77-78
National Security Command (NSC): creation of, 82; in Far South Thailand, 84-85; psychological operations of, 77; role of, 74, 83-84, 112. *See also* Mobile Development Units
North Thailand: beginnings of insurgency, 57-58; counterinsurgency problems, 98-100; external assistance to insurgency, 61-62; growth of insurgency, 60-61, 62; insurgent areas in, 58-59, 60; insurgent incidents, 58-60; objectives of insurgency, 59-60; Pakbeng Valley, 61; Tri-Province area (Phu Lom Lo), 58, 60, 61, 98, 148. *See also* Agriculture; Geography; Hill tribes; Resources
Northeast Thailand: beginnings of insurgency, 49; counterinsurgency problems, 97-98; government programs in, 102-104; growth of insurgency, 56-57; insurgent guidelines for, 53; insurgent incidents, 51, 52, 56; insurgent strongholds, 49-50, 52, 56, 57; neglect of, 6; weakness of insurgency, 52-53, 54-55. *See also* Agriculture; Geography; Minorities; Resources

Opium, 7, 8

Parliament, 9, 11, 15, 16, 17, 31
Per diem, 76, 80, 82, 91-92, 117
Phibulsongram, 15, 31
Police (Thai National Police Department, TNPD): behavior problems of, 102; Marine Police, 80; organization of, 78-80; Special Branch, 80; U.S. assistance to, 121-122; weaknesses of, 80. *See also* Border Patrol Police; Counterinsurgency; Provincial Police
Political parties: Democratic Party, 16, 19; organization and membership of, 37; United Thai Peoples Party, 16, 37

Political structure, 15-20; balance of power, 19; consensus in, 15; differences with communism, 36-37; the "establishment," 18; evolution of policies, 15; importance of individual in, 20; internal politics of, 15; lack of ideology in, 19-20; practice of "double-hatting," 18-19; role of military in, 16; U.S. knowledge of, 150. *See also* Constitution; Coups; Democracy; Parliament; Students
Praphas Charusathira, 16, 17, 18-19, 85, 88, 135
Prasert Sapsunthon, 31
Prasong Sukhum, 74
Pridi Phanomyong, 15
Provinces, 4-12; elections in, 16; problems of, 13; ties between, 14
Provincial Police: counterinsurgency role of, 91; organization of, 78-79; Police Patrol Project, 79; Special Action Forces, 79; strength of, 78-79; Tambon Police Station Project, 79; training program for, 116. *See also* Counterinsurgency; Police
Psychological operations: assessment of, 104-106; government programs for, 76-78; U.S. assistance for, 122, 125. *See also* National Information Psychological Operations Organization (NIPSO)
Public Relations, Department of, 77
Public Welfare, Department of, 8, 76

Radio Station 909, 77, 83, 105-106, 122
Regional Border Committee Organization (RBCO), 84, 100, 144
Resources, 5, 6-7, 8, 9, 11, 38
Royal Family, 8, 12
Royal Thai Air Force, 82
Royal Thai Army (RTA): counterinsurgency role of, 87, 91, 92, 97, 98-99, 100; counterinsurgency training of, 81; Joint Training Exercise 16, 97, 98; organization of, 80-81; U.S. advisors to, 124, 135. *See also* Counterinsurgency
Royal Thai Government (RTG): development programs of, 78; external problems of, 110-111; inattention to insurgency, 110, 111-112; intelligence efforts of, 54, 55, 63, 71, 97, 99, 100, 156; presence in villages, 55; response to insurgency, 51-52, 53, 61, 64-65, 86; socioeconomic problems, 108-110; stability of, 4, 13, 16; transportation program of, 14; weaknesses of, 106-107. *See also* Counterinsurgency; Foreign policy; Political structure
Royal Thai Navy, 82

Saiyud Kerdphol, 18, 85, 87, 112, 134, 135, 157
Sanya Dharmasakti, 17, 24, 112
Sarit Thanarat, 6, 33, 89
Sattahip, 12, 127
Seni Pramoj, 16
Solidarity Movement, 34
South Thailand. *See* Far South Thailand and Mid-South Thailand
Southeast Asia Treaty Organization (SEATO), 21, 71, 115, 120
Southern Coordination Center, 10
Students: anti-Americanism, 24-25; overthrow of government by, 17-18; political role of, 13, 18
Surikij Mayalarp, 85

Tanham, George. *See* U.S. Special Assistant for Counterinsurgency
Thanat Khoman, 21, 23, 111
Thanom Kittikachorn, 17, 18, 24

Unger, Leonard, 137, 142-143, 146, 161, 162
Unifying elements, 13-14
United States: agreements with Thailand, 21; assistance to Thailand by, 22, 111, 120; evaluating programs of, 167-168; influence on Thai economy, 108; opposition to Vietnam War in, 22-23; overhauling overseas activities, 163; overseas role of, 164-168; problems caused by, 22; reduction of forces by, 24, 111. *See also* Foreign policy; U.S. Embassy, Bangkok; U.S. Mission; and other U.S. agencies listed below
U.S. Advanced Research Projects Agency (ARPA): counterinsurgency research by, 117; Meo handbook, 141; organization of, 125; phase out of, 126; role of director, 125. *See also* Military Research and Development Center
U.S. Agency for International Development (AID), 74, 134. *See also* U.S. Operations Mission (USOM)
U.S. Air Force, 126, 127. *See also* Air bases; Civic action
U.S. Army, 126-127, 149; Special Forces, 123, 124-125, 148, 165
U.S. Central Intelligence Agency (CIA), 24, 127
U.S. Department of State, 138-139, 159-160
U.S. Embassy, Bangkok, 119-120, 131. *See also* Martin, Graham; Unger, Leonard

U.S. Information Service (USIS): assistance to Thais, 104; counterinsurgency role, 122; establishment of branch offices, 117; organization and programs of, 122. *See also* Mobile Information Teams (MITs); Psychological operations

U.S. Military Assistance Command, Thailand (MACTHAI): assistance to police, 147-148; Military Assistance Program (MAP), 117, 124, 134; organization of, 123-125; role of commander, 123. *See also* U.S. Army

U.S. Military Assistance Command, Vietnam (MACV), 24

U.S. Mission, Thailand: civilian sector of, 120-122; coordination problems of, 119, 142, 160-161; counterinsurgency plan of, 115-116, 116-117; counterinsurgency policy guidelines for, 145-146; counterinsurgency training programs of, 141; military sector of, 123-127; Mission Council, 137; regional coordination of, 142-144; role of ambassador in, 118-119. *See also* U.S. Special Assistant for Counterinsurgency

U.S. Operations Mission (USOM): assistance to Thais, 103, 104, 117, 147-148; budget for, 134; counterinsurgency role of, 121; organization and programs of, 120-122. *See also* Accelerated Rural Development (ARD); Police; U.S. Agency for International Development (AID)

U.S. Seabees, 121-122

U.S. Special Assistant for Counterinsurgency (SA/CI): achievements of, 161-162; assistance to Thais, 149; authority of, 161; committees of, 142; coordination problems of, 134-135; counterinsurgency policy guidelines paper, 144-149; Counterinsurgency Support Management Center, 133; De Silva's assessment of, 137-138; embassy contacts of, 144; establishment of, 120, 130-131; improvement of, 162-163; influence of, 134; intelligence efforts of, 135-136; liaison with Thais, 134-135; mission reporting by, 147; regional meetings, 143-144; resentment of, 135; reorganization by Tanham, 138-139; reorganization after Tanham, 150; role in village security, 136-137; study groups, 141, 145; Tuesday Group, 132-133, 139-140, 140-141, 147, 150, 162; view of Thai counterinsurgency, 132. *See also* Counterinsurgency; De Silva, Peer

U.S. Support and Advisory Group (USSAG), 24, 126, 127

Vietnam, 21, 32, 34, 35, 44, 48, 58, 92, 110, 111, 117, 120, 123, 127, 130, 135, 136, 138, 141, 147, 149, 153, 156, 157, 163, 164

Village Protection Units (VPUs), 64

Village Security Force (VSF). *See* U.S. Special Assistant for Counterinsurgency

Voice of the Malay Revolution, 67-68, 69

Voice of the Thai People, 34-35, 49, 60, 64, 69

Volunteer Defense Corps (VDC), 86-87

West Central Thailand: beginnings of insurgency, 63; counterinsurgency problems, 100; insurgent incidents, 63. *See also* Agriculture; Central Thailand; Geography; Resources